The Varieties of Joycean Experience

The Varieties of Joycean Experience

Tim Conley

Anthem Press
An imprint of Wimbledon Publishing Company
www.anthempress.com

This edition first published in UK and USA 2025
by ANTHEM PRESS
75–76 Blackfriars Road, London SE1 8HA, UK
or PO Box 9779, London SW19 7ZG, UK
and
244 Madison Ave #116, New York, NY 10016, USA

First published in the UK and USA by Anthem Press in 2021

Copyright © Tim Conley 2025

The author asserts the moral right to be identified as the author of this work.

All rights reserved. Without limiting the rights under copyright reserved above, no part of this publication may be reproduced, stored or introduced into a retrieval system, or transmitted, in any form or by any means (electronic, mechanical, photocopying, recording or otherwise), without the prior written permission of both the copyright owner and the above publisher of this book.

British Library Cataloguing-in-Publication Data
A catalogue record for this book is available from the British Library.

Library of Congress Control Number: 2025932544
A catalog record for this book has been requested.

ISBN-13: 978-1-83999-472-2 (Pbk)
ISBN-10: 1-83999-472-X (Pbk)

This title is also available as an e-book.

Cover illustration by Stephen Remus and
Natasha Pedros of the Niagara Artists Centre

Are you experienced?

—Jimi Hendrix

and after the lessions of experience I speak from inspiration
—*Finnegans Wake* (436.20–21)

CONTENTS

Acknowledgments ix
Abbreviations xi
Preface xiii

1. Categorical: "Meddlied Muddlingisms": The Uncertain Avant-Gardes of *Finnegans Wake* — 1
2. Narratological: "Whole Only Holes Tied Together": Joyce and the Paradox of Summary — 15
3. Compositional: Playing with Matches: The *Wake* Notebooks and Negative Correspondence — 31
4. Genetical: Revision Revisited — 41
5. Cerebral: "Cog It Out": Joyce on the Brain — 55
6. Mythametical: Waking "for an Equality of Relations" — 71
7. Scatological: Mixplacing His Fauces — 81
8. Thanatological: "Don't You Know He's Dead?": Postmortem Uncertainties — 95
9. Meteorological: Weathering the *Wake*: Barometric Readings of I.3 — 107
10. Hysterical-Exegetical: Petitions Full of Pieces of Pottery — 123

Bibliography 151
Index 159

ACKNOWLEDGMENTS

The word "Joycean" in this book's title denotes, among other things, a certain kind of reader or scholar. If pressed to give a definition, I would venture two: first, a Joycean is someone who may be said to be interested in Joyce, which is to say, in nearly everything; second, as more or less a general rule, Joyceans are a special, intelligent subspecies of *Homo ludens* to which one is honored to be thought to belong. Of this distinguished group I owe thanks to Austin Briggs, Bill Brockman, Catherine Flynn, Ronan Crowley, Ruth Frehner, the late Michael Groden, Frances Ilmberger, Onno Kosters, James Ramey, Gabriel Renggli, Genevieve Sartor, Sam Slote, and Ursula Zeller. And like just about every Joycean (and perhaps even more than most), I am especially indebted to Fritz Senn and the Zürich James Joyce Foundation.

My colleagues in the Department of English Language and Literature at Brock University have continually supported my work and provided a great environment in which to think, write, and teach.

For archival assistance I offer thanks to Squirrel Walsh of the Department of Rare Books and Special Collections at Princeton University Library and James Maynard of the Poetry Collection at SUNY-Buffalo.

All of the essays collected here have had previous lives, whether as talks or as publications in scholarly journals or edited volumes. Earlier versions of both "Meddlied Muddlingisms" and "Whole Only Holes Tied Together" appeared in the *James Joyce Quarterly*. "Cog It Out" first appeared in *Joyce Studies Annual*. "Playing with Matches" was published in *New Quotatoes: Joycean Exogenesis in the Digital Age* (ed. Ronan Crowley and Dirk Van Hulle (Amsterdam: Brill, 2016)): it was written as and remains a tribute to Geert Lernout. "Revisions Revisited" was a chapter in *Genesic Fields: James Joyce and Genetic Criticism* (ed. Genevieve Sartor (Leiden: Brill, 2018)). "Weathering the *Wake*" is a slightly revised version of an essay included in *Joyce's Allmaziful Pluralibities: Polyvocal Explorations of* Finnegans Wake (ed. Kimberly J. Devlin and Christine Smedley (Gainesville: University Press of Florida, 2015)). "Waking 'for an equality of relations'" was presented at an excellent panel on the politics of *Finnegans Wake* at the International James Joyce Symposium in Utrecht in 2014 and later published in *a long the krommerun: Selected Papers from the Utrecht James Joyce Symposium* (ed. Onno Kosters, Tim Conley, and Peter de Voogd (Amsterdam: Brill, 2016)). A shorter but no less disgusting version of "Mixplacing His Fauces" was presented—albeit apologetically—at the International James Joyce Conference in Toronto in 2017, and "Don't You Know He's Dead?" was presented at the Mexico City iteration of that conference in 2019, and was subsequently included in the volume *Joyce without Borders* (ed. James Ramey and Norman Cheadle). A *Wake*-focused (or obsessed?) version of "Petitions Full of Pieces of Pottery" was delivered as a keynote lecture at the "*Finnegans Wake* at 80" conference held at Trinity College Dublin in 2019. I salute all of the respectful editors and organizers.

My editor at Anthem Press, Megan Greiving, has been supportive of this book from its inception, and I thank her and her team for all of their work in producing it. I am also appreciative of the efforts and advice of the anonymous readers of the manuscript.

To my students, especially those of past *Ulysses* seminars and *Finnegans Wake* reading groups, this book is dedicated, with admiration and thanks.

ABBREVIATIONS

The following abbreviations are used in parenthetical citations throughout this book:

D	*Dubliners*
E	*Exiles*
JJA	*James Joyce Archive*
JJ II	*James Joyce*, by Richard Ellmann (2nd ed.)
FW	*Finnegans Wake*
Letters I	(ed. Stuart Gilbert)
Letters II, III	(ed. Richard Ellmann)
OCPW	*Occasional, Critical, and Political Writings* (ed. Kevin Barry)
P	*A Portrait of the Artist as a Young Man*
SL	*Selected Letters*
U	*Ulysses*

Details of specific editions used may be found in the bibliography.

PREFACE

Reviewing *Finnegans Wake* when it appeared in 1939, *The Irish Times* declared it "Endlessly Exciting in its Impenetrability"—a proper Irish backhand, that.[1] The apparent inevitability of hyperbole when it comes to discussions of that book is a subject perhaps worthy of a study of its own, but in this book, the emphasis is on how endlessly exciting Joyce's works are in their permeability: there is no single royal road by which one enters, but rather countless unexpected, obscure, and unlikely pathways for readers to discover and attempt—and which lead to just as many and varying degrees of enlightenment, dissatisfaction, amusement, and irritation.

The loose organizing principle to this collection of essays is the illustration of the available variety of critical approaches to Joyce's works, of which *Ulysses* and *Finnegans Wake* are here given the most attention. I hope that readers will find the absence of any grand and overarching thesis as refreshing as I did in assembling this book. What freedoms this offers the reader—not having to read the whole thing straight through, or even read the essays in the order presented—may well appeal to readers of Joyce, whose otherwise daunting enormities likewise allow their readers set their own pace and choose their own paths.

In recent years, I have taken to concluding a semester-long seminar on *Ulysses* first by congratulating the students on their achievement in having helped one another to read this notoriously complex book and then by making an unexpected and utterly unfair demand: going around the room, I ask each of them what *Ulysses* is *about*—what they would tell their mother or boyfriend or roommate who might ask such a question—and to make things worse, I limit their answer to a single word, and prohibit the repetition of answers. What this exercise reveals is the startling variety of possible answers. My students have offered as answers both grand and sometimes abstract concepts (*life, reality, time, thought*) and, more often, particular phenomena (*grief, movement,*

---

[1] "Sixteen Years Work by James Joyce: New Novel is 'Endlessly Exciting in its Impenetrability,'" *Irish Times*, June 3, 1939.

fatherhood, marriage, memory). In other such instances I have asked, sometimes in combination with the first question, what kind or genre of book *Ulysses* is, and again students give a wide assortment of answers: *epic* is not fixed upon as readily as when the class was just beginning, and when it is at the end, it seems to have new dimensions to its meaning; others suggest *comedy* or *ghost story* or *roman à clef* or *encyclopedia*, among other things, none of them entirely satisfactory not only to the class as a whole but to the very student who has given this or that answer. The first two essays in this volume take up these problems of categorizing and summarizing Joyce.

After that, the varieties bloom: cognition, death, equality, ecocriticism, bodily waste ... these "ten toptypsical readings" (*FW* 20.15) are offered together as a mixed bouquet. The pseudo-indexical classifications assigned to each essay ("Thanatological," "Ecocritical," etc.), which adopt an *Exagmination*-like terminology by way of Gilbert and Sullivan ("In short, in matters vegetable, animal, and mineral / I am the very model of a modern Major General") may aid the reader's selections.

This book's title's adaptation of a famous one by William James ought not to be taken to suggest that reading Joyce is a religion, even if some comparisons between the practice of the one and that of the other might prove insightful. Indeed, it is the understanding of reading Joyce *as* a practice, a human activity requiring a certain degree of commitment: time and effort (up to and including obsession) in the service of pleasure and illumination, which both underwrites the ongoing enterprise of critical study and necessitates it. This practice also encourages and even (I believe) requires the forging of communities. Yet it fosters doubt rather than faith, for the longer and more closely one reads Joyce, and the more one respects the variety of possible approaches, the less certain one becomes about any one approach, any one way of reading. As James observed in his study,

> To see a thing rightly we need to see it both out of its environment and in it, and to have acquaintance with the whole range of its variations. The study of hallucinations has in this way for psychologists been the key to their comprehension of normal sensation, that of illusions has been the key to the right comprehension of perception.[2]

Though there are specific terms in this pronouncement well worth challenging—"normal," most certainly, but also "key," as the last and longest essay included in this book will demonstrate—James's larger point retains its

---

[2] William James, *The Varieties of Religious Experience: A Study in Human Nature* (New York: Modern Library, 2002), 26.

force. It is from variety and variation, even unto apparent aberrations, that our best perspectives and understandings emerge.

My title also nods to Roland McHugh's *The* Finnegans Wake *Experience*,[3] an enigmatic phrase that is suggestive of a certain strange transformative quality to reading Joyce, a quality that eludes simple or even singular characterization, that calls for "every-tale-a-treat-in-itself variety" (*FW* 123.27–28). The essays collected here do not—cannot— encompass this experience, but I hope they might encourage further experience and inspire yet more variety of critical explorations.

---

[3] Roland McHugh, *The* Finnegans Wake *Experience* (Berkeley: University of California Press, 1981).

Chapter 1

CATEGORICAL

"Meddlied Muddlingisms": The Uncertain Avant-Gardes of *Finnegans Wake*

> MAN IN AUDIENCE: Mr. James Joyce, now, where would you put him?
> HOLLY MARTINS: Oh, would you mind repeating that question?
> MAN IN AUDIENCE: I said, where would you put Mr. James Joyce? In what category?
> —Dialogue from *The Third Man* (1949)[1]

I

Situating Joyce in relation to the avant-garde is a matter of affinity rather than affiliation, though this is no uncomplicated distinction. Another no less difficult distinction inherent in any discussion of this matter lies in the question of *whose* affinity is being discussed, for the taxonomy of authors is, if nothing else, a reflection of the expectations and agendas of readers, critics, teachers, and publishers. Joyce's separation from the contemporaneous avant-garde movements (among whose members he moved, amid whose writings he published) is the effect of a combination of authorial self-styling, biographers' spin, and a persistent but limiting conception of the avant-garde as more or less restricted and conspicuously marked social clubs. While certainly Joyce kept his distance from any orthodoxy, his demurrals are funny because they are often fantastical: when *Finnegans Wake* protests, "you're too dada for me to dance" (65.17), it's as though the town drunk were passing up an offered glass of wine with the excuse that the vintage was not quite his favorite year. It is far from easy to determine which is the greater: the reluctance of (justly) cautious scholars to fit Joyce within a specific avant-garde, or Joyce's own resistance to being "put" into a "category."

---

[1] *The Third Man*, dir. Carol Reed. Screenplay by Graham Greene, 1949.

"Avant-garde" ought to be understood as a political term rather than a political position, and this term is more often than not employed as retrospective identification. How is a given artist determined to be "avant-garde," "ahead of his time," "on the cutting edge," and so on? The process is just another subroutine in the designation of an "author function": if the novelist X is exemplary of a manner of novel that has become accepted as the norm, then Y, who writes a very different sort of novel from X, a sort that does not lend itself to ready emulation or is strikingly singular but cannot be ignored, requires a categorization that will instruct others that the manner of Y's novel is, according to one's views of the norms represented by X, either an experiment of uncertain value and in no need of repetition, or else an experiment that ought to inspire more such experiments. As arbitrary as this arrangement may be, its ideological force is very strong. It should not—should it?—be so difficult to imagine a world in which, say, the poetry of Ilarie Voronca held a more central place in the literary canon (more anthologized and republished, more often taught and studied, more acknowledged and quoted) than the poetry of Yeats. But difficult it is, and most especially for scholars, publishers, and all those professionally invested in the given day's Ponzi scheme of cultural capital that is the literary canon (and its environs, including more or less deterritorialized avant-gardes).

What is most important, then, in assessing the claims for and debates about this or that artist or work as avant-garde, is the conception of literary history behind them, in so far as they may be made out. Eric Hobsbawm, for instance, reports that "post-1917 developments [...] led to the bifurcation of Marxist aesthetic theory between the 'realists' and the 'avant-gardists'—the conflicts between Lukacs and Brecht, the admirers of Tolstoi and those of James Joyce."[2] Whatever the justice of this claim with respect to Marxist aesthetic theory (and it is surely little more than rough justice), Joyce would likely be almost as surprised to find himself associated with the "avant-gardists" in opposition with the "realists" as to hear that he and his work represent some sort of aesthetic nemesis to Tolstoy, of whose work Joyce was himself an admirer.

Finnegans Wake is no product of a specific avant-garde movement, as such, but as Marjorie Perloff has observed (and I will return to Perloff again later), "the identification of *avant-garde* with movements is not without its problems."[3] In studying affinities instead of affiliations, as I have proposed, it is useful

---

[2] Eric Hobsbawm, "Socialism and the Avant-Garde, 1880–1914," in *Uncommon People: Resistance, Rebellion and Jazz* (London: Abacus, 1999), 184.

[3] Marjorie Perloff, "Avant-Garde Community and the Individual Talent: The Case of Language Poetry." 2004. Online. http://marjorieperloff.com/stein-duchamp-picasso/avant-garde-community-and-the-individual-talent/ (accessed September 13, 2015).

to draw upon Jerome Rothenberg's conception of the avant-garde as "the work of individuals acting together—an effort somehow in common, even if performed by one."[4] More than any other of Joyce's books, the *Wake* is a collaborative production, in which a network of amanuenses, typists, translators, and correspondents was involved in the writing, constant rewriting, and publication. Without this network, the book would never have happened, or at least certainly not as we know it.

Moreover, the *Wake* is a mélange of avant-garde tendencies, albeit often as not in parody.

It might be argued that while the book is not avant-garde in the sense that it subscribes to the tenets of given brand's stated aesthetic program, it interacts with and translates such programs even as it rejects the brands. The *Wake* not only smirks at "futuerism" (130.01) and "expressionism" (467.07), it is in fact a catalog of dozens of "isms," more or less imaginary avant-gardes readily confused with entrenched political positions and worrying-sounding medical conditions, including "mienerism" (608.01), "cycloannalism" (254.26), "impulsivism" (149.11), "anteproresurrectionism" (483.10), "culotticism" (374.13), "hagiohygiecynicism" (353.08), and "liffeyism" (614.24). Joyce's ridiculing of the pretensions and extravagances of the contemporary avant-gardes is also that of his own writing ambitions and methods:

> after all his autocratic writings of paraboles of famellicurbs and meddlied muddingisms, thee faroots hof culchaw end ate citrawn woodint wun able rep of the triperforator awlrite blast through his pergaman hit him where he lived and do for the blessted selfchuruls. (303.18–24)

The "meddlied muddingisms" here are a muddled medley of modernisms and modern affectations: the automatic writings practiced by Georgie Yeats and those of the surrealists are cheek by jowl with Wyndham Lewis's *Blast* (and its propensity for alternatively "blasting" and "blessing"). One good bang at the typewriter ("rep of the triperforator")—that's all it takes—may strike a blow against not just the churls but even the Holy Roman Empire (founded by Charlemagne, St. Charles) and maybe the institution of literature itself (the ancient Library of Pergamum, origin of the word "parchment," can be glimpsed in "his pergaman"). And then there is the phrase "the faroots hof culchaw," not unlike the sort of parochial spelling that Pound tends to use in his letters, though the accent here is a very high sort of English. This is

---

[4] Jerome Rothenberg, *Poetics and Polemics, 1980–2005* (Tuscaloosa: University of Alabama Press, 2008), 261.

probably a reference to the play *The Fruits of Culture*, first performed in 1889, written by none other than that alleged anti-Joyce, Tolstoy.[5]

All of which is to state the point that this short essay intends to explore the slippery, persistent question of Joyce and the avant-garde—the *is he or isn't he* question—is more interesting (as a question) than any answer to it might be.[6] The history of its being framed and asked, and reframed and reasked (just as the questioner in *The Third Man* certainly does not mind repeating his question) is part of the history of Joyce's reception and influence, and its recurrence quite usefully makes the location of Joyce within the larger histories of literature and culture unfixed, always being determined and checked. A review of a few different critical and creative treatments of the relationship of *Finnegans Wake* to the avant-garde dating from the decade following its publication to today demonstrates how our understanding of this relationship depends upon the values we assign at any given point in time to any perceived "avant-garde," past, present, or continuous.

Here we are caught, though, between two opposing impulses, two conflicting senses of history that need to be acknowledged. There is no critical consensus as to whether or exactly how the term "avant-garde" is applicable to works produced decades after the decline of high modernism. Yet it may be that the avant-garde by definition rebels against constrictive localization in place and time, and instead insists upon a migratory, viral existence. Peter Bürger's much-discussed definition of the avant-garde as a negation of art as institution, commodity, and tradition has the virtue of being clear and to some extent useful, though it leaves the avant-garde perhaps uncomfortably proximate to a militant philistinism (are the rabid fanatics who have in recent years busied themselves with destroying ancient artifacts, temples, and sculptures in the Middle East constituents of an "avant-garde?") and it is unclear to what extent the avant-garde becomes, in spite of itself, a cultural institution in retrospect (the effect of academic study, Bürger's included).[7] However, Bürger offers an invigorating understanding of the avant-garde as not a means to an end, but a means to all means:

---

[5] The title is also translated as *The Fruits of Enlightenment*. Ellmann includes the play in a list of books that Joyce read in 1900 or 1901 (75). Of possibly greater interest to *Wake* studies than I am free to investigate here, *Fruits* is the story of peasants deceiving a landowner by means of a spiritualist séance.

[6] With magisterial authority, the first sentence of the "James Joyce" entry on Wikipedia—at least at the time of this writing—declares that he is "considered to be one of the most influential writers in the modernist avant-garde of the early 20th century." See https://en.wikipedia.org/wiki/James_Joyce (accessed September 2, 2015).

[7] In a scene in the mock-documentary *Borat* (2006), the gregarious hero from Kazakhstan asks the name of a New Yorker on the subway. The reply—"My name is Mind Your Own Fuckin' Business"—is perhaps the most avant-garde one possible. This is worth bearing in

it is in the historical avant-garde movements that the totality of artistic means becomes available as means. Up to this period in the development of art, the use of artistic means had been limited by the period style, an already existing canon of permissible procedures, an infringement of which was acceptable only within certain bounds. But during the dominance of a style, the category 'aesthetic means' as a general one cannot be seen for what it is because, *realiter*, it occurs only as a particular one. It is, on the other hand, a distinguishing feature of the historical avant-gardes that they did not develop a style.[8]

It might be argued that it was modernism, and not exclusively the avant-garde, that overthrew "the dominance of a style," and of course T. S. Eliot was excited and disquieted by the way that *Ulysses* "exposed the futility of all styles" (*JJ II* 528). But the exciting point here is that the outmatching of "permissible procedures" and "certain bounds" is not necessarily the province of one aesthetic or movement, nor is it necessarily short-lived. Paul Goodman asserts that "such a disruptive attitude [as that of the avant-garde] does not does not foster beautiful and finished works 'exemplary to future generations' (Kant): the writer is too busy with making an effect to give himself to the literary process."[9] The second part of this statement exemplifies how needlessly restrictive, almost abortive ideas of the "avant-garde" too often are. If the avant-garde permits even a glimpse of "the totality of artistic means," of possible future avant-gardes, then it is naturally not the "beautiful and finished works" or indeed any works as such that are "exemplary to future generations" but the process, and the process may itself ultimately become indistinguishable from the effect—as is the case with *Finnegans Wake*.

II

"Art is a community matter transcending the limits of specialization," declared the Hungarian artist László Moholy-Nagy in 1943.[10] As painter, photographer, sculptor, stage designer, educator, writer, and fugitive from

---

mind when we reflect on how for so many years, the very years when surrealists and others were fiercely declaring themselves, Joyce refrained from naming the book he was writing.

[8] Peter Bürger, *Theory of the Avant-Garde*, trans. Michael Shaw (Minneapolis: University of Minnesota Press, 1984), 18.
[9] Paul Goodman, "Format and Communication," in *The Paul Goodman Reader*, ed. Taylor Stoehr (Oakland: PM Press, 2011), 194.
[10] László Moholy-Nagy, "The Contribution of the Arts to Social Reconstruction," in *Moholy-Nagy*, ed. Richard Kostelanetz (New York: Praeger, 1970), 21. The phrase is italicized in the original.

ready categorization, Moholy-Nagy struggled against the separation of art from other human activities and discourses, against "art on a pedestal" and for its function as "a seismograph of the relationships of the individual to the world, intuitive re-creation of the balance between the emotional, intellectual and social existences of the individual."[11] Moholy-Nagy's embrace of *Finnegans Wake* as a central, inspiring part in this struggle is notably at odds with the "animosity and misunderstandings" the book faced at this time, when Joyce's last book was often pointed to as an example of art taking leave of life as it is lived.

In his essay on "Literature" in *Vision and Motion* (written just before his death and later included in Richard Kostelanetz's *The Avant-Garde Tradition in Literature* (1982)), Moholy-Nagy outlines a kind of curriculum for the student of not just the avant-garde but "all aspects of contemporary literature," a curriculum worth reproducing here in somewhat abbreviated form:

> (1) the tendencies of contemporary composers such as Stravinsky, Bartok, Schoenberg, Hindemith, Krenek, Milhaud, Copeland, Varèse and others [...] (2) simultaneists, futurists, as they appear in the work of Guillaume Apollinaire, F. T. Marinetti, Vladimir Mayakovski [...] (3) expressionists and proto-surrealists: August Stramm, Lajos Kassak, Franz Kafka, Yvan Goll, Ezra Pound, Gertrude Stein, Jean Cocteau, Blaise Cendrars, Bert Brecht, etc [...] (4) the dadaists: Tristan Tzara, Jean Arp, Hugo Ball, Richard Huelsenbeck, Kurt Schwitters, Ribemont-Dessaignes, etc [...] (5) surrealists and (6) James Joyce. Besides these more or less modern trends the student may study: (7) the historic background of world literature; (8) poems by children; (9) poetry of the psychotic.[12]

Joyce is a category unto himself, without further categorization. It is perhaps not surprising to find that Joyce is the single figure to whom Moholy-Nagy thereafter devotes the most space in his wide-ranging and well-informed essay. "Although the surrealists emphasized such a goal," Moholy-Nagy writes, "the new form of communication was not accomplished by them, but more by the dadaists and simultaneously even more by James Joyce."[13]

Moholy-Nagy sees in Joyce an opening up—a revelation—of Bürger's "totality of artistic means." The *Wake* is valuable because it is a resource, or

---

[11] Moholy-Nagy, "The Contribution of the Arts to Social Reconstruction," 21.
[12] Laszlo Moholy-Nagy, "Literature," in *The Avant-Garde Tradition in Literature*, ed. Richard Kostelanetz (Buffalo, NY: Prometheus Books, 1982), 78–79.
[13] Moholy-Nagy, "Literature," 127. On Joyce's awareness of surrealism, see Catherine Flynn, "'Circe' and Surrealism: Joyce and the Avant-Garde," *Journal of Modern Literature* 34.2 (2011): 121–38.

perhaps a meta-resource, even the kind of codebook for a new engineering that Donald F. Theall, directly recalling Moholy-Nagy, enthuses about.[14] The analogies to a machine invariably suggest a writing machine, and perhaps a perpetual writing machine, or at any rate one that has an obvious place in the future.

Moholy-Nagy's numbered curriculum might remind the reader of a well-known and remarkable passage from Borges:

> These ambiguities, redundancies, and deficiencies recall those attributed by Dr. Franz Kuhn to a certain Chinese encyclopedia called the *Heavenly Emporium of Benevolent Knowledge*. In its distant pages it is written that animals can be divided into (a) those that belong to the emperor; (b) embalmed ones; (c) those that are trained; (d) suckling pigs; (e) mermaids; (f) fabulous ones; (g) stray dogs, (h) those included in this classification; (i) those that tremble as if they were mad; (j) innumerable ones; (k) those drawn with a very fine camel's-hair brush; (l) etcetera; (m) those that have just broken the flower vase; (n) those that at a distance resemble flies.[15]

It is diverting to conjecture about correspondences between these two lists, and it is not at all difficult to see Moholy-Nagy's "James Joyce" category as comparable or even equivalent to either (h) or (j). Reading Borges's list, Michel Foucault reports, "kept me laughing for a long time, though not without a certain uneasiness that I found hard to shake off," and it drove him to consider the tensions between systems of categorization and the incongruous. In *Les Mots et les choses*, the book that came out of this consideration, Foucault observes a distinction between the reassurance of order that constitutes utopias, and the cognitive disturbance that is the essence of hetertopias: "disturbing, probably because they secretly undermine language, because they make it impossible to name this *and* that, because they shatter or tangle common names, because they destroy 'syntax' in advance."[16] This last phrase points directly to the initiatives of the avant-garde ("in advance") and perhaps particularly to Marinetti's Futurist vow to destroy syntax and set words free.[17]

---

[14] Donald F. Theall, "The Avant-Garde and the Wake of Radical Modernism," in *Contemporary Poetics*, ed. Louis Armand (Evanston, IL: Northwestern University Press, 2007), 57–66.

[15] Jorge Luis Borges, "John Wilkins' Analytical Language," in *Selected Non-Fictions*, trans. Eliot Weinberger (New York: Viking, 1999), 231.

[16] Michel Foucault, *The Order of Things: An Archaeology of the Human Sciences* (London: Routledge, 2002), xix.

[17] F. T. Marinetti, "Destruction of Syntax—Wireless Imagination—Words-in-Freedom," in *Modernism: An Anthology*, ed. Lawrence Rainey (Malden, MA: Blackwell, 2005), 27–34.

Moholy-Nagy's discussion of Joyce includes this striking illustration shown below:

What *is* this, exactly? A chart, a map, a diagram, a clock?[18] With lines dynamic splaying out from (or toward?) the "J.J." vortex and keywords like "Symbolic" and "Thunderword—Voice of God" and "Space–Civilization–Death," the whole thing resembles a futurist rendering of the kind of detailed Homeric schema that Joyce produced for *Ulysses* (though not for the *Wake*). Occasionally reproduced (especially online), it is very seldom closely studied or discussed;[19] it is often attributed to Moholy-Nagy, but is in fact the work of Leslie L. Lewis.

Certainly it represents an elaborate system. The seventeen chapters of the *Wake* are presented as "levels," immediately reminiscent of the

---

[18] Richard Kostelanetz not entirely satisfyingly but intriguingly labels it "a precursor of graphic criticism" (*More Master Minds* (Ridgewood, NY: Archae Editions, 2018), 215).

[19] One interesting exception is Clinton Cahill's remarks on "Illuminating the *Wake*" on the James Joyce Centre's blog (January 5, 2013): see jamesjoyce.ie/illuminating-wake-clinton-cahill-part-2.

topography of Dante's netherworlds (and perhaps this is a picture of a mountain, inverted or otherwise, seen from above). Four concentric circles count out the four books and stages in Viconian cycles. Along the top are five sigla, though we might quibble about their identifications, and twelve lines radiating from the center appear to enumerate themes (for lack of a better word). To my mind the most beguiling thing about this illustration is the blanks: the empty rectangles where nothing is written, the wordless circles between the circles. These suggest not only that the *Wake* may not be so neatly organized—and thus bring to mind Joyce's confiding to Beckett, "I may have oversystematized *Ulysses*" (*JJ II* 702)—but that the map is not already drawn, the interpretations already established. Arguably, the most important parts of *Finnegans Wake* are the margins that await the reader's own scribbles.

III

In the course of defending Joyce from any association with the chaotic campaigns of dada in his essay "*Ulysses*, Order, and Myth," Eliot makes a point of rejecting the influence of Joyce's work as "an irrelevance": "A very great book may have a very bad influence indeed; and a mediocre book may be in the event most salutary. The next generation is responsible for its own soul; a man of genius is responsible to his peers, not to a studio full of uneducated and undisciplined coxcombs."[20] Of course Eliot's is in effect a moral argument (the evaluation of "great" is somehow connected with the "soul"), and as such may hold water, but his plumping for the individual poet over tradition (or traditions) is coldly ahistorical. If it is true that any conception of history that precludes even the consideration of a changeable future is suspect, then likewise any workable notion of "tradition" has to remain somewhat open, even at time synonymous with possibility. When Moholy-Nagy calls Joyce "the vessel of very old knowledge and very new hunches,"[21] he highlights not only how Joyce both observes and reinvents tradition but also how Joyce, as a "vessel," carries things forward. This is very different from the conception (fearfully held by Eliot and others) of Joyce as a terminal point.

In 1977, David Hayman observed both the marginal, neglected status *Finnegans Wake* seemed to have and the inspiration it offered to later writers,

---

[20] T. S. Eliot, "*Ulysses*, Order, and Myth," in *Selected Prose*, ed. Frank Kermode (London: Faber and Faber, 1975), 175–76.

[21] Moholy-Nagy, "Literature," 132.

"the invitation to perpetuate creation."[22] Joyce's book, Hayman opines in an essay that was reprinted in Richard Kostelanetz's anthology *The Avant-Garde Tradition in Literature* (1982), "is not yet the model and integrated source it could and may become," though he adds that "the declared Joycean bias of Arno Schmidt, Philippe Sollers, Maurice Roche, and the Brazilian concrete poets is something more than a straw in the wind—if something less than a tradition."[23] Hayman's "Joycean bias" is distinguished from the Eliotic trigger-word "tradition," but he nonetheless confidently predicts that "there will be more of it" in future writing.[24] Joyce represents a kind of initiative—an advance guard—that has not yet been adequately realized. Here again we see the "avant-garde" not as a stated position but a new direction, typically acknowledged in retrospect and primarily by those who have pursued a similar direction.

That Hayman's focus is predominantly on ("experimental") fiction unduly narrows the appreciation of the *Wake*'s influence. More than thirty years later, we can affirm Hayman's prediction and make additions to Hayman's list. For example, Caroline Bergvall's polyglottal hybrid poetries adapt Joyce's "abnihilisation of the etym" (*FW* 353.22) to a process of genetic splicing. In *Goan Atom* (2001), Bergvall examines Dolly, who is with Wakean simultaneity at once a woman, a doll, and a cloned sheep. This excerpt gives a taste:

Sgot
a wides lit
down the lily
sgot avide slot
donne lolly to a head
less cin
dy slots in
       to lic
Kher shackle
good dottersum
presses titbutt
on for the Puppe's
panoRama[25]

---

[22] David Hayman, "Some Writers in the Wake of the *Wake*," in *In the Wake of the* Wake, ed. David Hayman and Elliott Anderson (Madison: University of Wisconsin Press, 1978), 4.
[23] Hayman, "Some Writers in the Wake of the *Wake*," 5.
[24] Hayman, "Some Writers in the Wake of the *Wake*," 37.
[25] Caroline Bergvall, *Goan Atom* (San Francisco: Krupskaya, 2001), 23–24.

Reading Bergvall's poetry is remarkably akin to the multifarious, contradictory sort of exegesis involved in reading the *Wake*. The variations of word fragments, like the parts of an unassembled doll (think Hans Bellmer), are suggestive but never definitive. Dolly's vagina is a slot for a vending machine or perhaps a pornographic mutoscope, through which the viewer may watch ("avide" contains the Latin *videre*, whence "video") Dolly cavort with Cindy (the world "slut" is hinted at between "slit" and "slot"). "Puppe" is the Pope, but also German for "doll" (and one might pronounce it as the French *poupée*), and in all the anatomical confusion the orifice in question might turn out to be poopy. Or perhaps that slit "down the lily" is a surgical opening in her belly, and we are watching some kind of birth ("dottersum" leaves the gender of the offspring unknown). Bergvall's probing of the politics and poetics of reproduction[26] is reciprocal to the new means of production opened by the *Wake*.

In the Wake of the Wake, the anthology that Hayman edited with Elliott Anderson, excerpts from writers such as Christine Brooke-Rose, Raymond Federman, John Cage, Hélène Cixous, Samuel Beckett, and Gilbert Sorrentino are gathered as examples of "texte scriptible," writing that engenders writing. While Hayman's notion of "texte scriptible" undoubtedly has several sources, one of the most significant to consider here is his own groundbreaking work in the textual evolution (later to be called the "genetics") of the *Wake*. "Although it has been described as a work of destruction," Hayman begins his introduction to *A First-Draft Version of* Finnegans Wake (1963), "James Joyce's *Finnegans Wake* was designed as a triumphant reconstruction."[27]

In interview with Hayman, Philippe Sollers admits, "I don't think one can improve on *Finnegans Wake* when it comes to multiple meanings." Asked about his own use of musicality rather than polysemy, Sollers says:

> As far as musicality goes, my text may use means which seem less rich than Joyce's, but it is never a question of fragments, or passages taken out of context or cited. Any time you try to pull something out of the fabric, the whole thing will slip out of your hands, melt. One *can* take passages from the *Wake*.[28]

---

[26] For more on this subject, see Tim Conley, "Auguries: The Stuff of Modernism," *Hyperion* 8.2 (2014): 71–81.
[27] David Hayman, *A First-Draft Version of* Finnegans Wake (London: Faber and Faber, 1963), 3.
[28] "An interview with Philippe Sollers," in *In the Wake of the* Wake, ed. David Hayman and Elliott Anderson (Madison: University of Wisconsin Press, 1978), 128.

In understanding his own work to have a precarious integrity or wholeness that differs from the *Wake*, which has "multiple meanings" and passages that can be "taken," Sollers might be judging his own writing to be less generous, less instructive than Joyce's. In any event, the *Wake* is characterized as something that can be "taken," transmitted, without its being diminished, and without its effect on other work being so overwhelming as to deprive that other work of its own difference. The *Wake*'s influence may be viral, but not assimilative nor merely self-reproducing.

IV

Finally, I return to Marjorie Perloff, who has written extensively on the poetry and poetics of the avant-garde, both of the heyday of modernism and of today, the heyday of uncertainty. In the 2004 essay I quoted earlier, Perloff asks whether Stein, Joyce, or Beckett can be "'avant-garde' without being part of a movement":

> The concept of individual genius, it seems, dies hard. Does this mean that the term *avant-garde* has become meaningless? Not at all. The dialectic between individual artist and avant-garde groups is seminal to twentieth-century art-making. But not every "movement" is an avant-garde and not every avant-garde poet or artist is associated with a movement. What we need, it seems is a more accurate genealogy of avant-garde practices than we now have.[29]

No contest on this last point, but the odd thing is that Perloff should ask about Joyce, who is something of an uncertain quantity in her work. He has never appeared as a focal subject in any of her many books and essays; he comes and goes in passing mentions (usually references to *Ulysses* or *Finnegans Wake*), the occasional rhetorical question or list of names.[30] There is a palpable reticence about Joyce in her work, and Perloff seems to operate under a working assumption about Joyce as an avant-garde writer, though she does not, as she has for Eliot and Gertrude Stein, among others, actually make the case for it.[31]

---

[29] Perloff, "Avant-Garde Community and the Individual Talent: The Case of Language Poetry."

[30] The closest thing to a study of Joyce in Perloff's work, as far as I am aware, is the chapter comparing Pound's and Joyce's epistolary styles in *The Dance of the Intellect: Studies in the Poetry of the Pound Tradition* (Evanston, IL: Northwestern University Press, 1985), 74–87.

[31] See Marjorie Perloff, "Avant-Garde Eliot," in *21st-Century Modernism: The "New" Poetics* (Malden, MA: Blackwell, 2002), 7–43, and Marjorie Perloff, "Poetry as

To point this out is neither to hector nor to presume to dictate a subject to Perloff, whose work I admire; rather, it is to measure what this lacuna (or perhaps the very Joycean word "hesitancy" is more apt) suggests about the way scholarship currently views Joyce's relation to the avant-garde. Perloff's declining to tackle this question, if I may call it that, may have a number of reasons about which we might speculate, but it ought not to be simply assumed that Perloff takes Joyce's avant-garde status for granted. Perloff recounts that she did write an undergraduate thesis on "James Joyce and the Stream-of-Consciousness Novel," a fact which she presents as a symptom of being "like most students, much more interested in fiction than in poetry."[32] If Perloff's subsequent conversion to poetry is taken to be the reason for her "hesitancy" on the avant-garde qualities or status of Joyce, can or ought we to infer (or simply wonder) whether prose or the novel is generally less likely to be avant-garde than poetry? And this raises the old problem of the indeterminable genre of *Finnegans Wake*, which Joyce did not refer to as a "novel" and many have likened to poetry. Cue again the man in the audience with his question about categories.

Ulysses has become a touchstone and even provided a structural basis for experimental writings of the past two decades; writings that might well be termed avant-garde, including novels such as Andrew Lewis Conn's *P* (2003) and Vanessa Place's *La Medusa* (2008) and poetry such as Lisa Jarnot's "What In Fire Did I, Firelover, Starter of Fires, Love?"(2003) and Kenneth Goldsmith's *Fidget* (2000).[33] Perloff has written enthusiastically about at least two of these four authors, and it is worth noting that Joyce's prose novel can beget work that is called poetry, even when it looks like prose:

> Goosebumps appear all over body. Elbows on knees. Hands rest on chin. Eyes stare straight ahead. Forefingers push on eyelids. Red seen with streaks of green. Dots of many colors. Horizontal stripes appear in a field. Eyes ache from behind eyeballs. More pressure applied. Bluish ghostlike images of veins seen through closed eyelids. Eyes view retina and pupil. Press hard. Colors darken. Veins become white. Swirling red dots seen. Pain behind eyeball.[34]

Word-System: The Art of Gertrude Stein," in *The Poetics of Indeterminacy: Rimbaud to Cage* (Evanston, IL: Northwestern University Press, 1981), 67–108.

[32] Marjorie Perloff, "Becoming a Critic: A Memoir," in *Poetics in a New Key: Interviews and Essays*, ed. Jonathan Y. Bayot (Chicago: University of Chicago Press, 2013), 3.

[33] Andrew Lewis Conn, *P* (Brooklyn: Soft Skull Press, 2003); Vanessa Place, *La Medusa* (Tuscaloosa: University of Alabama Press, 2008); Lisa Jarnot, "What in Fire Did I, Firelover, Starter of Fires, Love?" in *Ring of Fire* (Cambridge: Salt, 2003), 11–12; Kenneth Goldsmith, *Fidget* (Toronto: Coach House Books, 2000).

[34] Goldsmith, *Fidget*, 39.

Goldsmith's *Fidget* approximates a "stream of consciousness"—though as the quoted passage demonstrates, it is hardly a gentle flow—by recounting in excruciating detail the author's every bodily movement in the course of a single day. The fact that that single day happens to be June 16, 1998 changes the complexion of the enterprise: the naive attraction to the quotidian turns out to be a self-consciously literary feat, not just an experiment in personal biometry but a kind of oblique rewriting of a high modernist masterpiece. Does this instance of cross-purposes, in which literary tradition serves as cultural capital, invalidate or qualify claims that *Fidget* is avant-garde? The tendency to imitate *Ulysses* (even if in parody) is different from the "taking" from *Finnegans Wake* (which might well be inimitable) that we have seen by Moholy-Nagy and Lewis, Bergvall and Sollers, and this is perhaps what is meant when the *Wake* is judged more "avant-garde" than *Ulysses* at this point in literary history. Indeed, the *Wake* may teach critics and writers alike how to stop worrying about taxonomies and categories—not just "novel" and "prose" and "poetry" but also "traditional" and "avant-garde"—or at least to see them precisely as anxieties.

The enthusiasms and hesitancies of the writers outlined here suggest a continuing—and continually wavering—struggle to "categorize" the *Wake*, to situate it within or without the avant-garde of its years of composition, and to connect it with whatever plausible avant-gardes have emerged since. The *Wake*'s potential lies outside of itself: its request of the reader, now mild, now brusque—"To pass the grace for Gard sake!" (377.30–31)—is ever before us, *avant nous*. It is ready to be avant-garde if we are.

Chapter 2

NARRATOLOGICAL

"Whole Only Holes Tied Together": Joyce and the Paradox of Summary

> Was that in the air about something is to be said for it or is it someone imparticular who will somewherise for the whole anyhow?
> —*FW* 602.06–08

I

While teaching a survey course in American literature some years ago, I encountered a truly puzzling student essay. In lectures, I had remarked (or thought I had remarked) that the Puritan Anne Bradstreet's poetry was generally apostrophic, that the occasions for her verses were usually a feeling of absence or loss. We noted her animal imagery in, for example, "In Reference to Her Children, 23 June, 1659."[1] One of the assigned essay topics asked students to discuss "either the importance of separation and absence or the use of animal imagery" in one or two of Bradstreet's poems. One student, apparently disregarding the word "either" and misreading a conjunction for a preposition, wrote about the absence of animal imagery in "A Letter to Her Husband, Absent upon Public Employment."[2] Where the zodiacal-astronomical conceit of the poem aptly expresses the paradox of feeling loneliness and unity simultaneously, the essay flatly stated that horses, chickens, and the like would be completely out of place. "I here, thou there, yet both but one"[3]: indeed, what room is there between this couple for a symbolically charged buffalo, say, or even a wee fruit bat?

---

[1] Anne Bradstreet, "In Reference to Her Children, 23 June, 1659," in *The Works of Anne Bradstreet*, ed. Jeannine Hensley (Cambridge, MA: Harvard University Press, 1967), 232–34.
[2] Anne Bradstreet, "A Letter to Her Husband, Absent upon Public Employment," in *The Works of Anne Bradstreet*, ed. Jeannine Hensley (Cambridge, MA: Harvard University Press, 1967), 226.
[3] Bradstreet. "A Letter to Her Husband, Absent upon Public Employment," 226.

A comic misunderstanding, certainly—the absurdity of the argument rivals Monty Python, an astute literary theorist I will bring up again later in this essay—but it was not easy for this instructor to explain, in written comments returned with the paper, what was wrong with this approach, besides the easy initial chiding for not following instructions. Intuitively, perhaps, it makes more sense, is of clearer purpose, to discuss what is *in* a given poem than what is *not*, and words to this effect were what I wrote, with hesitation, to the student. That hesitation, however, has remained. Is the act of analysis necessarily predicated upon a subject invested with some sense of presence or even reality? To affirm such a definition lands the scholar of literature in a highly paradoxical position, since one who studies fiction studies events that did not happen, and in some instances, never could. We can, like Don Quixote, descend into the darkest caves, chat with the ghost of a knight, and then express doubt about whether the phantom was not, as the Don puts it, "enchanted into the bargain"[4]—without, of course, stooping to confess our own quixotic state of enchantment. If fiction requires suspension of disbelief, does not criticism also? Is literary critique best understood as negative analysis, the study of that which is not—or even, ad absurdum, the study of that which is not within that which is not?

This essay does not, of course, propose to answer these large questions in any absolute manner. Instead, I hope to show how the works of Joyce echo and restate such questions within their narrative fabric. Specifically, I want to consider how the very concept of the summary suffers an epistemological body blow from texts such as *Ulysses* and *Finnegans Wake* expressly because these texts are removed from and effectively resist definition; in fact, they resist having a coherent, singular subject to define.[5] The counterintuitive strategies behind this resistance—a surfeit of information, qualification, and contrary information that cannot be totaled—thus have to do with identity and how it is measured, regulated, controlled. Just as Bloom declines to end his declarative statement on the beach "I ... AM. A" for, ostensibly, lack of room, Joyce's texts reject a definitive statement (*U* 13.1258–64).[6] The *Wake*'s mock-Cartesian

---

[4] Miguel de Cervantes, *Don Quixote*, ed. E. C. Riley, trans. Charles Jarvis (Oxford: Oxford University Press, 1998), 619.

[5] *A Portrait of the Artist as a Young Man*, it might be objected, is readily summarizable—"Stephen Dedalus grows up in words"—because of its genre. Portraits are (visual) summaries of their subjects. The painter may evoke and effectively encapsulate the character and qualities of such and such a figure by either allegory (the loyal dog eyeing its master will always do in a pinch) or luminous detail (the undone button and the dirty nails speak volumes).

[6] In *Finnegans Wake*, where all names and descriptions are provisional at best, "this old boy" who is recurrently referred to rather than actively present, is said to be "not all there,

formula, "cog it out, here goes a sum," turns Bloom's incomplete assertion inside out (*FW* 304.31).

Consciousness becomes an unextraordinary mechanism; the Latin verb for "I am" becomes an addition problem; and the singularity of both the speaker and the phenomenon that the utterance is supposed to underline (and, one could argue, summarize) is rejected (*a* sum, not *the* sum). If subjectivity can be understood as a plurality, and these works maximize the subjectivity of their interpretations by confounding summary (both within and without the text), the subjectivity of a text is thus measured by the elusiveness or absence of its subject.

One can more readily imagine a discussion of or essay on "the absence of Ulysses in *Ulysses*" than one on "the absence of Oliver Twist in *Oliver Twist*." By the same token, if one were to ask whether the title *Finnegans Wake* provides an accurate summary of what happens in that book, an honest reader would succumb to a series of equivocations and such fine semantic quibbles as to make Bill Clinton, who wondered what "is" is, seem forthright: "well, it depends on what you understand by *Finnegans*, and what you take *Wake* to mean. And I would need to know by what criteria an 'accurate summary' is adjudged. In fact, everything depends on what you mean by 'happens.'"[7] Joyce radically, persistently reminds us that when we talk about fiction, indeed when we enter into any literary discourse no matter the critical tenor or approach, we are quixotically discussing "that which is not" and when we attempt to summarize *Ulysses*, for example, we become inside-out historians, students of unreal

---

and is all the more himself since he is not so" (*FW* 507.01, 03–04). Like Tim Finnegan, Jesus Christ, and Schrödinger's cat, he is simultaneously dead and not dead (more on this specific question in a later essay in the volume), an "everybody" of contradictions who resists direct and conclusive signification.

[7] Fritz Senn likewise wonders about "that signifying copula 'is'" in "Dogmad or Dublioused?" (*Joyce's Dislocations: Essays on Reading as Translation*, ed. John Paul Riquelme (Baltimore, MD: Johns Hopkins University Press, 1984), 103). In surveying the long-standing problem of whether *Finnegans Wake* can be spoken of as having a narrative, Margot Norris in "Possible Worlds Theory and the Fantasy Universe of *Finnegans Wake*" suggests that "Possible worlds theory could abet a more rigorous analysis" of the book (*James Joyce Quarterly* 44.3 (2007): 471). While I agree that this route may offer some or even many useful vistas from which to view the *Wake*, I am reminded of Jorge Luis Borges's preference for H. G. Wells over Jules Verne because the latter wrote about "probable things" while the former deals in "mere possibilities, if not impossible things" ("The First Wells," in *Other Inquisitions, 1937–1952*, trans. Ruth L. C. Simms (Austin: University of Texas Press, 2000), 86). Here I am concerned not with the probabilities of what Joyce writes about but with what is (the range of the) impossible in his writing and how we might consider what he does *not* write about, if we can, in contradistinction to the often-noted problem of saying just what he does write about.

events, however vividly detailed they may be. In case we forget or, if you like, "suspend" this idea, we are reminded by the seemingly precise mechanism of this novel that there is no foundation for the details.[8]

I have remarked elsewhere on how strange it is to observe that so much of *Finnegans Wake* scholarship, even to date, amounts to descriptive guides and wobbly paraphrases.[9] Moreover, so much of Joyce's work depends upon what does not happen, what does not take place. Rudimentary but ever-tantalizing examples include what the queer old josser is "doing" in the field (*D* 26) and whether Alf Bergan, like Don Quixote, saw the ghost of Paddy Dignam, unaware of his having been buried earlier that day. Such ellipses and absences are not simply minor exceptions to an otherwise seamless or comprehensive totality. Rather, they point us to "the incertitude of the void," a phrase repeated in "Ithaca" (*U* 17.1014–15): Joyce's universe is not only "decentered," as Margot Norris was the first to point out, but, like the universe we live in, is mostly made of empty, negative space.[10] Molly Bloom's watchword is "yes," but that is simply how she herself proceeds energetically from the unknown to the known through the incertitude of the void: "the greatest earthly happiness" may be to answer "a gentlemans proposal affirmatively" but "my goodness theres nothing else" (*U* 18.744–45). Between the text and the events, the signification and the signified, and even between the words themselves yawns that same void—itself the starting point for *Finnegans Wake*: "In the buginning is the woid" (*FW* 378.29). Despite the

---

[8] A brief digression on "suspension": this metaphor has held a central position in theories of reading from Samuel Taylor Coleridge's well-worn phrase "suspension of disbelief" in *Biographia Literaria or Biographical Sketches of My Literary Life and Opinions* (in *The Collected Works of Samuel Taylor Coleridge*, ed. James Engell and W. Jackson Bate (Princeton: Princeton University Press, 1983), 312) to Roland Barthes's conception of the reader as a dangling man, "faisant couper la corde qui le pend, au moment où il jouit" in *Le plaisir du texte* (Paris: Éditions du Seuil, 1973), 15: "cutting the cord that suspends him at the moment at which he climaxes" (my translation). Of interest here is the significance of the void below the suspended reader: we who engage in protracted critical discourse about this void, the emptiness of fiction otherwise known as "that which is not," should have sympathy for the cartoon character Wile E. Coyote each time he dashes off a cliff and continues to move forward through the air until, and only until, he notices the absence of terra firm beneath his feet, at which point he unfailingly looks at us, the viewers of his catastrophe, with a look of stupefying grief, and then promptly plummets. Could it be that the measure of truly engaged literary criticism is how far the critic can run beyond the cliff's edge before acknowledging gravity?

[9] See Tim Conley, "'Oh Me None Onsens!': *Finnegans Wake* and the Negation of Meaning," *James Joyce Quarterly* 39.2 (2002): 233–49, as well as *Joyce's Mistakes: Problems of Intention, Irony, and Interpretation* (Toronto: University of Toronto Press, 2003), 17–19.

[10] See Margot Norris, *The Decentered Universe of "Finnegans Wake": A Structuralist Analysis* (Baltimore, MD: Johns Hopkins University Press, 1974).

"excess of signification" in the *Wake*, Sam Slote observes, "there remains a profound absence of a single unifying and over-riding meaning."[11]

"Disnarration," however handy a term for instances of variations within or between narratives or metanarratives, presupposes a (potential if not actual) "narration" that may be privileged for its truth-value (even if only degree) or some similar value (aesthetic, say, or political). Does Bergan's account of having seen Dignam "not five minutes ago [...] as plain as a pikestaff" (*U* 12.323–24) constitute a "disnarration" or just a delusion (and, as Bergan himself might ask, what's the difference?).[12] The more one considers the problem, the more puzzling it becomes: the only character who can support Bergan's claim is Willy Murray, himself a most elusive quantity. Not only does Willy Murray not appear anywhere else in the novel apart from this conversational mention in Barney Kiernan's, but the coincidence of his name's similarity with that of Joyce's own uncle, William Murray, thought to be the model for Richie Goulding, makes him seem as much a will o' the wisp as M'Intosh. Bob Doran's subsequent sobs for a hybrid "poor little Willy Dignam" (*U* 12.388–89) are perhaps not quite so ridiculous as they first appear to be. We do not have a precise antonym for summary (and "dissummary" is too clumsy to contemplate), but, interestingly, the *Oxford Thesaurus* suggests "detail" and "story" as options.[13] As usual, Joyce encourages or even necessitates a reexamination of critical terms, even (especially) those most likely to be taken for granted.

II

The word "summary" comes from the Latin *summus* or "highest": "when the Romans counted up the columns of figures they worked from the bottom upwards, and put the total on top—whence the use of the expression *rēs summa*, literally 'highest thing,' for 'total.'"[14] Summarizing is, by its very etymology, an imperialist gesture. It is an act of confinement of—despite the implied meaning of addition and accumulation—reduction. Also lurking in the word's history is the second meaning of Stephen Dedalus's "two masters," for the *summa* is the form of orthodox gloss made most famous by Thomas Aquinas in the thirteenth century (*U* 1.638); in the pages of his *Summa*

---

[11] Sam Slote, "Nulled Nought: The Desistance of Ulyssean Narrative in *Finnegans Wake*." *James Joyce Quarterly* 34.4 (1997): 534.
[12] This expression retains its morbid association in the *Wake*: "as plane as a poke stiff" (*FW* 296.29–30).
[13] See *The Oxford Thesaurus*, 2nd ed. (Oxford: Clarendon Press, 1997).
[14] John Ayto, *Dictionary of Word Origins* (New York: Arcade, 1990), 510.

Theologicæ, Aquinas wrestles with the questions of polysemy in scripture and rejects such potentially troublesome niceties as "ambiguity or any other kind of mixture of meanings."[15] Joyce, at one time an Aquinan disciple, contests the formation and reification of *doxa* and authorizes interpretations of *Ulysses* and the *Wake* by openly mixing meanings, having columns of figures fail to add up, and making summary a risible endeavor.[16] The word "summary" not only suggests that a text is tractable, consistent, and—by implication—worthy of study and ideologically sound, but it also effectively imposes those qualities.

Eloise Knowlton has called Joyce scholarship "a project of colonization, of taming a wilderness, of turning a 'jungle' into a 'map,'"[17] and summarizing Joyce seems to me the most aggressive and fruitless of colonial methods, a kind of scorched-earth approach. Consider, for instance, John Gordon's *"Finnegans Wake": A Plot Summary*. By its author's own admission "thoroughly reductive,"[18] Gordon's book begins with an emphasis on symbols that, despite the ambivalence that Joyce criticism had at that time begun to show toward such approaches to the *Wake*, seems to him of essential importance. Gordon compares this ambivalence to that legendary rejoinder, "sometimes a cigar is just a cigar," attributed to Sigmund Freud and customarily offered to anyone who fails to see a signifier as anything other than a means of signifying something else. For Gordon, the world of *Finnegans Wake* is "a world not of 'cigars'

---

[15] Thomas Aquinas, *Summa Theologicæ*, trans. Thomas Gilby (London: Eyre and Spottiswoode, 1964), 1:39.

[16] The *Wake*'s tale of the Gracehoper and the Ondt dramatizes the way that extremes meet: "the next time he makes the aquinatance of the Ondt after this they have met themselves, these moushical unsummables, it shall be motylucky if he will beheld not a world of differents" (*FW* 417.07–10). Ever the dogmatist and partisan, the Ondt is "a conformed aceticist and aristotaller" (*FW* 417.16): he can always be summarized and is himself nothing but categories and systems of organization. Against him, Joyce poses the Gracehoper, who "tossed himself in the vico" (*FW* 417.05–06), just as Joyce challenges the verticality and linearity of summary and Aquinas with the dizzying circularity of Giambattista Vico.

[17] Eloise Knowlton, *Joyce, Joyceans, and the Rhetoric of Citation* (Gainesville: University Press of Florida, 1998), 5. One of the central reasons why students of *Finnegans Wake* are so often frustrated by Roland McHugh's *Annotations to "Finnegans Wake"*—at least as often as we are indebted to it—is its sense of scale. McHugh operates on the assumption, implied by his book's form, that every page of the *Wake* can be annotated within its own spatial arrangement and, thus, that the meanings and interpretations of the *Wake* can be confined within the dimensions of the *Wake* itself. Note that this is entirely contrary to Sigmund Freud's point about condensation within dreams and the potentially infinite expansion that analysis may yield; see Freud, *The Interpretation of Dreams: The Standard Edition of the Complete Psychological Works of Sigmund Freud*, ed. James Strachey et al. (London: Hogarth Press, 1900), 4:383.

[18] John Gordon, *"Finnegans Wake": A Plot Summary* (Dublin: Gill and Macmillan, 1986), 1.

but of this or that cigar."¹⁹ Gordon's *Wake* is a plot-driven novel, with as exact a setting as *Ulysses* (Chapelizod on Monday, March 21, 1938); the strangeness of its form and its linguistic aberrancy are presumably not part of this singular "plot," since they are not discussed.

By "this or that cigar," Gordon means that Joyce "generates, as opposed to receives" meanings, but this distinction is itself the kind of false binary that the *Wake* (and even, to a lesser extent, *Ulysses*) rejects.²⁰ Bloom's "knockmedown cigar" in the "Cyclops" episode is not, for the reader, just a cigar (*U* 12.502): the book's "mythological method" invites us to see the cigar as a spear capable of blinding a giant.²¹ Has the reader generated this meaning or received it? Reading is surely an inextricably dialectical process of reception *and* generation, in which each word's associations react in relation to those of every other word. Summary, by contrast, requires a detachment from the text and represents a forceful compression, a violence like that voiced by Malvolio when he desires to "crush" words to his will in *Twelfth Night*.²² Reading allows for freer associations than summary can and even permits uncertainty—everything a cigar might be and, in *Finnegans Wake*'s scheme of marrying opposites, all that it might not. Summary is addressed to the non-reader and seeks to replace reading—close, but not cigar.

It is worth considering Freud's principle of condensation here, particularly since the earliest and many subsequent attempts to summarize the *Wake* characterize it as a dream narrative, as though this gesture were a diagnosis that rationally establishes the interpretive procedures required.²³ Yet psychoanalytic critique itself faces a categorical impasse in this case, because it cannot isolate a unified subject from its interpretation. In reaction to the discourse of psychoanalysts, the most oneiric works of modern art—which is to say, those most formally committed to dreamlike states of being—are themselves

---

[19] Gordon, *"Finnegans Wake": A Plot Summary*, 2–3.

[20] Gordon, *"Finnegans Wake": A Plot Summary*, 3. This distinction is also inconsistent with all that we now understand about how Joyce wrote—or compiled—the *Wake*, as discussed in later essays in this book.

[21] See Hugh Kenner, *Joyce's Voices* (Berkeley: University of California Press, 1978), xii.

[22] William Shakespeare, *Twelfth Night, or What You Will*, in *The Norton Shakespeare*, 2nd ed., ed. Stephen Greenblatt et al. (New York: Norton, 2008), 1793–846.

[23] John Bishop, himself a proponent of this line of attack, remarked over thirty years ago that "one of many reasons why Joyce's repeated claims about *Finnegans Wake* have seemed so improbable for so long is that people have customarily treated the book, at Joyce's invitation, as the 'representation of a dream' —doing so, however, as though dreams took place only in theory, and without concretely engaging the very strange and obscure question of what a dream is" (*Joyce's Book of the Dark: "Finnegans Wake"* (Madison: University of Wisconsin Press, 1986), 6).

analyses of dreams, reworkings, and remediations more or less in progress. Dreams, in Freud's memorable phrase, are "brief, meagre and laconic,"[24] but none of these adjectives applies to *Finnegans Wake*. Freud writes, "If a dream is written out it may perhaps fill half a page. The analysis setting out the dream-thoughts underlying it may occupy six, eight or a dozen times such space."[25] Seldom scrutinized, the supposition behind this uneven ratio of dream content to (external, post facto) analysis betrays the fact that Freudian *Traumbedeutung* is a contradiction in terms, since it is the dream that is "written out," the pleasantly compact summary, that is analyzed, and not the dream itself. Slavoj Žižek observes how, in Freud's view, "the meaning of a dream [...] [is] to be sought in some detail unconnected with its totality (interpretation *en détail* versus the hermeneutic interpretation *en masse*)."[26] The totality, like the emotion that the dreamer experiences, is for Freud chimerical and misleading.

Ulysses seems a less obvious problem for psychoanalysis but only if the expanding divide between depiction and event or between perception and fact can be ascribed to the workings of a specific consciousness. The popular wisdom that the novel is written in a stream of consciousness or as an interior monologue handily warrants this necessary predication of a psychological subject but similarly requires passing over in silence all of the various narrative loopholes, inconsistencies, and questions about whether and why each word and structural turn can be ascribed to a recognizable, represented source: for example, who or what subject decides when to swing from one conversation in the cemetery to another; which headline is to be used before the event it serves in "Aeolus"; or, for that matter, what title should be given to the novel itself.[27] It is effectively misleading to claim, in the way that back-cover copy or a crammer's guide might, that "*Ulysses* presents Dublin as seen by Leopold Bloom," but, if rather less snappy, it is perhaps slightly more accurate to suggest that "*Ulysses* presents certain ways of seeing the ways that Dublin is perhaps seen by Leopold Bloom." That these formulae, no matter how qualified and precise, fail to convey anything tangible, let alone summarize the novel, is demonstrated by the fact that no one ever says of *Hamlet* (for example)

---

[24] Freud, *The Interpretation of Dreams*, 4:383.
[25] Freud, *The Interpretation of Dreams*, 4:383.
[26] Slavoj Žižek, *The Parallax View* (Cambridge: Massachusetts Institute of Technology Press, 2006), 229.
[27] Both the appealing thought-games about the effects of this or that further turn of the narrative screw (what would Molly Bloom have titled *Ulysses*, or what if the reader glimpsed one of those "interpolations" of the "Wandering Rocks" episode in, say, the "Sirens" episode?) and the insouciance with which both film versions of *Ulysses* not only omit details and change perspectives but cut entire episodes point to how perversely difficult it is to change the overall shape of the novel.

that "it presents Denmark as it is seen by Prince Hamlet," though, of course, one could justly say just that.

To make a summary and to psychoanalyze both require a plausible, finite subject. The joke about the psychiatrist who charges for each of the schizophrenic's multiple personalities highlights this limitation.[28] It has to be exactly "this cigar," not "this or that cigar" (like "the sum," rather than the more ambiguous "a sum"), for the same reason that the psychiatrist needs to know to whom the bills are to be sent. If Joyce's predilection for the multiplication of manifestation of selves (psychomachia) complicates analysis by overcrowding the couch, his equal (and often, especially in the *Wake*, simultaneous) fondness for enantiodromia, the collapsing together of opposites, prevents any of these manifestations from being apprehended in isolation, or even in distinction from any of the others. That is, it is not merely that there are too many analysands in the office for the analyst to give them attention but, effectively, no analysand at all, only the untenable plurality of decentralized symptoms.[29]

III

It is disarming to observe that the words "summary" and "summarize" do not appear—or do not appear as such, one feels compelled to qualify—anywhere in either *Ulysses* or *Finnegans Wake*. This is notable because we sense the depth and scale of these works, have measured or at least approximated their vast lexical armory, and have come to expect anything and perhaps everything in their pages.[30] There are a few telling instances where we come close to this word in these texts, and I will examine some of these illustrative "near-misses" in *Ulysses*.

Perhaps the first such instance is the title of young Cyril Sargent's copybook, "*Sums*" (*U* 2.128). Stephen Dedalus watches the boy struggle with this subject—one that Joyce himself was never particularly good at (a point to which I will return in a later essay) and even in *Ulysses* there is frequent trouble

---

[28] There are currents in contemporary philosophy (particularly and most intriguingly cognitive philosophy) indicating that the very phenomenon of the "self" is a neural illusion. See, for example, Thomas Metzinger's *The Ego Tunnel: The Science of the Mind and the Myth of the Self* (New York: Basic Books, 2009).

[29] The insinuation I am risking here is this: psychoanalytical approaches to *Finnegans Wake* are bound to be psychoanalytical approaches to a reader (real or imagined) of the *Wake*. Thus the *Wake*'s seemingly defensive cry, "I can psoakonaloose myself any time I want" (*FW* 522.34–35) is truly something of a booby-trap.

[30] It is a more unusual absence than, say, that of orangutans in Anne Bradstreet's poems and thus more potentially worthwhile to investigate.

with the correct addition of numbers—and, ever the solipsist, compares himself to the boy:

> Like him was I, these sloping shoulders, this gracelessness. My childhood bends beside me. Too far to lay a hand there once or lightly. Mine is far and his secret as our eyes. Secrets, silent, stony sit in the dark palaces of both our hearts: secrets weary of their tyranny: tyrants willing to be dethroned.
>   The sum was done. (*U* 2.168–73)

The matter of Stephen's contemplation has won much critical attention; the terse, stand-alone sentence that cuts it short has not. Viewed in isolation, this last sentence is, admittedly, not terribly interesting, but its context is part of a larger pattern. Note that the plain syntax, monosyllabic words, and decisive tone of the subsequent sentence are entirely at odds with Stephen's style of interior monologue, almost as though it stands as a reply, even a kind of rebuke. Stephen's thoughts of the physical and perhaps spiritual "gracelessness" are redolent of the sentimentalism that Robert Scholes, echoing Clive Hart, argues is an important part of Joyce's narratives, Stephen's arch, Miltonic syntax notwithstanding.[31] These secrets are the heart's captive tyrants, "willing to be dethroned," the individual's counterpoint to the "gratefully oppressed" masses (*D* 42). Repeatedly in the novel, Stephen's alleged freethinking perversely leads him to captivity and incarceration.

The phrase "[t]he sum was done" is also occlusive. Although Sargent has presumably worked out this problem for himself, in imitation of Stephen's example, the use of passive voice here nonetheless raises doubts and makes the action seem miraculously performed without agency; nor does Joyce reveal what the sum itself is. The glimpsed "sloping figures" (corresponding with the "sloping shoulders") are of no greater help (*U* 2.129), since the phrase both conceals the particular numbers and prompts the reader to think of another meaning for "figures"; by the time "the symbols moves in grave morrice" and become "unsteady" (*U* 2.155, 164), the reader is more confused by these animated abstractions of the subject than young Sargent when he began. Whereas Stephen's "hard" riddle about the fox and his grandmother is presented fully and directly, with question and answer—though the connective logic between them remains to be seen—the "very simple" problems of arithmetic, the methods applied to them, and their solution are pointedly never brought into focus (*U* 2.100, 174).

---

[31] Robert Scholes gave a keynote address entitled "Sentimental Jimmy" at the Joyce conference at the University of Tulsa in June 2003; he then wrote an introductory note, "Introduction to James Joyce's Sentimentality" (*James Joyce Quarterly* 41.1 (2003–4): 25–26), to Clive Hart's "James Joyce's Sentimentality" published in the same issue (26–36).

Compare this scene with a moment from "Scylla and Charybdis." Near the end of Stephen's algebraic argument, he focuses on "the note of banishment" that appears "in infinite variety everywhere" in William Shakespeare's plays (*U* 9.999, 1012). Once again, Joyce ends Stephen's monologue with a four-word sentence: "Judge Eglinton summed up" comes right after "[h]e laughed to free his mind from his mind's bondage" (*U* 9.1016–17). Here also, the act of making a sum is directly connected to bondage, those mind-forged manacles Stephen cannot quite escape. In this instance the word "sum" has a legal connotation, and John Eglinton has farcically become a judge (a precursor to the trial fantasy of "Circe"): there is a grim finality to "summed up" that is diametrically opposed to the Bloomian, convivial, and circumlocutional phrase "[p]reparatory to anything else" (*U* 16.01).[32] Eglinton pronounces judgement in the case at issue: Shakespeare is "all in all" (*U* 9.1018–19), a purloined phrase that is, depending on your point of view, either deep with Shakespearean significance or the kind of shallow cliché one expects to hear at board meetings and read in annual reviews—smug rhetorical invocations of "the big picture."

Yet there is no "all" to speak of in *Ulysses*, except as an abstraction. Right after Mrs. Purefoy has safely delivered her child, the chronicler of "Oxen of the Sun" muses on the portents: "In sum an infinite great fall of rain and all refreshed" (*U* 14.521–22). Joyce counters the word "sum" with "infinite"—a glaring mathematical contradiction—in the same manner that he empties Eglinton's summing up of any definite value or meaning with the infinite tautology, "all in all."[33] Again, the preceding image is one of captivity: while Mrs. Purefoy is made to spawn seasonally, her husband and sons net fish further downstream: "catches a fine bag, I hear" (*U* 14.521). The portrayals of childbirth and the Purefoys' marriage, in particular, are of as grimly cyclical a routine as any in Joyce.

In each of these instances, the act of making a sum or summary judgement (confining and reducing constitutive elements of experience) is ironically controverted by affirmations of freedom and infinitude. This pattern outlines a daunting realization about the act of interpretation that comes upon Bloom in "Ithaca":

What qualifying considerations allayed his perturbations?

---

[32] We may think here of the "laconic" interpreter described in Joyce's 1907 essay "Ireland at the Bar," who summarizes all of the accused man's anguished protestations and explanations as "no, 'your worship'" (*OCPW* 145–47).

[33] *Finnegans Wake* delights in this habit: the cheerfully heretical phrase "thank God, they were all summarily divorced" (*FW* 390.18–19), for example, resounds the theme of bondage and liberation.

> The difficulties of interpretation since the significance of any event followed its occurrence as variably as the acoustic report followed by the electrical discharge and of counterestimating against an actual loss by failure to interpret the total sum of possible losses proceeding originally from a successful interpretation. (*U* 17.342–47)

The meaning of the phrase "the total sum of possible losses" is remarkably hard to grasp (as is, to a lesser extent, "[t]o have sustained no positive loss" (*U* 17.352)), and one wonders how one can but fail to interpret it. Bloom's reflections on his day have much to do with loss, both positive loss and possible losses, if there is a tangible distinction between the two. These operations are more complex than rote addition, for *Ulysses* ultimately suggests that human beings are more than the sum of their experiences or even of their conscious thoughts. They are unquantifiable—impossible to "sum up" or comprehend "all in all."

IV

In a number of his essays, Hermann Broch suggests that Joyce is one of the few modern artists who achieves "an immediate grasp of the world totality," which is, in Broch's view, the goal for "a genuine work of art."[34] Broch, who fled the Nazis with Joyce's help, does not equate "Totalität" (totality) with "totalitarian" the way Theodor W. Adorno does,[35] though he expresses some concern about Joyce's approach at the end of "Joyce and the Present Age":

> the nearer he comes to the goal of a totality in which he does not believe, the narrower and more restricted becomes the net of symbols and associations in whose multiplicity all existence is to be imprisoned; and the more fundamentally the work of art undertakes the task of totality, without believing in it, the more threatening the peril of the infinite becomes […][36]

---

[34] See Hermann Broch, "Hugo von Hofmannsthal and His Time: Art and Its Non-Style at the End of the Twentieth Century," in *Geist and Zeitgeist: The Spirit in an Unspiritual Age*, trans. Michael P. Steinberg, ed. John Hargreaves (New York: Counterpoint, 2002), 170.

[35] Adorno's extended argument with "totality" may be observed in many of his works but is arguably most trenchant in *Negative Dialectics*, trans. E. B. Ashton (New York: Continuum Books, 1973).

[36] Hermann Broch, "Joyce and the Present Age," in *Geist and Zeitgeist: The Spirit in an Unspiritual Age*, trans. Maria Jolas, ed. John Hargreaves (New York: Counterpoint, 2002), 94.

Broch's anxiety seems abstract, but the abstraction *is* the anxiety. Peering into "Anna Livia Plurabelle" and finding it "indescribably beautiful," Broch is worried that Joyce is becoming virtually ineffable, presenting a universe rich in uncertain meanings "in which he does not believe."[37] Joyce's "net of symbols and associations" is, like all nets, "only holes tied together" (*FW* 434.22).

The same point is a concern, though for almost precisely opposite reasons, for Fredric Jameson, who says of *Ulysses*, "if there was ever an attempt to mold an image of social totality, it was that."[38] Jameson understands the novel to be a failed image, however: an exemplary instance of a trend in modernism's unresolvable "crisis in the possibility of representing a social totality."[39] While this flat supposition of breakdown between intention and act seems a little like reading *Hamlet* as a comedy that Shakespeare did not quite pull off, the pressing problem here is to consider whether "totality" signifies a product or a process. Both Broch and Jameson conceptualize totality as a "goal," but *Ulysses* expressly and repeatedly doubts such concepts:

> —The ways of the Creator are not our ways, Mr Deasy said. All human history moves towards one great goal, the manifestation of God.
> Stephen jerked his thumb towards the window, saying:
> —That is God.
> Hooray! Ay! Whrrwhee!
> —What? Mr Deasy asked.
> —A shout in the street, Stephen answered, shrugging his shoulders. (*U* 2.380–86)

Raphael's famous depiction of Plato arguing with Aristotle is recast in this scene, with Mr. Deasy pointing heavenward and Stephen to the earthly scene at hand, as Stephen takes Mr. Deasy at his word: if God is a goal, he is no more momentary than a hockey goal, one of a continuous series. Rather than representing a "manifestation," *Ulysses* manifests: both it and *Finnegans Wake* multiply potentialities, understanding the notion of the infinite as neither a "peril" nor as a realizable "goal," but simply as a given fact of the universe, the last plausible line of young Stephen's address (*P* 253).

It is worth noting, finally, that "totality" is also frustrated by Joyce's peculiarly complicated textual production and history. Fritz Senn has pointed out that long after Joyce's canonization has been repeatedly reenacted and

---

[37] Broch, "Joyce and the Present Age," 82, 94.
[38] Fredric Jameson, *Jameson on Jameson: Conversations on Cultural Marxism*, ed. Ian Buchanan (Durham, NC: Duke University Press, 2007), 84.
[39] Jameson, *Jameson on Jameson*, 142.

reconfirmed, "we do not have what would be a matter of course for most authors—a complete, uniform, well-edited edition of Joyce's complete works."[40] Certainly the unholy legal whirlwind of the Joyce estate still has its chilling effects, even as copyrights have gradually been falling by the wayside, and putting "well-edited" and "Joyce" together has been known to start academic wars and overthrow noble minds. I wonder, however, whether this state of affairs does not reflect a more fundamental quality of our readings of Joyce. We do not see or conceive of him as a whole; nor, I submit, do we critically respond to him wholly. Some years ago, I heard John Bishop say, during a conference's lunchtime *Finnegans Wake* reading group, that the passage we were then reading was a "key passage" in the book—although, he added in the same sentence and to my relief and admiration, "as they all are": *every* passage is a key passage in the *Wake*. The *Wake* cannot be cogently discussed or represented as the sum of its parts because the parts themselves *are* the whole; the book is everywhere divisible.

Our situation in trying to "sum up" Joyce is, I think, best dramatized by Monty Python's "All-England Summarize Proust Competition." In this parody of a gameshow, the host (who persistently squawks the name as "Prowst") explains that "each contestant has to give a brief summary of 'A La Recherche de Temps Perdue,' once in a swimsuit and once in evening dress."[41] A "Proustometer" displays the progress (or its lack) of each of the competition's three very different finalists through the seven volumes of the novel. Naturally, none of the contestants makes any real headway in the mere 15 seconds allotted them, but it is the variety of their approaches and failures that make the sketch a cautionary tale for the literary critic. The first finalist hurriedly tells of "the forfeiture of innocence through experience" and "the reinstatement of extra-temporal values of time regained" before the gong cuts him off and the host summarizes the summary: "A good attempt there but unfortunately he chose a general appraisal of the work, before getting on to the story [...] A good try though and very nice posture."[42] The second contestant eagerly but nervously stammers out half-descriptions of a setting. (Although he is pushed aside by the host, his rating on the Proustometer is noticeably higher than the previous contestant's.) Finally, a choir of firefighters opens a contrapuntal madrigal with the phrase "Proust in his first book wrote about, wrote about, wrote about..." but get no further.[43] None of the contestants

---

[40] Fritz Senn, letter to the editor, *James Joyce Quarterly* 41.1/2 (Fall 2003–Winter 2004): 325-26.

[41] *Monty Python's Flying Circus: Just the Words* (London: Methuen Press, 1989), 2:105.

[42] *Monty Python's Flying Circus: Just the Words* 2:106.

[43] *Monty Python's Flying Circus: Just the Words* 2:107.

wins, but the Proustometer conspicuously reaches its highest level by far with the choir.

Approaches to summarizing Joyce could generally be grouped into the three kinds represented by these poor contestants: thematic overtures, plot and/or character sketches, and what might be called a chorus of hapless deconstruction. Jacques Derrida's arresting idea that *"il n'y a pas d'hors-texte"*—"there is nothing outside of the text" or "there is no outside-text"[44]—is itself perverted by Joyce's "holey" writ: the discontinuities of *Ulysses* and the gaps in the *Wake* suggest that there is nothing inside the text either. Caught between "the peril of the infinite" and "the incertitude upon the void," we may find that my former student's strategy—to concentrate on what is not, or seems not, to be in Joyce's texts—is very possibly the best one. Though many critical histories (such as Jameson's) would have us see modernist writers like Joyce constructing totalizing narratives (which we can then, cushioned with the comfort of retrospect, find either incomplete or overbearing), the reverse may be true: Joyce represents "the total sum of possible losses" in what his works do not do, do not represent, do not include, and do not even summarize. And it is this Joyce, the incomplete and uncollected Joyce, who liberates us, as partial readers of parts, similarly to fly past the nets of summaries and totalizing readings.

To sum up: *James Joyce did not write about, write about, write about …*
(*Gong.*)

---

[44] Jacques Derrida, *Of Grammatology*, trans. Gayatri Chakravorty Spivak (Baltimore, MD: Johns Hopkins University Press, 1967), 158.

Chapter 3

COMPOSITIONAL

Playing with Matches: The *Wake* Notebooks and Negative Correspondence

I

If there is a more disorienting kind of reading than one encounters with *Finnegans Wake*, it is found in Joyce's *Wake* notebooks, and the differences between these two forms of reading are worth investigating. To the much-asked and much-fumbled question of how we read *Finnegans Wake*, Finn Fordham has outlined seven different interpretive approaches to the book: Structural, Narrational, Theoretical, Inspirational, Philological, Genetic, and Exegetical.[1] As helpful as these (sometimes porous) categorizations are, these are distant evaluations, perceived by standing back from the text. In other words, they are "macro" views of reading, implicitly predicated on the text's being a functional object (a book, literary in character, perhaps a novel) rather than, say, an indeterminate thing (some sort of "writing") or even a kind of cognitive environment, while what I am asking about here is the "micro" view, the immediate predicament of a reader faced with an unusual and often bewildering form of writing. The difference is between seeing the forest and seeing the trees. Let us, for the duration of this discussion, insofar as it is possible, be arborists rather than forest inspectors.[2]

On this "micro" level, *Finnegans Wake* requires its reader to suspend if not abandon recognition as a reliable operating principle. A more or (often) less familiar sequence of letters or sounds will provoke a reaction of "almost— but not quite," and after a while, as Clive Hart has remarked, "the mind's ear takes part-writing for granted, the mind's eye is fixed in a permanent state of multiple vision."[3] Positive identification (X = Y) is supplanted by

---

[1] Finn Fordham, *Lots of Fun at Finnegans Wake: Unravelling Universals* (Oxford: Oxford University Press, 2007), 7–33.
[2] For the unanswerable insult "Crrritic!" the German translation of Beckett's *Godot* uses "Oberforestinspektor!"
[3] Clive Hart, *Structure and Motif in "Finnegans Wake"* (Evanston, IL: Northwestern University Press, 1962), 34.

negative correspondence (X ≠ Y, but X is *not altogether unlike* Y). A sentence found in some other book, a sentence such as "Napoleon was imprisoned on the island of St. Helena until his death," causes a reader to directly associate each word with some workable definition within a field or cluster of personal associations with that word ("Napoleon" might well be the painted profile of the Emperor for one reader, or a Bugs Bunny character to another, while "imprisoned" may require more imagination than memory for anyone who has never been incarcerated, and so on). A *Wake* sentence, by contrast, frustrates our internal search engines (asked for "Harlyadrope" (*FW* 89.19), Google initially balks: "Did you mean: *halyard rope?*"), for the terms of the *Wake* are of a perpetual difference: never quite this, and yet not altogether not that, either. Take this apposite sentence from III.3, the vocabulary of which is not nearly so bizarre as much elsewhere: "What can't be coded can't be decorded if an ear aye sieze what no eye ere grieved for" (482.34–36). One can hear tangled together a homily ("what the eye can't see the heart can't grieve for" (see *U* 15.1998)), and song lyrics ("What can't be cured, sure, / Must be endured, sure" (see *P* 74)), but in fact the *Wake* line is neither: again, almost—but not quite. The most positive (and positivist) identification claim for these resemblances as allusions or sources is akin to identifying this or that ingredient in a stew. And a stew is by definition a composition, a process, and not simply a combination of ingredients.

Genetic inquiries do not dispel or obviate the problem of negative correspondence; rather, probing the history of notes, drafts, and revisions repeatedly illustrates how capricious is context, how elusive are origins, and how much more rather than less complex and poorly understood are an author's (and perhaps especially Joyce's) imaginative processes. Attempting to establish the history of the text in the finest detail proves to be strikingly like that of reading the *Wake* itself: an alternately thrilling and maddening kind of archaeology, a matter of building unseen and unheard-of dinosaurs or lost cities out of mismatched fragments of which—each time the would-be archaeologist completes the assembly of a plausible model of meaning or origin—there are always too many left over. Textual genetics, for better and worse, helps us locate and index more of these fragments of an imaginable whole. As Jerome McGann has shrewdly argued, "[t]he ideal interpreting agent can know the presence of the whole but never the sum of the parts."[4]

And this brings us to the notebooks, and the question of how independently they can be read, each from the other or indeed any from the *Wake* itself. So far as I know, no one has yet ventured a claim for any given *Wake* notebook as

---

[4] Jerome McGann, *A New Republic of Letters: Memory and Scholarship in the Age of Digital Reproduction* (Cambridge, MA: Harvard University Press, 2014), 78.

a literary work in its own right, as has been done for Joyce's early collection of "epiphanies" or the notebook known as *Giacomo Joyce*.[5] This is perhaps a missed opportunity, if only because reading these texts in this novel way might instructively challenge persistent assumptions about authorial intentions and their stability. The microscope of genetic studies shows that the author's creative process is no singular organism but composed of a host of processes in interaction.[6]

Stridently averse to any notion that any textual error or inconsistency is anything but diametrically opposed to Joyce's intentions, Danis Rose contends that the *Wake* notebooks are not "part of the draft record": "They [the notebooks] belong to a purely compilational phase of the work in progress antecedent to the act of composition. To put it another way, the words were not Joyce's until they left the notebook page."[7] This distinction between "compilation" and "composition," made all the more spurious with the emphasis of "purely," is at least partly the result of a narrowly teleological reading of the range of *Wake* documents solely and exclusively as a unified "draft record." Against it we might invoke Blanchot's consideration of when writing begins: "to write, one has to write already."[8] More precisely (or less enigmatically), we might say that any given history begins where its historian decides, and for this reason alone readers and critics ought to be wary of zealous attempts to cement a starting point.[9]

---

[5] Although the "Scribbledehobble" notebook is exceptional for having an affectionate nickname, there has been no case made for its being anything other than a satellite text to the *Wake*. The other possible exception is the alleged ur-*Wake* text, *Finn's Hotel*, as discerned (and long insisted upon) by Danis Rose, but this is an instance not of reading a given notebook as a narrative in itself, but of signs and constituent parts of another narrative. For a diverting computational analysis of Rose's claims, see James O'Sullivan, "*Finn's Hotel* and the Joyce Canon," *Genetic Joyce Studies* 14 (Spring 2014).

[6] The plurality and variety of these processes are crucial, and a monolithic or linear hermeneutics that reifies *a* process ought to be avoided. In "Joyce and the Case for Genetic Criticism," Jed Deppman calls for a critical approach that is "less a practice of geology or archeology subservient to authorship and more a form of open-ended comparative inquiry [...] less about information and more about dynamic, catalytic processes [...] the narratology of contemporary genetics, is worth more attention than it has received" (*Genetic Joyce Studies* 6 (2006)).

[7] Danis Rose, *The Textual Diaries of James Joyce* (Dublin: Lilliput Press, 1995), 180.

[8] Maurice Blanchot, *The Space of Literature*, trans. Ann Smock (Lincoln: University of Nebraska Press, 1989), 176.

[9] So too Rose's distinction between words that are "Joyce's" and those that are "not Joyce's" is neither tenable nor useful when it comes to the *Wake*, by its own admission "the last word in stolentelling" (*FW* 424.35), and its relationship to its "sources" (textual or otherwise). I have elsewhere discussed at greater length the book's "multiple" authorship: see *Joyce's Mistakes: Problems of Intention, Irony, and Interpretation*, 40–58.

It may be that "cloisterphobia" (VI.B.4.4.184), "any fille in a fog" (VI.B.4.4.196), and "To-thank amen" (VI.B.4.4.206) are "not Joyce's" words, as Rose has it, but I suspect that this will be rather difficult to prove. Positing the notebooks as raw material to the magic cookery of drafts underestimates both Joyce and the notebooks. In the same (untranscribed and unpublished) notebook from which the three items I have just quoted come, and which notebook I'd like to retain as focus for the remainder of this discussion, we find a number of early as well as fully-fledged Wakean puns. "Missisliffi" (VI.B.4.4.209), for example, is ready to jump into this typescript emendation: "and she was stout and struck on dancing and her muddied name was Missisliffi" (*JJA* 47:199 (Yale 9.1–15); see *FW* 159.11–13). Joyce put "austereways" and "wasterways" (VI.B.4.4.320) together and inserted into a page proof the phrase "austereways or wasterways, in roaming" (*JJA* 47:202 (Yale 9.2–3); see *FW* 153.22–23), bisecting the more direct punning path "Allrouts run through Room" (almost "all roads lead to Rome"—but not quite). And it is hard to imagine a source other than Joyce himself for "the fetter, the summe, and the haul it cost" (VI.B.4.4.337; *JJA* 47:212 (Yale 9.3–3); see *FW* 153.31–32). The notebooks sometimes blur plausible distinctions between origin and response, a point to which I'll return.

II

Notebook VI.B.4 in many ways represents a fascinating period in the history of the *Wake*'s evolution. Joyce filled it in the first four months of 1929, close to a midpoint in the process as a whole and by which time the method and madness of that process—the polylinguistic hybridity of the text, the author's habit of collecting all sorts of bric-a-brac from various and often unexpected sources—were well established. This was also the time in which the French translation of *Ulysses* appeared (February), a German translation of *Anna Livia Plurabelle* had begun (though it would take a long time to complete), and *Our Exagmination* was falling into place (e.g., Vladimir Dixon's letter of complaint to "Mister Germ's Choice"—which Ellmann wrongly supposed was "obviously composed if not written by Joyce himself but never acknowledged by him"—is dated February 9, 1929 (*Letters III* 187–88)): it was published in late May, by which time Joyce was already conceiving of a follow-up volume. Apart from eye troubles and family matters, Joyce was most occupied with *Tales Told of Shem and Shaun* for its publication by Black Sun Press that summer, and after some delay ("I believe something went wrong in the factory" (*Letters I* 286)) Joyce's recording of an excerpt from *Anna Livia Plurabelle* eventually appeared. Thus, when Joyce was scribbling in VI.B.4, the promotional campaign for "Work in Progress" was in full swing—Joyce's letters to Weaver during this period are full of notices and plans on this score—and effectively became inseparable from the composition of the book itself.[10]

Joyce was not exactly kidding when he wrote, on a postcard of April 26, 1929, to Harriet Shaw Weaver: "You will scarcely recognise my fables now" (*Letters III* 189). "At some point," writes David Hayman, Joyce's "enthusiasm" for additions and revisions "took over and the changes ballooned. The prime example of this is the material [...] that eventually filled fifteen extra sheets [...] enormously swelling his question 1 (Finn MacCool)" of the quiz that is I.6.[11]

> Since there are no rough versions of some of the typed additions, we may assume that Joyce was composing as he dictated. That the holographs surround the typescript suggests that he became impatient with the typing process or decided to proceed with his revision in the typist's absence, sometimes with the help of an amanuensis. The process must have been a complicated one. The results are unlike anything found elsewhere in the *Wake* archive. (xv)[12]

One example of a typed revision without extant "rough versions" has its first appearance in VI.B.4: the memorable *Portrait*-parody opening of "The Mookse of the Gripes"—"Eins within a space and a wearywide space it wast" (*FW* 152.18–19) was once upon a time "Somes amid a space + a very whit [?] space it was" (VI.B.4.4.250). Somewhere along the way, perhaps the undocumented way, it changed (I will say more about this in the next essay in this book). The notebooks are not the drafts, the drafts are not the proofs, the proofs are not the *Wake*. Again, as McGann says, even if we might know "the presence of the whole," we can never know "the sum of the parts."

There are few letters in the published record from the period of VI.B.4, perhaps because Joyce was so concentrated on his work—and by extension, perhaps because in a sense that work then effectively supplanted the writing of letters by fulfilling that particular writerly need. We might read VI.B.4 as

---

[10] Previously I have written that *Our Exagmination*, "like the notebooks [...] is part of a conceptual meta-text rather than just a complementary or satellite para-text" ("Introduction," *Joyce's Disciples Disciplined: A Re-Exagmination of the 'Exagmination' of 'Work in Progress'"* (Dublin: University College Dublin Press, 2010), xvii).

[11] An earlier version of I.7 appeared in *transition* 6 (August 1927).

[12] David Hayman, "Preface," *JJA* 47, vii–xxi. Ellmann notes that a January 26, 1929, letter to Stanislaus was "probably typed by Joyce, who was learning to use a typewriter" (*Letters III* 186n3), so we might entertain the notion that Joyce's becoming "impatient with the typing process" is not unconnected with this education, or even (tricky though it may be to imagine!) that Joyce may have attempted some of the typing himself.

itself a kind of letter to himself (or "himself"), a way of communicating with (and feeding) "Work in Progress," itself a letter (or "litter") that answers by appropriating, echoing, and distorting what the notebook has offered. That is, the notebook is a participant in a conversation (or correspondence), and we can compare the responses found in other *Wake* documents, including but not limited to and not even necessarily centralizing or privileging the published *Wake* itself, and sometimes deduce or guess as to what the notebook is repeating or responding to. This way of reading the notebook also reminds us that (1) not every element of a conversation functions as a response to a specific utterance, (2) not every element of a conversation provokes a definite response, and (3) the possibility of error, or of the absence of an ascertainable reason for omissions and oversights in transmission, cannot be altogether dispelled.

Indeed, the entire compositional network of "Work in Progress" can be envisioned and understood as a postal system (much like the way that the *Wake* can be read as a garbled transmission about misdirected mail). As in all postal systems, many messages are unanswered (the puzzling ratio of uncrossed-out items in notebooks to crossed-out ones) or mislaid (e.g., corrections to one stage of proofs for one publication are not in turn conveyed to a subsequent typescript). And postal systems do not cease (there is no "Mission Accomplished"): every letter crosses paths with another.

III

Even more than reading the *Wake* itself, reading the *Wake* notebooks can feel like a process of reconstruction and remembering ("where have I heard that—or something quite like that, but not—before?").[13] The words, some recognizable and others not, flash out at us without definite contexts, and we try to connect one with another. At length what begins as groping in darkness becomes something akin to a "memory match" game, in which the more cards are revealed, the more matches are made. The key difference, however, is that obtaining exact "matches" is not the task, however satisfying it is to locate a convincing source for a notebook entry in some other work. By entering a word, phrase, or passage into a notebook, Joyce changes it, makes it a part of something different from whence he found it. Subsequent drafts and emendations are again further alchemical transformations, misrememberings and mismatchings.

---

[13] Besides their own, it is Joyce's memory that readers (and especially genetic readers) are reconstructing, so in a sense the *Wake* is an effort at resurrection.

VI.B.4 includes, as R. J. Schork's discussion of the notebook observes,[14] various names of popes and points on papal ascension, to be added to the seals of the magisterial Mookse's office; but it also contains lists of insect names and entomological terms from various languages (such as "tchela = bee" (VI.B.4.4.315), later metamorphosed to "ptchelasys" in "The Ondt and the Gracehoper" (*FW* 417.23), the breezy catchphrases of financiers (such as "my capital is safe" (VI.B.4.4.211) and "earn while you learn" (VI.B.4.4.185)), and deities and phrases pulled from E. A. Wallis Budge's 1895 translation of *The Egyptian Book of the Dead* (such as "god at the top of staircase" (VI.B.4.170): see *JJA* 47: 267; *FW* 131.17). Here too is a pronounced interest in mathematics: equations, geometric diagrams (including a faintly sketched equilateral triangle being born between two circles sharing one radius length (VI.B.4.4.306, and of course *FW* 293)), borrowings from Euclid.[15] (In Joyce's next notebook, VI.B.27, the fascination with insect names and mathematics continues.) And a very particular point of astronomy briefly comes into focus (VI.B.4.4.292 and 293):

Saturn
30 years   [crossed out in red]
lithium   [crossed out in red]
1/8 dense E

And on the next page:

snowball
gasometer   [crossed out in red]
albedo   [crossed out in blue]

"30 years" refers to the orbital period of the planet Saturn, whose atmosphere's density is one-eighth that of the earth. As one of the solar system's gas giants, Saturn might be characterized as a "gasometer," and its famous rings are made of large "snowballs." "Albedo" is a term from astronomical

---

[14] R. J. Schork, "Genetic Primer: Chapter I.6," in *How James Joyce Wrote Finnegans Wake: A Chapter-by-Chapter Genetic Guide*, ed. Luca Crispi and Sam Slote (Madison: University of Wisconsin Press), 124–41.

[15] In a letter of April 26, 1929 to Harriet Shaw Weaver, Joyce complains, "I was awake nearly all last night trying to solve a problem in elementary mathematics—all this for a word or two" (*Letters III* 189). A month later he reports the same sleepless fixation, "being up sometimes till 1.30 fooling over old books of Euclid and algebra" (*Letters I* 280).

photometry: the composition of planets may be determined by study of their surface's reflectivity. One of Saturn's moons, Enceladus (first seen in 1789), has a notably high albedo.

In a letter to Weaver dated May 28, 1929, Joyce connects "the old earwig" with "Time, Saturn" (aka Cronos, the father who devours his children), "which, as you will see, I introduced into the *Ondt and Gracehoper*" (*Letters I* 281). In fact the integration of these Saturn notes first occurs in "The Mookse and the Gripes." Here is the handwritten draft of the relevant passage:

> he's as globeful as a gasometer of lithium and luridity and it ^he^ was thirty ^thrice ten^ anular years before he got ^wallowed^ round Raggiant Circos. (*JJA* 47:267; see *FW* 131.35–132.01)

"Albedo" is crossed out in blue rather than red, because it was added at a different time to a different part of the *Wake*, and became "albedinous" (414.36–415.01) in "The Ondt and the Gracehoper." Either Joyce is getting mixed up here or—and these are not necessarily mutually exclusive propositions—we as readers may have to think carefully about how there are different and perhaps even counterintuitive or contradictory sequentialities for the different but oddly overlapping processes of imagining, composing, and reading "Work in Progress" and *Finnegans Wake*. At any rate, one has to wonder just what Joyce means by "introduce."

Saturnity, associated here with the overpowering father-figure HCE, is just another instance of the *Wake*'s theme of false substitution, a kind of negative correspondence. Saturn does not consume the son who will overthrow him, but a stone put in his place ("tree-stone" in Joyce's translation), while Jacob usurps Esau's inheritance by means of a hairy subterfuge (only Joyce's twins can tell the difference: "I know His Heriness" (*FW* 351.31)). VI.B.4, like all the notebooks, comprises the selection processes of the author, and in turn, also of the reader, as they both try to decide, like Saturn and Isaac, what to consume, where to bestow one's blessing.

But to return to "matches," albeit of another kind. Another peek into this notebook (VI.B.4.155 and 156):

> In less time than it takes to—[crossed out in red]
> foyer brigade   [crossed out in red]
> flintlock
> Bryant + May

And on the next page:

fusee
friction match
phosphorous
sesquisulphide
phossy jaw
matchmaker   [crossed out in blue]
aspen peeler [crossed out in blue]

Bryant and May, a British matchmaking company founded in 1861, is probably best known (or infamous) for its being the target of an 1888 East End labor strike by "Match-Girls," female employees who fought for better working conditions. Regularly exposed to white phosphorous, these women were subject to various health risks, among them phosphorous necrosis of the jaw, known as "phossy jaw," a disfiguring and often deadly affliction. In 1898, the "friction match" was invented, which replaced the use of white or yellow (and the less toxic red) phosphorous with phosphorous sesquisulfide.[16] The victimized workers might be memorialized in the *Wake* as "soft youthful bright matchless girls" (*FW* 134.23).

Where did Joyce get this information? Perhaps he was reading a newspaper report about Bryant and May: in 1926 the company merged with the Swedish Match Company to form the British Match Corporation, and in 1929 it expanded its phosphorous sesquisulfide production by forming the A & W Match Phosphorous Company.[17] Or he might have been scouring an encyclopedia (the *Britannica* was a favorite hunting ground), in which case he probably went between entries in order to collect all of these different data. The associations (or "matches") that can be guessed at, at any rate: in the course of military technology's history, the flintlock replaced the matchlock (not just an instance of word association, for the theme of substitution quietly repeats here). "Foyer brigade" is in the same "cooked" (rather than "raw") category

---

[16] See Louise Raw, *Striking a Light: The Bryant and May Matchwomen and Their Place in History* (London: Continuum, 2009).

[17] It is pleasing to speculate (or imagine) that Joyce might have been contemplating Ivar Kreuger, "the Match King," the polyglot charmer behind the Swedish Match Company and the architect of what one historian has called "the financial scandal of the century," as a possible source for or incarnation of his own fallen King Hosty. Kreuger's fraud, precipitated by the stock market crash, which occurred six months after the period Joyce was using VI.B.4, wasn't fully exposed until 1931. See Frank Partnoy, *The Match King: Ivar Kreuger and the Financial Scandal of the Century* (London: Profile Books, 2009).

as "Missisliffi": it may be a pun that occurred to Joyce, or it may be purloined from some uncertain source.[18] And might the blank that follows "In less time than it takes to" be filled in with "strike a match"? This passage from VI.B.4 is all about how cause and effect stretch out so very far from the twinkling of an instant that distinguishes them; how strikingly disproportionate are the time and effort behind production and long-term effects to workers to the momentary, easy, and minute gesture of lighting a match.

The possible contexts and negative correspondences that I have just sketched out bear no small resemblance to the ways that one might read a poem, or part of a poem, and I would suggest that reading Joyce's notebooks as poetry,[19] or at any rate as a kind of literary work themselves, offers a richer appreciation of Joyce's writing processes than merely designating such texts as instrumental data in service to the more important *Wake*, as "raw" material, "not Joyce's" writing. Opening rather than closing interpretations both of the *Wake* and themselves, the notebooks present a reading experience made up of guesswork, pattern detection, and comparative readings, not unlike but all the same different from that found in the *Wake*. "Match of a matchness" (*FW* 294.17), that is, not much of a muchness. Almost—but not quite.

---

[18] The pun of "foyer brigade," for better or worse, does not reach the published *Wake*. "Matchmaker" and "aspen peeler" were transmuted into the expanding first question of I.7: "put a matchhead on an aspenstalk and set the living a fire" (*JJA* 47:267; *FW* 131.13–14). "In less time than it takes to" is presumably the basis for "in less time than it takes a glaciator to submerger an Atlangthis" (*FW* 232.31–32), but I have not tracked down (or not yet convinced myself of) the instance of its adoption from the notebook.

[19] It is likely more advantageous than has been hitherto discussed to read the notebooks aloud, to hear them, as one is advised to do with (and in) the *Wake*: "As you sing it it's a study" (*FW* 489.33) or, in other words: *hear it, learn it*.

Chapter 4

GENETICAL

Revision Revisited

> the revise of him and in fact not an ideal
> (*FW* 161.18–19)

Once upon a time—or, to be somewhat more specific, one day in the early months of 1929—Joyce wrote this phrase in a notebook:

> Somes amid a space + a whit [?] space it was (VI.B.4.250)

This, as hearty readers of *Finnegans Wake* will recognize, is the earliest version of what will become this:

> Eins within a space and a wearywide space it wast ere wohned a Mookse. (*FW* 15.18–19)

And readers of *A Portrait of the Artist as a Young Man* will recognize that as rather similar to this:

> Once upon a time and a very good time it was there was a moocow coming down along the road and this moocow that was coming down along the road met a nicens little boy named baby tuckoo (*P* 5)

But what exactly is the relationship between these three texts? To what extent is it correct or even adequate to call the second a "parody" of the third? By the same logic, can we call the second also a kind of parody of the first? And is it safer—or even riskier still—merely to state that what we are looking at are three different versions of the same text? Especially significant, and especially vexing, is the fact that all three of these passages are revisions of revisions, that there is no extant origin point for this writing (we have no opening to *Stephen Hero*, a damaged fossil).

Genetic inquiry is above all else the determination of the relationships between texts that are in some sense variants of one another, though these determinations can remain as provisional as the relationships can be multidimensional. Other hermeneutic methods might well envy the weight of documentary evidence that genetic studies depend upon and in turn the provability that they can claim as a result, yet it is this very room for uncertainty and contrary possibilities that identifies such studies as a form of literary criticism. Just as a reader comparing a translation to an original may trace any number of other possible renderings, while the unfortunate translator must commit to a single choice, the genetics scholar can entertain and explore various hypotheses without, unlike his poor cousin, the textual editor, having to choose just one and live with it. Fixing a text—in the double sense of restoring and stabilizing it—is the editorial mandate, not in and of itself the impetus for genetic research.

This insufficiently acknowledged but crucial subjectivity[1] of genetic studies can be glimpsed with a little probing of its preferred terminology, which, as technical or precise as it might appear, bend and blur on closer inspection. The term "revision," the focus of this essay, is no answer in itself to the questions raised above, because it denotes a specific kind of writing, understood to be functionally distinct from note-taking, on the one hand, and composition as such, on the other. If one text is recognized as a parody of another—as Joyce's "Eins within a space" might well be of his earlier "Once upon a time"—this would seem to invalidate its being what Zachary Leader calls, perhaps a little huffily, "revision proper," a class apart from "metaphorical" or "intertextual" revisions.[2] Setting aside the fact that the very phrase "revision proper" smacks of something one might find in the "Eumaeus" episode, it is odd to suppose that there is not a significant measure of metaphor in the necessarily comparative study of the stages of a given written work's development ("genetics" is itself a metaphor, as is so much of the language it employs). Of greater concern, though, is how the understanding of "intertextual" as an improper sort of revision deprives the notes, drafts, proofs, and other documents at issue in an author's revising of any status as "texts" themselves, presumably retaining that title for the "completed" or published version.[3]

---

[1] Both Finn Fordham (in *I Do I Undo I Redo: The Textual Genesis of Modernist Selves* (Oxford: Oxford University Press, 2010)) and Dirk Van Hulle (in *James Joyce's "Work in Progress": Pre-Book Publications of Finnegans Wake Fragments* (London: Routledge, 2016)) connect the process of revision with an emergent selfhood and subjectivity which is itself a "work in progress."

[2] Zachary Leader, *Revision and Romantic Authorship* (Oxford: Clarendon Press, 1996), 16.

[3] French formulations of *critique génétique* provide the term "avant-textes," which at least affords some distinction, though in some respects this (teleologically loaded) distinction generates problems similar to those found in discussions of "influence" and "precursors." There is a sense in which those texts neither included in the "final" version nor published by the author might just as well be called "après-textes" (as indeed they sometimes are). See *Genetic Criticism: Texts and Avant-Textes*, ed. Jed Deppman, Daniel Ferrer, and Michael

It is this assumption, the reification—or perhaps it is an outright fetishization—of a "final" (and sometimes "authorized" for good measure) version, that is the basis for the definition of revision as "post-compositional change," to use Hannah Sullivan's phrase. "At the simplest level," according to Sullivan, the writer who revises his or her work has three choices:

1. "to add material, so the final version is longer than the first draft"
2. "to delete, so it is shorter"
3. "to substitute, producing a first and final draft of similar length"[4]

Apart from those (fewer and fewer) writers paid by the word and undergraduates scrambling to meet an assignment's minimum length, it seems improbable that many authors think primarily in these terms. In fact, this formula smacks of a crude sort of determinism, along the lines of my confidently predicting that either you will eat lunch tomorrow or you won't: it is true as far as it goes, but it is a statement so lacking in commitment and detail as to be of little or no value. Just as my prediction says nothing at all about your own individual habits, Sullivan's choices elide the particular thinking and particular significance behind particular revisions, which is after all the business of genetic research and criticism.

Sullivan articulates another, equally broad and equally specious facet of "revision" when she identifies revision as a means by which to discover its opposite, writing that represents the author's "natural" style. Of the stylistic differences between one book by Joyce and other, Sullivan has this to say:

> *Portrait*, which can be regarded as a revision of *Stephen Hero* in only the second, extrinsic sense, is much more condensed [...] On the whole, the textual history of *Portrait* and *Dubliners*, with its style of "scrupulous meanness," shows that additive revision and a pushing of styles and genres to their limit was not so much Joyce's "natural" or organic style of writing (as "piecing together" seems to have been for Eliot), as a deliberate choice made for *Ulysses*.[5]

Revision is, in this view, at once a departure from a "natural" writing and a measure of that departure. The notion that Joyce's method of writing may

---

Groden (Philadelphia: University of Pennsylvania Press, 2004), especially the introduction (1–16) and the essay by Louis Hay (17–27).

[4] Hannah Sullivan, *The Work of Revision* (Cambridge, MA: Harvard University Press, 2013), 15.

[5] Sullivan, *The Work of Revision*, 175.

have changed over the years never arises;[6] nor are the implications of the suggestion that there is a writing that is without "deliberate choice" explored. If all of this seems very curious, it may be because a central part of Joyce's achievement as a writer lies in his denaturalization of style, but it is also because Sullivan explicitly minimizes the significance of one kind of revision (i.e., one kind of textual relationship, that of *A Portrait* as a revision or rewriting of *Stephen Hero*) while she inflates that of another ("deliberate" additions to drafts of *Ulysses* are unlike and reveal the "natural" writing of earlier texts) without any convincing justification for doing so.

Recognizing that "revision" is a slippery and idiosyncratic term prompts the question whether "revision" as a concept or a process means the same for one writer as for all others. I argue that revision is an editorial fiction, a more or less necessary working understanding of writing as a paradigm—an understanding that may be by different degrees assumed, inferred, and/or imposed. Again, the genetic critic significantly differs from the textual editor in that the former has the luxuries of being able to entertain more than one such paradigm, to acknowledge gaps in these models of textual evolution and present multiple conjectures about them, and to make greater allowance for inconsistencies (Joyce's or one's own). In what follows I want to think about the value and difficulties of determining relationships between texts and ultimately offer some cautionary notes about what we talk about when we talk about "revision."

Recurrent Origins

Kurt Vonnegut once remarked that the surest way to break a writer's heart is to tell him how much you loved his first book. What did Joyce think of his first novel in the years when he was writing his last book? Of course, we cannot know what exactly Joyce was thinking when he wrote "Somes amid a space" in his notebook, but we can speculate, with whatever biographical or textual rubrics to guide those speculations—*not* as an effort to fix meaning within a frozen historical moment, or even to isolate some privileged "intention," but to trace patterns within the long history of Joyce's writing.

---

[6] The logic here reminds me of the character in the 1980 film *Airplane!* who, while travelling by air with her husband, makes worried mental notes about his apparently inconsistent behavior: "Jim never has a second cup of coffee at home …" and later, "Jim never vomits at home …." Themselves a kind of revision or parody of television commercials for coffee, these scenes nicely demonstrate how a behavioural norm is sought by an observer's anxiety. Earlier work acts as the same comparative and privileged basis as "at home" for Sullivan, who is effectively saying, "Jim never revises like that at home …."

To probe the question of why or in what connection Joyce was thinking of *A Portrait* at this moment, we need to map out several contexts. At the time when Joyce added the first phrase into his notebook, he was at an altogether industrious stage in his literary career. The hesitation that had slowed "Work in Progress" (later the *Wake*) only a little over a year before was past and the blending of composition and revision was now speeding up. At the same time, the textual universe of Joyce was expanding with the French translation of *Ulysses* (February 1929) and the planned publication of *Our Exagmination Round His Factification for the Incamination of "Work in Progress,"* the book of essays that, as its title might suggest, obviated little of the obscurity of Joyce's work. This notebook was used in making revisions and additions to the text for the publication of *Tales Told of Shem and Shaun* by Black Sun Press that summer.

The "Somes amid a space" note feels out of place in the notebook, surrounded as it is by names and niceties of insect anatomy and parasite behaviors: "ticks," "pincer," "pulex irritans," "larva," and "find a host." A good percentage of this material gets into the *Wake* in some form or (most often) another. For example, the tasty phrase "flea's gizzard" eventually gets digested into this passage:

> involving upon the same no uncertain amount of esophagous regurgitation, he being personally unpreoccupied to the extent of a flea's gizzard anent eructation, if he was still extremely offensive to a score and four nostrils' dilatation. (*FW* 558.02–06)

R. J. Schork connects these notes with Aristophanes's satire on Socratic philosophy, *The Clouds*, in which one of the headier research projects seeks "to determine whether a gnat's buzzing is caused by wind expelled through its trachea and mouth or through its intestines and anus. By means of a convoluted argument Socrates proves that the flatulent gnat 'has a bugle up its ass.'"[7] Small matters, it must be agreed, but the phrase with which we began is all about the very small: "whit space" denotes the space of the tiniest particle, and "somes" might just come from trypanosomes, the blood parasites responsible for such delights as sleeping sickness, and some of which are transmitted by fleas. And then with just a quick nod to Aristotle, and his ideas of the inorganic, spontaneous generation of tiny things that creep—

> the flea is generated out of the slightest amount of putrefying matter; for wherever there is any dry excrement, a flea is sure to be found. Bugs

---

[7] R. J. Schork, *Greek and Hellenic Culture in Joyce* (Gainesville: University Press of Florida, 1998), 209.

are generated from the moisture of living animals, as it dries up outside their bodies. Lice are generated out of the flesh of animals. (Aristotle's *History of Animals*)

—off we can leap to this scene in *A Portrait*:

> A louse crawled over the nape of his neck and, putting his thumb and forefinger deftly beneath his loose collar, he caught it. He rolled its body, tender yet brittle as a grain of rice, between thumb and finger for an instant before he let it fall from him and wondered would it live or die. There came to his mind a curious phrase from Cornelius a Lapide which said that the lice born of human sweat were not created by God with the other animals on the sixth day. But the tickling of the skin of his neck made his mind raw and red. The life of his body, illclad, illfed, louseeaten, made him close his eyelids in a sudden spasm of despair: and in the darkness he saw the brittle bright bodies of lice falling from the air and turning often as they fell. Yes; and it was not darkness that fell from the air. It was brightness.
>
> *Brightness falls from the air.*
>
> He had not even remembered rightly Nash's line. All the images it had awakened were false. His mind bred vermin. His thoughts were lice born of the sweat of sloth. (*P* 196–97)

Joyce's mind, still breeding vermin in 1929, recalls his lousy first novel while making notes about mandibles and pupation. *Finnegans Wake* cheerfully refers to "his perusual flea and loisy manner" (516.09–10). Since the *Wake* is itself a parasitical monster, nourishing itself on all kinds of texts, why shouldn't it do the same with Joyce's own? At this point, the connection's made and the thesis writes itself, right?

Well, *maybe*. This whole line of inquiry is a kind of speculation quite similar to the "plotsome to getsome" (*FW* 312.18) method by which we read the *Wake*: making tenuous connections, always in progress, watching and listening for further substantiation while expecting imminent contradiction. The only absolute, whether in meaning or in verification, lies in the absolute absence of absolutes.

It may well be that the placement of "Somes amid a space" in the notebook is not indicative of any direct textual connection between sources. How limited, how often uncertain is our understanding of how and why Joyce takes notes: what strikes him as "noteworthy," and then why a note—sometimes just a word, usually no more than a fragment of a phrase—should graduate, almost certainly to be transformed, to a place in a draft or manuscript, perhaps itself to become a revision. The note-taking for "Work in Progress" seems quite unlike the "epiphanies" that the younger Joyce collected, moments of transformative immediacy, specificity, "thisness." If the epiphanies are the building blocks of narratives like *Dubliners* and *A Portrait*, by comparison the often brief and always disjunctive notes for the *Wake* seem like mere granules—seventeen years of sandcastle-building. (Even the term "notes" seems like rather a comedown from the highfalutin "epiphanies.") The epiphanies are conceptually, expressively dramatic—they are composed of speakers, gestures, scenarios—and whatever else it might manifest, there is nothing exactly *dramatic* about a word like "larva." Nobody in the *Wake* notebooks is saying "flea's gizzard," and no action happens to or because of a flea's gizzard. Yet there is an intractable, extraordinary and perhaps even ineffable "thisness" to "flea's gizzard," an utterly distinct conception, an image that is entirely in the mind's eye, and a unique set of sounds. The same may or may not be said of "larva" (or, to take other random bites from the notebook with which I began, "Spanish prisoner," "shirtfront wickets," or "upholsterer"). This or that reader may have a strong resonance with "larva," the way that the word "foetus" cut into a desk "startle[s] [Stephen's] blood" (*P* 75): a personal, somatic reaction; a historic, aesthetic moment.

Contemplation of the material constitution of art—the ideal or simply the credible ingredients or media—remains bound to any conceptual or even metaphysical definition of art throughout Joyce's writing career, though perhaps we can gauge some shifting perspective as to whether the ingredients or media at issue are weighed as ideal or simply credible. Stephen Dedalus's question about the "man hacking in fury at a block of wood" *(P* 180), taken from a list of such aesthetic conundrums in Joyce's 1903 Paris notebook,[8] is as much about the hacking and the block of wood as it is about the man's artistic intention or lack thereof. The question is not answered in *A Portrait* but *Finnegans Wake* responds with garbled Pythagoras: "*Eggs squawfish lean yoe nun feed marecurios*" (*FW* 484.36). This is a homophonic rendering of *Ex quovix ligno non fit Mercurius*: "you can't make a Mercury out of just any piece of wood." Yet "any piece of wood" seems to be the very principle of the *Wake*'s composition. The wooden cow produced by furious hacking is the apparatus contrived by Daedalus to allow mare-curious Pasiphae to have congress with a bull, after which Joyce turns his attention to the maker of a wooden horse and, with the *Wake*, a hobbyhorse, perpetually rocking.

---

[8] Robert Scholes and Richard Kain, eds. *The Workshop of Daedalus: James Joyce and the Raw Materials for* A Portrait of the Artist as a Young Man (Evanston, IL: Northwestern University Press, 1965), 55.

The disconcertingly lateral associations governing (if that is the word) Joyce's note-taking have this in common: a pronounced sense of their being part of an ongoing conversation with other texts ("sources" as well as other notes, other notebooks, drafts, and manuscripts). In the essay preceding this one, I sought to demonstrate why it is neither plausible nor particularly useful to rigidly distinguish (as Danis Rose does, for example) accumulation from composition; that is, to distinguish notebook writings from composition per se. Here I would like to extend this argument from note-taking to revisions, to caution against setting "revisions" as a clearly delineated, tertiary operation. Doing so neglects the fascinatingly multidirectional, recursive paths that Joyce's writing (and especially "Work in Progress") takes.

The Case of the Prigged Portrait

Let's compare another pair of passages from *A Portrait* and *Finnegans Wake*:

> Like a scene on some vague arras, old as man's weariness, the age of the seventh city of christendom was visible to him across the timeless air, no older nor more weary nor less patient of subjection than in the days of the thingmote. (*P* 141)

> It scenes like a landescape from Wildu Picturescu or some seem on some dimb Arras, dumbs as Mum's mutyness, this mimage of the seventyseventh kusin of kristansen is odeable to os across the wineless Ere no œdor nor mere eerie nor liss potent of suggestion than in the tales of the tingmount. (Prigged!) (*FW* 53.01–06)

I remember coming across the first passage in my first reading of *A Portrait* as an enthralled student and being struck by my inability to decide whether what I was reading was a finely wrought sentence of sensation or a patch of purple prose, an example of circumlocution mixed with abstraction. This uncertainty, I confess, abides even now, and this uncertainty thus extends itself into any reading of the second passage. What is striking about these two passages, taken together, is how little—relatively speaking, and bearing in mind that this is Joyce we are talking about—has changed: the one text simply reads like a clunky translation of the other. From "vague" to "dimb," the journey is from one field of obscurity to another. The specific mutations (my favorite is the shift from "patient of subjection" to "potent of suggestion") take care not to dismantle or obscure the earlier version, a degree of care that is noticeably different from much of Joyce's modus operandi in the *Wake* years. If Joyce's "Work in Progress" revisions are almost habitually unconcerned with previously set themes, structures, and patterns, this "revision" of *A Portrait* acts as a challenge both to any fixed or absolute formulation of "how Joyce revises" and to any facile differentiation between "post-compositional change" and some other, secondary, improper form of revision.

Is the second passage a parody of the first? At any rate it is literally a re-vision, a seeing again of a poetic vision. "Arras" is surely a loaded word, invoking *Hamlet* and sounding out "arse," pointing readers behind, where perhaps some unseen author is lurking. "Wildu Picturescu," perhaps the most extravagant addition, cues us to think of Oscar Wilde and his own portrait-novel *The Picture of Dorian Gray*. Is Joyce acknowledging, in retrospect, the influence of Wilde on *A Portrait?*—for the first passage is a Wildean sentence, both in cadence and vocabulary. Or is Joyce remarking on how overcooked this Wilde-influenced sentence is by throwing it back in the oven? Is "Prigged!" a self-accusation or a confession of having been too enamored or influenced by Wilde, or even of having stolen from him (a *prigger* is a seventeenth-century word for "thief")? Or is someone being identified as a prig—Stephen Dedalus, perhaps (and plausibly so), and/or maybe the young Joyce upon whom Stephen is based, and/or even the author of *A Portrait?*

Joyce's interest in Wilde represents a continuity (rather than a constant, for his perspective changes) from *A Portrait* through *Ulysses* and into the *Wake*.[9] This continuity or through line provides genetic criticism with a valuable vantage point from which to observe how Joyce's writing is ever a rewriting, both of his own texts and Wilde's, sometimes together. Interestingly, the *Wake*'s occasional snickers at this or that "poor trait of the artless" (*FW* 114.32) are directly concerned with origins. "Eins within a space" is one example, and "Once upon a grass and a hopping high grass it was" (516.01–02), but Joyce also revisits this verse of self-location—

Stephen Dedalus is my name,
Ireland is my nation.
Clongowes is my dwellingplace
And heaven my expectation. (*P* 12)

—to produce this rather more muddled index of names and addresses: "Awabeg is my callby, Magnus here's my Max, Wonder One's my cipher and Seven Sisters is my nighbrood" (*FW* 248.34–35). Joyce's rewriting of Wilde, though,

---

[9] Surprisingly, the depths of this ongoing evaluation of and conversation with Wilde have not been anywhere near fully sounded in Joyce criticism. Doctoral students kicking over stones looking for thesis subjects take note: there is no book-length study of the two authors.

goes further back. The evolution of Stephen's villanelle in *A Portrait*, shown in such deliberate stages, illuminates how deeply the process of writing intrigues Joyce and is his true subject:

> Are you not weary of ardent ways,
> Lure of the fallen seraphim?
> Tell no more of enchanted days. (*P* 183)

As Yeatsian as these lines might seem, they are at least as Wildean, echoing as they do Wilde's 1894 poem "The Sphinx": "Why are you tarrying? Get hence! I weary of your sullen ways, / I weary of your steadfast gaze, your somnolent magnificence."[10]

Joyce becomes more and more self-conscious about the "Wildu Picturescu" effect in his writing in a way that makes it more than an abstract "anxiety of influence": Joyce's reading (and rereading) of Wilde becomes a means of retrospection, a look into a cracked lookingglass or at an enchanted portrait of the artist as an other. Yet another pairing of passages fortifies this connection. Take this conversational scene from *Dorian Gray*:

> "You talk books away," he said, "why don't you write one?"
>
> "I am too fond of reading books to care to write them, Mr. Erskine. I should like to write a novel certainly, a novel that would be as lovely as a Persian carpet and as unreal. But there is no literary public in England for anything except newspapers, primers, and encyclopaedias. Of all people in the world the English have the least sense of the beauty of literature."
>
> "I fear you may be right," answered Mr. Erskine. "I myself used to have literary ambitions, but I gave them up long ago. And now, my dear young friend, if you will allow me to call you so, may I ask if you really meant all that you said to us at lunch?"
>
> "I quite forget what I said," smiled Lord Henry. "Was it all very bad?"[11]

And hear this same invitation to write, the same gesture of disowning one's "theory" in *Ulysses*:

---

[10] Oscar Wilde, "The Sphinx," in *The Complete Works of Oscar Wilde* (London: Collins, 1991), 841.

[11] Oscar Wilde, "*The Picture of Dorian Gray*," in *The Complete Works of Oscar Wilde* (London: Collins, 1991), 45–46.

Do you believe your own theory?

—No, Stephen said promptly.

—Are you going to write it? Mr Best asked. You ought to make it a dialogue, don't you know, like the Platonic dialogues Wilde wrote. (*U* 9.1065–69)

Shakespeare is not the only ghost haunting the library in "Scylla and Charybdis." That the episode itself is "like the Platonic dialogues Wilde wrote" is Joyce's ironic form of citation. Joyce's "rere regardant" self-representation is fused with his repeatedly taking the measure of Wilde: his judgment of himself remains as open to revision as his judgment of that earlier writer.

For Wilde's judgment of Joyce, though, we must turn to Hester Travers Smith's 1923 book *Psychic Messages from Oscar Wilde*. Speaking through an Ouija board one summer's night, Wilde's unperished spirit appraised *Ulysses* as an "involuntary" work.[12] It is remarkable for a disembodied spirit to pronounce a living writer not to be in possession of himself. Joyce, as Sam Slote has detailed,[13] found irresistible ore in both Smith's book and Frank Harris's biography of Wilde, and notes on both filtered into the *Wake*. His first notes from Smith's *Psychic Messages*—or more likely, a review of it—appear in a 1924 notebook. These include the following:

planchette
Mr V—
taps or writes
Oscar's sister Isola
°Sir Wᵐ Wilde ⊓   (VI.B.14.186)

Interestingly, the association that Joyce's placement of the sigla makes between HCE and Wilde's father and the happy coincidence that Wilde had a sister named Isola means that we can infer that Wilde is aligned with one of the sons—presumably the wastrel aesthete Shem, since the very next note links Shaun with the "medium" or psychic who is "impersonating" a "third party."

---

[12] Hester Travers Smith, *Psychic Messages from Oscar Wilde* (London: T. Werner Laurie, 1923), 40.

[13] Sam Slote, "Wilde Thing: Concerning the Eccentricities of a Figure of Decadence in *Finnegans Wake*," in *Probes: Genetic Studies in Joyce*, ed. David Hayman and Sam Slote (Amsterdam: Rodopi, 1995), 101–22. See also Van Hulle, *James Joyce's "Work in Progress,"* 18–19.

Joyce's "revision" of this psychic event is behind the séance in III.3, in which the voices of son(s) and father are imitated and ultimately confused:

> Old Whitehowth he is speaking again. Ope Eustace tube! Pity poor whiteoath! Dear gone mummeries, goby! Tell the woyld I have lived true thousand hells. Pity, please, lady, for poor O.W. in this profundust snobbing I have caught. Nine dirty years mine age, hairs hoar, mummery failend, snowdrift to my ellpow, deff as Adder. I askt you, dear lady, to judge on my tree by our fruits. (*FW* 535.26–32)

Shem produces art both from the filth of his body (just as the spectral Wilde denounced *Ulysses* as a "great bulk of filth"[14]) and the works of other artists that he appropriates for revision: "but with each word that would not pass away the squidself which he had squirtscreened from the crystalline world waned chagreenold and doriangrayer in its dudhud" (*FW* 186.06–08). Shem is his own Dorian Gray, revealing himself even as he tries to conceal himself and moving closer to death ("dudhud") even as he reaches for immortality for or through his art ("that would not pass away"). This sui generis theme is undercut, however, when Joyce winks at Balzac's *Le peau de chagrin* in "chagreenold" as a reminder that Wilde's novel took its subject from another novel. All writing is rewriting; to revise is to compose.

A World of Differents

Having observed Joyce's wont to return to origins (his own and those of writing) and this enduring textual relationship with Wilde, we can return to this essay's Wildean point of origin, that moment in 1929 when Joyce wrote "Somes amid a space" in his notebook and when he had just turned 47 years old. Oscar Wilde was 46 when he died. Joyce's letters from the time of this notebook are full of health concerns, and mortality was obviously heavy in his thoughts. For some time he had been entertaining the strange idea that James Stephens, an Irish writer with a name (and perhaps a birthday) too good to be true, could take over the writing of this unfinished book. In fact, this idea coincides with his introduction of this "prigged" passage into the evolving text of "Work in Progress." Joyce inserts the *Portrait* parody and Wilde reference together, at the same time, in notes made in early 1927 onto a late 1923 typescript (Figure 1) (see *JJA* 45:187).

---

[14] Smith, *Psychic Messages from Oscar Wilde*, 39.

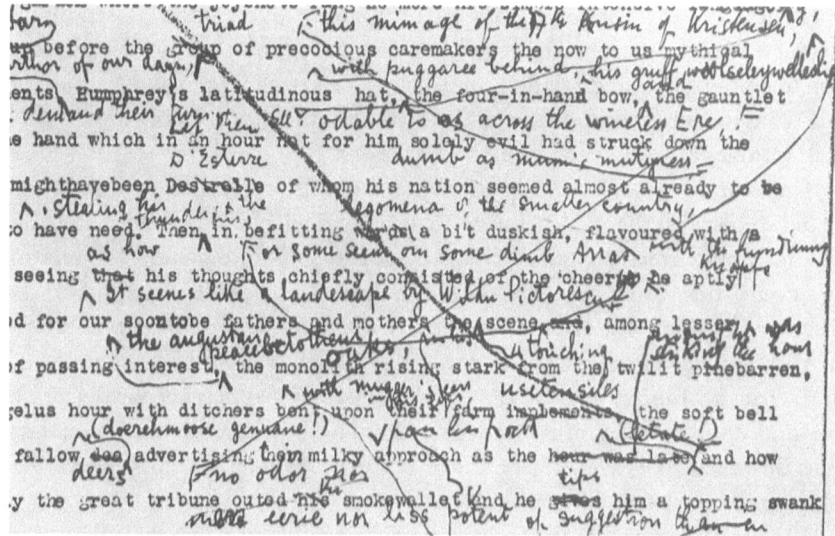

Figure 1 1923 typescript with Joyce's handwritten additions (*JJA* 45:187)

On the subsequent fair copy Joyce made only minor changes:

> It scenes like a landescape from Wildu Picturescu Like some ^or some^ seem on some dimb Arras, dumbs as Mum's mutyness, this mimage of the seventyseventh kusin of Kristansen is odeable to os across the wineless Ere no odor ^œdor^ nor mere eerie nor liss potent of suggestion than in the tales of the tingmount. (*JJA* 45:203)

"Prigged!" is added to the second typescript (March–April 1927), but now we must ponder whether and how to distinguish "correction" from "revision," for Joyce seizes upon some of the typist's deviations and reinstates his earlier text, but not all such instances.

> It scenes like a landescape from Wildu Picturescu or some seem on some dimb Arras^,^ dumbs as Mum's mutyness^,^ this mimage of the seven^t^yseventh kusin of kristansen is odeable to os across the wineless Ere no œdor nor mere eerie nor liss potent of suggestion than in the tales of the tingmount. ^Prigged!^ (*JJA* 45:226)

That lowercase "k" in "kristansen" introduced by the typist survives through two subsequent sets of galleys for *transition*, which Joyce later used for instructions to the printer of *Finnegans Wake*, in which book one finds "kristansen." Rose and

O'Hanlon, in their "Restored" edition, recapitalize "Kristansen," discrediting several waves of revision. They make no allowance for a collaborative dimension to composition and revision, in which Joyce's declining to alter or correct this "k" is an acceptance of the change: presumably they see only Joyce's eyesight troubles at work (bad vision, bad revision).

There are of course a startling number of instances such as this in the textual record of the *Wake*—but what exactly do I mean by "this?" Do we call this non-correction, non-revision, tacit revision, ambiguous revision? In any event, this range of variation within the acts generally categorized as "revision" unsettles the foundations of any attempt at a set or comprehensive formula for the classification and handling of such transitions between texts. In so far as revision is in some sense a signification of difference between one text and another, caution is needed in deciding how "difference" manifests or is observed. It is also important to consider—again, carefully—whether "difference" perhaps differs from "change."

All critical approaches necessarily have their inherent dangers, and genetic criticism, illuminating and invaluable as it is, is no exception. A certain kind of historical determinism that seeks to preclude or invalidate interpretations—for example, insisting that the range of meanings for a given portion of text is fixed within the moment it is written—is obviously a many-headed Scylla worth avoiding. But there is a Charybdis, too; a whirlpool that I have been arguing has as its center a definition of revision that is universal or one-size-fits-all, applied a priori to any writer or text. Joyce, the master rewriter, broadens our ideas of "revision" with his continuous and recursive stream of text. The uncertain, polyvalent, and shifting relationships between his various texts—whether that be work published or unpublished, ostensibly "finished" or admittedly "in progress"—prompt us to rethink our narrow conception of revision as (exclusively) *marked* instantiations of (exclusively) *authorial* decree; to question the "post-compositional" as a class of writing entirely, perceptibly distinct from "composition"; and to be ever aware that these conceptions and distinctions, limit or can even deny the very relationships between texts that genetic studies seeks to discern.

Chapter 5

CEREBRAL

"Cog It Out": Joyce on the Brain

> He affirmed his significance as a conscious rational animal proceeding syllogistically from the known to the unknown and a conscious rational reagent between a micro and a macrocosm ineluctably constructed upon the incertitude of the void. (*U* 17.1012–15)

I

Consciousness studies today has become a deeply divided discourse. The first division lies within the problem of disciplinary and discursive territoriality, which in some instances approaches chauvinism: philosophers may claim seniority, having mulled over the meaning of thought throughout and even as recorded history, while incomparably better-funded cognitive scientists can approach this last unexplored frontier with the swagger underwritten by split atoms, decoded genomes, modern miracles. This situation underscores the caution that every conscious person is an authority on consciousness, a caution worth bearing in mind but which is perhaps overstated, since one could say that every breathing person is an authority on oxygen, with more or less the same significance. Second division: there are generally reckoned to be two kinds of approaches to consciousness, dualism and materialism. The former view, most famously hypothesized by Descartes, absolutely cleaves mind from matter, while the latter view suggests that the hunk of electrified meat lodged in my skull is inseparable from the processes by which I formulate and write this sentence. (Note that these are approaches, not models, and very wide-open approaches at that. Indeed, proposed materialist models for consciousness can seem to differ as much as the two approaches themselves do.) And finally, a third, cataclysmic division: among these sects, both philosophers and scientists, dualists and materialists alike, there are those who firmly hold that consciousness is unknowable, that the workings of consciousness are precisely that which consciousness cannot fathom.

So what has this to do with literature, let alone James Joyce? Nothing at all, if one can believe Raymond Tallis, who in a *Times Literary Supplement* screed entitled "The Neuroscience Delusion" rejects the entire notion of "neuroaesthetics" (he does not seem to be familiar with the term "cognitive poetics,"[1] but that's probably just as well). He rightly points out that neuroscience is very, very far from a fait accompli—though of course that is tautological, since scientific inquiry is understood by definition to be an ongoing pursuit—but he also assumes that its purported findings and developments provide an a priori foundation not only for the recent interest among authors and scholars in cognitive research but for any kind of indication or suggestion as to what consciousness is or how it works that might be discerned in literature. Here is how he concludes:

> Neuroaesthetics is wrong about the present state of neuroscience: we are not yet able to explain human consciousness, even less articulate self-consciousness as expressed in the reading and writing of poetry. It is wrong about our experience of literature. And it is wrong about humanity.[2]

Tallis hammers out an overture to the first division I mentioned: human consciousness is one thing, literature is another, and, strangely, "humanity" may be something else altogether. I'd like to note in passing the oddity of the phrasing "articulate self-consciousness as expressed," to be returned to later. Although Tallis rejects the use of neuroscientific ideas in interpretations of poetry—in the same way, incidentally, that he rejects *any* theoretical approach or "fashions," as he calls them, in a *totally wicked* use of retro-80s reactionary lingo[3]—he evidently cannot even imagine any other sort of contact between these discourses and forms.

---

[1] See, for example, Peter Stockwell's *Cognitive Poetics: An Introduction* (London: Routledge, 2002).

[2] Raymond Tallis, "The Neuroscience Delusion," *Times Literary Supplement*, April 9, 2008. http://entertainment.timesonline.co.uk/tol/arts_and_entertainment/the_tls/article3712980.ece?&EMC-Bltn=CUEGU8 (accessed June 10, 2012).

[3] A brief example (stop me if you've heard this one before):

> Like hypochondriacs, theory-led critics find what they seek: so Jane Austen and the Venerable Bede are alike in representing the hegemony of the colonizer over the colonized, the powerful over the powerless, or the voiced over the voiceless; or in their failure to acknowledge the fictionality of the bourgeois fiction of the self. The fashions have moved on. Structuralist, post-structuralist, psychoanalytical (Freudian, Lacanian), historical materialist, Marxist approaches look pretty dated. "Literary studies" at the cutting edge has woken out of some of its most ambitious appropriations, though they are still inflicted on students.

And so on.

This outright balking at even the idea of cooperative discussion and exchange between literary studies and what is emphatically branded neuro*science* is reminiscent of how Alan Sokal, in explicating every joke and jape of his infamous 1996 hoax essay, "Transgressing the Boundaries: Toward a Transformative Hermeneutics of Quantum Gravity," ultimately reveals his own bias not merely against inaccuracy but concerning form.[4] Of a footnote in the essay that states "The intimate relations between quantum mechanics and the mind-body problem are discussed by Goldstein," Sokal offers this concise disparagement: "Goldstein's book on the mind-body problem [...] is an enjoyable *novel*."[5] For Sokal and Tallis, it is taken for granted, even if it is not explicitly stated, what a novel is and what it can do, and at least one of the things it apparently cannot by definition do is contribute in any truly meaningful way to scientific discourse as they conceive it. At best a novel might illustrate in an entertaining way a concept that is validated by science (and science does not write novels). This is a tedious argument—if argument it may be called—but its naked prejudice provides possible means for its circumvention. For the duration of this paper, I propose to relax literary-specific taxonomies and reflexes and consider, for instance, *Ulysses* as a human product and nothing more definite or exclusive than that, without pretending that it is something it clearly isn't. Even Sokal would have to admit, in these circumstances, that *Ulysses* shares more common properties with a scientific paper than it does with a vase of flowers. In the case of *Finnegans Wake*, about which Victor Llona's statement "I don't know what to call it but it's mighty unlike prose"[6] still has a sympathetic ring, very little effort might seem needed in this regard. However, in probing these distinctions between science and philosophy as well as the divisions within consciousness studies, we may come to realize that Joyce's own "new science" of the *Wake* is, like Vico's, a conception of history, but one that turns inward, a recursive conception of the conception of history ("the curse of his persistence the course of his tory will have had been having recourses" (*FW* 143.11–12)), and as such constitutes an experiment in modeling the mind.[7]

---

[4] Sokal's essay was originally published in *Social Text* 46/47 (1996): 217–52, and later included as an appendix in Alan Sokal and Jean Bricmont, *Fashionable Nonsense: Postmodern Intellectuals' Abuse of Science* (New York: Picador, 1998), 212–58, followed by comments and an afterword; the latter is used for citations here.
[5] Sokal and Bricmont, *Fashionable Nonsense*, 219, 262. Italics in the original.
[6] Victor Llona, "I Dont Know What to Call It but Its Mighty Unlike Prose," in *Our Exagmination Round His Factification for Incamination of Work in Progress* (New York: New Directions, 1972), 93–102.
[7] That is, the *process* of modeling the mind: the suggestion here is not that *Finnegans Wake* is a finished model, or otherwise embodies an exclusive theory of consciousness, but rather that Joyce's text enacts ways of thinking. A good example is the key term "recursive,"

It doesn't take long for the reader of cognitive research and theory (both philosophical and scientific, though these distinctions are truly blurry) to notice how provisional and semantically loaded the claims tend to be, how reliant upon anecdote and analogy and highly conditional experiments, how much metaphor is both subject and style—even when, as in the case of Gilles Fauconnier and Mark Turner's *The Way We Think*, such authors aver otherwise.[8] In other words, the discourse shares a good deal in common with the language of narrative studies generally, and specifically with studies of Joyce, which are usually attenuated to "plurabilities" of meaning and accustomed to, if not always easy with, conceptual paradoxes and tentative conclusions. "Sifted science will do your arts good," the *Wake* sagely advises (440.19–20), and sifting between narrative studies and consciousness studies does some good, too, as literary criticism of Joyce may be usefully instructed by various theories of mind, and in turn the scientists and philosophers behind those theories may find that Joyce's own expositions of mind challenge and enrich our understanding of the problem of consciousness by compelling their reader to be aware of the irregularities of her own process of comprehension. Joyce never lets us forget what a strange thing it is to be thinking at all: to be bound within "the incommensurable categorical intelligence situated in the cerebral convolutions" (*U* 17.1767–68).

II

Daniel C. Dennett concludes his 2005 book *Sweet Dreams: Philosophical Obstacles to a Science of Consciousness* by citing an "echoic capacity" as the most tangible and perhaps the defining feature of consciousness. He then unexpectedly refers to "the Joycean machine in our brains," an expression never defined or made clear—indeed, this is the only reference to Joyce in the book, and while "Joycean machine" appears in the index, "Joyce, James" does not.[9] The origin of the phrase lies in Dennett's earlier book, the boldly titled *Consciousness Explained* (1991), but there, too, its valences are obscure. Dennett does not,

---

which Michael C. Corballis, among others, holds to be the crucial cognitive property of modern humans, directly linked to recursion in language (see *The Recursive Mind: The Origins of Human Language, Thought, and Civilization* (Princeton, NJ: Princeton University Press, 2011)). Both *Ulysses* and the *Wake* are significantly recursive, allowing echoes to act as elaborations and by degrees making the reader more and more aware (or less and less unable to ignore) that the text seems constantly to rewrite itself.

[8] Gilles Fauconnier and Mark Turner, *The Way We Think: Conceptual Blending and the Mind's Hidden Complexities* (New York: Basic Books, 2003).

[9] Daniel C. Dennett, *Sweet Dreams: Philosophical Obstacles to a Science of Consciousness* (Cambridge: MIT Press, 2006), 171–72.

for example, specify a particular work by Joyce, and a short mention of the "meandering sequence of conscious mental contents famously depicted by James Joyce" conceals so much behind that word "famously."[10] Yet even before one probes the dimensions of what is concealed there, a number of immediate questions arise.

Why Joyce, specifically? Why not, say, Proust, another keen student of how the mind works,[11] or any other writer? Is there some difference to be inferred between a Joyce machine and a Joycean machine? Why a "Joycean machine in our brains" and not "a Joycean text in our brains," since it is unlikely that one would refer to "a Mozartian machine" rather than "a Mozartian symphony"? Is there something mechanical about Joyce, mechanical in the way that consciousness is allegedly mechanical, or thought of as mechanical? What's "Joycean" about consciousness? In the course of exploring these questions, I'd like to suggest that Dennett's invocation of Joyce in this context is more appropriate—because more fruitful—than he himself supposes, and as a corollary to this point I'd argue that parallels between Joyce's work (and how we experience and talk about it) and the phenomenon of consciousness (and how we experience and talk about it) provide enriching avenues and insights for the mutual benefit of the students of both.

Dennett's use of Joyce is presumably either analogical or metaphorical, though it is never made clear exactly which, or even confirmed that isn't meant otherwise. Yet this central reference to Joyce in his model and "explanation" of consciousness is all the stranger for his surprisingly lusterless conception of fiction:

> Perhaps some people are deeply perplexed about the metaphysical status of fictional people and objects, but not I. In my cheerful optimism I don't suppose there is any deep philosophical problem about the way we should respond, ontologically, to the results of fiction; fiction is *fiction*; there *is no* Sherlock Holmes.[12]

The "results of fiction" is not a phrase often encountered; it sounds like a slip for "results of the experiment," though presumably because "fiction is *fiction*" (an altogether vacuous tautology with the same emphasis as Sokal's "is

---

[10] Daniel C. Dennett, *Consciousness Explained* (Boston: Little, Brown, 1991), 214.
[11] See Jonah Lehrer, *Proust Was a Neuroscientist* (Boston: Houghton Mifflin, 2007). This book is neither a particularly strong argument for the general case I am making here nor a literary study of much value, but the hostility it has aroused, akin to the sort of attack Tallis is making, is of interest here.
[12] Dennett, *Consciousness Explained*, 79.

an enjoyable *novel*"), the "results" are always the same and/or negligible. It is tempting to set this aside as an unfortunate hiccup, of no great bearing on the matter at hand, but 350 pages later Dennett, having argued against the most enduring vestiges of Cartesian dualism even as they manifest in materialist arguments, pronounces the self, as we discern it, a "center of narrative gravity." To the possible objection that centers of gravity "aren't real; they're theorists' fictions," Dennett answers:

> That's not the trouble with centers of gravity; it's their glory. They are magnificent fictions, fictions anyone would have been proud to have created. And the fictional characters of literature are even more wonderful. Think of Ishmael, in *Moby-Dick*. "Call me Ishmael" is the way the text opens, and we oblige. We don't call the text Ishmael, and we don't call Melville Ishmael. Who or what do we call Ishmael? We call Ishmael Ishmael, the wonderful character to be found in the pages of *Moby-Dick*.[13]

Here's a question: what do we call a real person who calls himself Sherlock Holmes? Or can someone be called Ishmael and something else too? Here I'm thinking of Adaline Glasheen's ever-pertinent question, "who is who when everybody is somebody else?"[14] and how among the other standard precepts of narrative that *Finnegans Wake* dismantles is the notion of stabilized, unified *character*. For example, Emma Woodhouse is always and consistently Emma Woodhouse even as Jane Austen allows her heroine to mature and develop: she gradually becomes an older, wiser, and ultimately affianced Emma Woodhouse, but she is never Jane Fairfax, though in some respects and at certain points she might be compared with Jane Fairfax. The *Wake*'s dream-logic erases such a distinction, so that everybody (the "hero" of the book) is somebody else. Dennett, however, holds that fiction has no "metaphysical status," but he is remarkably pliable when reading it—he calls the narrator of *Moby-Dick*, who does not exist but is nonetheless wonderful, Ishmael just because he's told to—and what's more, he (perhaps inadvertently) raises the question of who or what creates (his word) the self? Do I make me just by thinking I do? How unexpectedly Cartesian of me.

Since *Moby-Dick* appears to be little more than a random example, an indicator of a general trend rather than a specific case, and because Dennett himself refers to "Joycean" as a vaguely phenomenological measure (and I am

---

[13] Dennett, *Consciousness Explained*, 429.
[14] See Adaline Glasheen, *Third Census of* Finnegans Wake (Berkeley: University of California Press, 1977).

arguing here that the vagueness can be dispelled, for the idea of the "Joycean machine" has much promise), we might instead consider *Ulysses* in this context (though *Moby-Dick* is itself a great deal more complex on this score than Dennett allows). Whom do I call Ulysses? The text, of course, but it's not impossible that Leopold Bloom could be given this name, along with the various other appellations he seems to collect as the book goes on. Or ought I to call him "Mr. Bloom," as he so often is, though by whom and why are precisely the sorts of questions that Dennett's invocation of Joyce (rather than a "Melvillean machine") usefully provokes. Who or what narrates the story? For Dennett, contemplating consciousness, you are the narrative of yourself and "your existence depends on the persistence of that narrative."[15] The question that must follow is: what is narrative? And obviously this is where literary studies can lend a hand, and the study of Joyce's narrative experimentation provide useful complications for pat assumptions and theories.

One of the general and recurrent problems with cognitive literary studies, it seems to me, is that the literary texts selected for examination tend to be construed as *normative*, as representative of a given genre or mode of literature as they are reflective of ordinary cognitive processes. In *On the Origin of Stories*, a book that scorns "Theory" for "evocriticism," an umbrella term that includes cognitive studies of literature, Brian Boyd explains that his case studies (Homer's *The Odyssey* and Dr. Seuss's *Horton Hears a Who!*) were not selected "because they bear out evolutionary themes in which I have a prior investment, but simply as supremely successful stories as near as I can get to narrative's phylogenic and ontogenic origins."[16] If the logic of that artificial selection posing as natural were not in itself questionable, Boyd adds that, but for lack of space, he would have included discussion of "other highly successful stories, a Shakespeare tragedy (*Hamlet*) and comedy (*Twelfth Night*), a classic novel (*Pride and Prejudice*), a modernist novel (Joyce's *Ulysses*), and a postmodernist text (Spiegelman's *Maus*)."[17] We are back to the Sokal problem of a priori labels for texts (*Ulysses* is a modernist *novel*) that bespeak a priori definitions, understandings, and limitations.[18] This is exactly why the problem of the "Joycean machine" rather than the "Joycean novel" is so compelling.

---

[15] Dennett, *Consciousness Explained*, 430.

[16] Brian Boyd, *On the Origin of Stories* (Cambridge, MA: Harvard University Press, 2009), 389.

[17] Boyd, *On the Origin of Stories*, 389.

[18] One sign of the infancy of consciousness studies (and by extension, cognitive literary studies) lies not only in the normative-making examples and case studies that it too often favors, but in its choosing never to study itself. Just as it has been frequently observed that Freud is glaringly bad at psychoanalyzing himself, and early anthropology did not

It is an understatement to say that Joyce is interested in cognitive processes:[19] indeed, Joyce's ambivalence about psychoanalysis may be understood as symptomatic of an interest in the human mind beyond the discursive, systematized confines of psychology. In the same way that *Finnegans Wake*'s attempt to rediscover a language of languages can be viewed as demonstrating an awareness of how superficial the differences between particular languages are in light of the genetic predisposition to language encoded within us, Joyce's ambition is to understand not just the software of the individual but the hardware of the species. Seemingly counterbalanced against Joyce's interest in consciousness, in what makes the self distinctive and aware of its distinctiveness, is the fact that, if we look at Joyce's work as a continuum, we notice that the trajectory is a gradually more radical disintegration of selfhood and subjectivity. On the one hand, there is the structural motif of development that Joyce likes to combine with the appreciation of narrative as perspective. Thus *A Portrait* is not just a book about learning but a book that emulates learning, and *Finnegans Wake* is itself a sort of universal primer, by which we "learn from that ancient tongue to be middle old modern to the minute" (270.17–18). On the other hand, however, with each subsequent book, the uncertainty about the sources and integrity of the data provided or found becomes more and more acute: what Hugh Kenner named the "Uncle Charles Principle"—an idiosyncratic kind of free indirect discourse—graduates from apparent exception to rule.[20]

---

recognize the length of shadow it cast over its ostensible subjects, students of cognition do not—yet—consider their own enterprise as a cognitive process worthy of study.

[19] Accordingly, the body of criticism on Joyce and consciousness is gargantuan; but with our focus here we can distinguish a little and leave aside those works with a predominantly *psychological* understanding of consciousness to take note of the following examples and the variety of their approaches to the subject: Richard Ellmann, *The Consciousness of Joyce* (New York: Oxford University Press, 1977); David Herman, "Cognition, Emotion, and Consciousness," in *The Cambridge Companion to Narrative* (Cambridge: Cambridge University Press, 2007), 245–59; Tom Simone, "'Met Him Pike Hoses': *Ulysses* and the Neurology of Reading," *Joyce Studies Annual* (2013): 207–37; Tim Conley, "'Are You to Have All the Pleasure Quizzing on Me?' *Finnegans Wake* and Literary Cognition," *James Joyce Quarterly* 40.4 (2003): 711–27; Alexandra Anyfanti, "Time, Space, and Consciousness in Joyce's *Ulysses*," *Hypermedia Joyce Studies* 4.2 (2003–4), online. In 2011, an entire conference was held at the Sorbonne on the theme "Cognitive Joyce: The Neuronal Text," which eventually led to the publication of *Cognitive Joyce*, ed. Sylvain Belluc and Valérie Bénéjam (Cham, Switzerland: Palgrave, 2018).

[20] Hugh Kenner, *Joyce's Voices* (Berkeley: University of California Press, 1978), 15–38. Kenner's term is drawn from the striking use of the word "repaired" in this sentence from *A Portrait of the Artist as a Young Man*: "Every morning, therefore, uncle Charles repaired to his outhouse but not before he had creased and brushed scrupulously his back hair and brushed and put on his tall hat" (50). "Repaired" is of a fine Victorian vintage, expressive of a man of Stephen's uncle age and efforts at dignity and propriety.

A vivid example of this development is Joyce's use of the word "literally" in two sentences written years apart. The pregnant and much-studied first sentence of "The Dead" ("Lily, the caretaker's daughter, was literally run off her feet" (*D* 175)) offers an ironic correspondence between "Lily" and "literally," both in the repetition of sounds and in the implication that this ill-chosen adverb somehow reflects Lily's own thinking. The story as a whole has to do with the slippery division between the literal and the figurative, demonstrated by how the very phrase "the dead," which both begins the story as its title and ends it as the last words, manages to have both literal and figurative referents simultaneously. What seems like the same ploy in the "Eumaeus" episode of *Ulysses* turns out to be a much cloudier affair: when Stephen tells Bloom when he last dined, Bloom is said to be "[l]iterally astounded at this piece of intelligence" (16.1578). Whereas one *can* be literally run off one's feet, "literally astounded" is just as much a puzzle as the inverse proposition it invokes—being *figuratively* or *metaphorically* astounded—which may very well describe the state of the reader at this point. Not only can this locution not be as assuredly linked with a source consciousness in the way that "literally run off her feet" at least arguably can (claims that Bloom himself is the narrator of this chapter seldom square with similar claims about earlier chapters, altogether different in style,[21] and though it might make more sense to say that *a version of Bloom* narrates "Eumaeus"—the Beaufoy Bloom, we might say—such a qualification only magnifies rather than eliminates the problem of knowing "who," literally or otherwise, uses "literally"), its meaning cannot be as clearly comprehended as expressive of a character who has misused "literally."

Yet for the most compelling of current directions in consciousness studies, this is not a paradox, or at least it is of a piece with a series of counterintuitive observations and propositions. Trying "to isolate i from my multiple Mes" (*FW* 410.12) turns out to be just the problem the *Wake* presents it as: subjectivity is an effort of separation of sensations and meanings. That is, consciousness is not so much a quality as a process, not a given but a work in progress. Dennett's "Joycean machine" chugs along so long as the brain lives, constantly absorbing material for ongoing interpretations, the so-called "stream of consciousness." He writes:

---

[21] There is a comparable though less paradoxical use of "literally" in "Nausicaa": "His dark eyes fixed themselves on her again drinking in her every contour, literally worshipping at her shrine" (13.564). However, this "literally" operates in much the same way that Lily's does (i.e., as a kind of fantasy: Gerty might wish that the dark stranger were "worshipping at her shrine" just as Lily's being "run off her feet" may well reflect her own romantic frustrations, obliquely suggesting the proverbial "swept off her feet"), so it need not necessarily be attributed to Bloom.

> one of the fundamental tasks performed by the activities of the Joycean machine is to adjudicate disputes, smooth out traditions between regimes, and prevent untimely *coups d'état* by marshaling the "right" forces. Simple or overlearned tasks without serious competition can be routinely executed without the enlistment of extra forces, and hence unconsciously, but when a task is difficult or unpleasant, it requires "concentration," something "we" accomplish with the help of much self-admonition and various other mnemonic tricks, rehearsals [...] and other self-manipulations.[22]

The martial and political language here stems from Dennett's insistence that there is no central seat of power or authority within the mind, a point that does tie in with such Joycean problems as the open question of who narrates *A Portrait*, or the more labyrinthine speculations and arguments about the role of an "Arranger" in *Ulysses*.[23] A committed Darwinian, Dennett knows that a function or effect need not signify a role, and the dislocated adjudication process that he outlines sounds the same chord as Fritz Senn's notion of the "autocorrective" text:

> *Ulysses* is probably the first consistently autocorrective work of literature—and the interconnections depend in part on the time of the reading [...] But the more we absorb the more skeptical we can also become about what, so far, we thought we knew for certain.[24]

For these reasons, Joyce's reader cannot truly assume the role of "decider." Dennett wryly borrows this epithet from George W. Bush, who once firmly announced, "I'm the decider."[25] Instead, the reader must navigate a steady stream of doubts. Understanding consciousness as a collaborative network will appeal to those of us who see authorship as a plurality (of motives, of voices, of productions), as *Ulysses* suggests and *Finnegans Wake*—"even more rigorously autocorrective"[26]—emphasizes.

---

[22] Dennett, *Consciousness Explained*, 277.

[23] See David Hayman, Ulysses: *The Mechanics of Meaning*, revised ed. (Madison: University of Wisconsin Press, 1982), 84, and Patrick McGee, *Paperspace: Style as Ideology in Joyce's Ulysses* (Lincoln: University of Nebraska Press, 1988), 72–74.

[24] Fritz Senn, *Joyce's Dislocutions: Essays on Reading as Translation*, ed. John Paul Riquelme (Baltimore: Johns Hopkins University Press, 1984), 69. See also H. Porter Abbott, "Unnarratable Knowledge: The Difficulty of Understanding Evolution by Natural Selection," in *Narrative Theory and the Cognitive Sciences*, ed. David Herman (Stanford: CSLI Publications, 2003), 143–62.

[25] Dennett, *Consciousness Explained*, 229.

[26] Senn, *Joyce's Dislocutions*, 69.

Ulysses represents the thinking processes of an uncertain number of people, but, perhaps more significant than this unascertainability (again an echo of the decentralized sources of thought) is how the reader's own thinking cannot fall altogether into step with the process represented. Bloom's mistaking of the first word of "Blood of the Lamb" in the leaflet given to him early in "Lestrygonians" is recognized by him as a mistake ("Bloo. Me? No" (8.08)) before the reader can do so. Because this mistake cannot originate with the reader, who does not "see" the text of the leaflet as and when Bloom does, the reader does not "correct" Bloom the way she well might when she finds him fumbling to articulate the definition of metempsychosis, or how black responds to heat; rather, she has to figure out how to get it both wrong *and* right, and appreciate how both readings coexist. A dictatorial decider who cannot see any value in *x* after selecting *not-x* as the correct or preferred term will unjustly adjudicate a variety of such disputes in the novel, which is to say that such a reading method would be astonishingly insensitive to the possibilities *Ulysses* invites its readers to evaluate and enjoy—*continuously*. Nearly every word and phrase of *Finnegans Wake* likewise requires that the reader see the jumbled words as they are (i.e., as gobbledygook: a word like "painapple" (167.15) has no clear meaning or referent), then as they are not (on second thought, "painapple" sounds like "pineapple"), and then again as they are (although "painapple" does sound like "pineapple," it is not "pineapple"), and so on: reading becomes—like consciousness—a work in progress. Perhaps the conception of consciousness as a series of recognitions should be retooled with this example of the experience of reading the *Wake*, so as to see consciousness instead as a non-linear back-and-forth between contrary recognitions.

We might take up the starting point of Stephen's aesthetic theory in *A Portrait*: "in order to see that basket [...] your mind first of all separates the basket from the rest of the visible universe which is not the basket. The first phase of apprehension is a bounding line drawn about the basket to be apprehended" (*P* 178). Just as modern art dispels the fixed "bounding line," Joyce's subsequent books progressively problematize the task of separating basket from not-basket by making such acts of apprehension provisional, doubtful, and often subject to change or even outright contradiction. When is the "phase of apprehension" completed? The questioning refrain of *Finnegans Wake*, "when is a man not a man," highlights—in both its persistence and its persistent variations—how continuous, evolving, and doubtful the distinguishing of one perception from another is in the process of meaning-making.

Dennett's ultimate proposal of a "Multiple Drafts model" for consciousness also has a nicely Joycean feel to it. Instead of a "Cartesian Theater" in which the aloof decider neatly collates sensory data called "qualia," Dennett suggests that "there are just Multiple Drafts composed by processes of content fixation playing various semi-independent roles in the brain's larger economy" (431). Dennett's designation of the "Multiple Drafts model" as a "Joycean machine" appears to be predicated on the "stream of consciousness" narrative in which a character's impressions are subject to perpetual revision in light of previous and subsequent impressions, even to the point of reshaping or entirely distorting the first impression (Bloom's Beaufoy/Purefoy confusion is a relatively straightforward example), but such a model is also notably akin to our more and more compulsively comparative and textual-genetic methods of rereading Joyce. The network of texts, errata, and possible meanings that we refer to as Joyce, as convenient shorthand, is so various and vast that when someone refers to Joyce, even very broadly, it ought to be understood that only a narrow perception of the incomprehensible because pragmatically unassimilable whole is being referred to, though that understanding does not necessarily invalidate the particular claims being made. So too with conscious experience.

There is another attractive, hotly contested theory about consciousness that does not contradict Dennett's but is rather more the stuff of "hard science," if no less speculative for that. Physicist Roger Penrose, later joined by anesthesiologist Stuart Hameroff, holds that consciousness is a quantum mechanical phenomenon. In this view (without getting distractingly technical), the phenomenon of consciousness is directly comparable and perhaps altogether equivalent to the phenomenon of quantum physics, as it is observed on a subatomic level. Thus, everything depends upon the brain's providing the conditions in which very tiny particles can attain superposition, the utterly boggling point at which they can violate the most rudimentary, observable, and intuitive rules of matter by being in different places at the same time. This particular theory is of interest to this discussion precisely because *Finnegans Wake* anticipates it: in its pages, time and space are repeatedly warped and a given character is simultaneously dead and alive, then and now, here and also there. The *Wake*'s "quantum theory" (149.35), however tongue-in-cheek that expression may appear, may ultimately signify that this puzzling, discontinuous, and counterintuitive book affords greater insights into the workings of the human mind than is usually credited.

Consider the disorientation caused by this passage, and note that this disorientation is not simply or at least significantly attributable to syntactic convolution and/or (literally) non-referential vocabulary:

> A space. Who are you? The cat's mother. A time. What do you lack? The look of a queen.

But what is that which is one going to prehend? Seeks, buzzling its brains, the feinder. (*FW* 223.23–26)

Where the reader of *Ulysses* can, however tentatively and sometimes unconvincingly, connect brief, disjointed sentences such as these with the supposition that they reflect the variegated, spontaneous impressions of and responses to specific experiences within a single consciousness—effectively seeing in such lexical rapids a stream of consciousness rather than wandering rocks—there is no such assurance for the reader of the *Wake*, which text always seems (as here) to be asking who is speaking and of what or whom is being spoken.[27] The reader who considers that this passage appears to be part of an extended outline or description of a play ("*The Mime of Mick, Nick and the Maggies*" (219.18–19)) must admit that such a context allows the suggestion that these lines represent a dialogue only to logically compromise that very context, since (1) no words are spoken in a mime or dumbshow, (2) Joyce's customary punctuation for spoken words, the tiret, is absent, and (3) it is not at all clear who is speaking to whom, and the breaks between sentences and the one between paragraphs do not help. Distorted allusions to fairly paternalistic proverbs ("She is the cat's mother," "A cat may look at a king [or queen]," "Seek and ye shall find") underline the state of confusion rather than dispel it, so that the reader can only (again, tentatively and perhaps without absolute conviction) posit a connection between these sentences and so claim a continuous understanding (or grasp, "prehend") of the text with the supposition that they reflect the variegated, spontaneous impressions of and responses to specific experiences within a single consciousness—not that of a character in the text, however, but the reader's own. The only unifying consciousness in the *Wake* is the one that experiences all of these discontinuities, just as the human mind may generate the sense of selfhood to unify, as best as it may, the deluge of partial, contradictory information it receives. By these lights, then, Dennett's assertion about how "existence depends on the persistence of that narrative" becomes that much more tangible, if the rather abstract term "existence" is refined to mean a working state of awareness, itself a serviceable illusion of continuity, "ineluctably constructed upon the incertitude of the void."

---

[27] This passage might be usefully compared with Stephen's riddle in "Nestor" about the fox and his grandmother (2.101–115). Critics have generally preferred to treat Stephen's riddle as a collection of psychologically rich associations and symbols; as though, in fact, it were an isolated outbreak of *Finnegans Wake* within *Ulysses*. But the essential hermeneutic difference is again apparent: Stephen's riddle is just that, Stephen's riddle, and all such interpretations draw upon this assumption as capital. No such basis underwrites interpretive ventures about the "time" of "the cat's mother."

III

Let me return to Raymond Tallis, who, you'll recall, claimed that we are unable to "articulate self-consciousness as expressed in the reading and writing of poetry." The redundancy of the phrase highlights the meaninglessness of the statement: we cannot express what is expressed in poetry? If not, it's because we don't have to: the poem already does that. The poem is, if you like, an enactment of consciousness (and not just a conscious act, like the construction of a chair or the preparation of a milkshake), even an extension of consciousness, in the way that a printed dictionary is an extension of memory. All the same, though we might call *Ulysses* or *Finnegans Wake* a "Joycean machine" and compare its "mechanical" operations to the workings of the human mind, I remain unsure whether the by now customary likening of consciousness to a machine is not itself a reductive framework.[28] The *Wake* phrase borrowed for my title, "cog it out, here goes a sum" (304.31) mocks the facile and cruel mechanization of Cartesianism, just as it carefully inserts the indefinite pronoun "a" to suggest the provisional, non-exclusive sum the ever-adding mind never actually possesses.[29] Indeed, it seems to me—and the sheer breadth of Joyce scholarship underscores the point—that, contra Tallis, we do and can study Joycean machines very well and in a number of enlightening ways.

The use of Joyce as a case study or kind of simulation experiment in consciousness studies is, interestingly, as ambivalent as it is frequent, and this may be because it is not easy to say just what a "Joycean machine" does, even if it seems to emulate in this or that respect the workings of the mind. In a breathtakingly ambitious—and sometimes frustrating—study of how the divided brain (though not quite the one diagnosed by Julian Jaynes years before[30]) has shaped Western civilization and culture, Iain McGilchrist argues that the

---

[28] Similar caution was voiced by Norbert Wiener:

> if we insist too strongly on the brain as a glorified digital machine, we shall be subject to some very just criticism [...] I have said that in a digital machine there is a *taping*, which determines the sequence of operations to be performed, and that a change in this taping on the basis of past experience corresponds to a learning process [...] in considering the problem of learning, we should be most wary of assuming an all-or-none theory of the nervous system, without having made an intellectual criticism of the notion, and without specific experimental evidence to back our assumption.
> (*The Human Use of Human Beings: Cybernetics and Society* (Boston: DaCapo Press, 1954), 65–66)

[29] On the ways that Joyce's works actively resist acts of "summing up" and gestaltic interpretations, see the second essay in this collection.

[30] Julian Jaynes, *The Origin of Consciousness in the Breakdown of the Bicameral Mind* (Boston: Houghton Mifflin, 1976).

logical but atomizing left hemisphere has come to dominate our perceptions and thinking. In his survey of the cultural shifts in this "Western" imagination since the Middle Ages, he gives modernism a stern rebuke for having "experimented, unsuccessfully in my view, with abandoning" the idea of a cohesive, intuitive, shared language—not the lexical structures of the left brain but the holistic arrangements of the right.[31] McGilchrist contends that the suggestion

> that meaning is not in the words themselves, but needs further decoding to be unlocked, was something of a dead end, an interesting culturohistorical document, like Joyce's *Finnegan's Wake* [sic], rather than powerful poetry—although its borrowings make it gleam in places like a magpie's nest.[32]

One need not take sides of the left-versus-right question that is McGilchrist's thesis to see how confused an admiration-by-way-of-rejection this is of Joyce. The implied categorical opposition between "an interesting culturohistorical document" and "powerful poetry" is hard to fathom, and the attribution of the idea that "meaning is not in the words themselves" to Joyce ignores everything he ever said about the *Wake* (never mind the aforementioned work of scholars). In effect, what the above passage says is "*Finnegans Wake* is sort of remarkable but alas it does not fit my theory"—and while such a lame exemption warrants ridicule, it ought to be remembered how many times just such a gesture is made in literary histories of narrative. Whereas scientists like Tallis and Sokal recognize cultural artifacts (such as "a novel") as outside of, distracting from, or even essentially contrary to the phenomenon of consciousness and any reasonable investigation of it, McGilchrist sees culture as both cause and effect, as much creating the mind as it is a creation of it, a view which—if only he would notice!—Joyce's work enthusiastically shares: "But the world, mind, is, was and will be writing its own wrunes for ever, man, on all matters that fall under the ban of our infrarational senses" (*FW* 19.35–20.01).

The assertion that it is incorrect to suppose that "meaning is not in the words themselves, but needs further decoding to be unlocked," while it flies in the face of what is known about how the mind necessarily deciphers text and finds meaning in relations, may also be indicative of a favored model

---

[31] Iain McGilchrist, *The Master and His Emissary: The Divided Brain and the Making of the Western World* (New Haven, CT: Yale University Press, 2009), 421.

[32] McGilchrist, *The Master and His Emissary*, 422. One could argue that McGilchrist's undisguisedly adverse conception of modernism in general is itself the product of the narrow kind of left-brain interpretation of which he despairs.

of narrative that excludes differences and experimentation. If "narrative" is understood to have such fixed elements as causal plot, distinguishable and stabilized characters, certain unities of time and place, and so on, *Finnegans Wake* will be written off, as McGilchrist has done, as some sort of aberration, and if this rigid conception of a "traditional" or "normal" narrative is the only one to be drawn upon in discussions of consciousness and literature, it is those discussions that will be the poorer for it. Yet if the unlocking of meaning is itself narrative—if, as Stephen Dedalus, thinking of Aristotle, ponders, "thought is the thought of thought" (*U* 2.74)—then it is those works of literature that most complicate and expand our experience of the act of reading that may likewise complicate and expand those valuable discussions.

In case my argument's first claim, that Joyce studies and consciousness studies can learn a good deal from one another, seems overinflated (here's another literature professor who has the gall to suggest that literature has anything to say about anything other than literature!), it's worth pointing out that commonplaces that hold that to understand childhood one can read *Alice in Wonderland* or *Huckleberry Finn*, or that to read Dante is to understand medieval Italy, are never thought to diminish the complexity of such subjects as childhood or medieval Italy. If this point is granted and some "sifting" of science and art is attempted, this essay's second claim about the reciprocal benefits that Joyce's associative, recursive, and multiple-draft networks (especially those of *Ulysses* and *Finnegans Wake*) and the exciting consciousness research of the past twenty years hold for each other becomes an impetus for further discussion and illuminating connections—or as the *Wake* has it, "increasing, livivorous, feelful thinkamalinks" (*FW* 613.19).

Chapter 6

MYTHAMETICAL

Waking "for an Equality of Relations"

> These last have wrought but one hour, and thou hast made them equal unto us, which have borne the burden and heat of the day.
>
> —Matthew 20:12

> Rarely equal and distinct in all things.
>
> — *FW* 306F7

I

Regular or prolonged exposure to *Finnegans Wake* has significant social consequences. These effects—unlike, say, the bleary-eyed hipness achieved by binge viewing of entire television seasons, which thereafter fuels knowledgeable exchanges and valuable cultural fluency—seem to alienate their subjects from the world. Reading everyday functional texts such as street signs, telephone directories, and restaurant menus becomes unexpectedly strange and difficult, and—let's be honest—the chances of finding someone with whom to puzzle over the riddles of the *Wake* and giggle through the protracted bouts of puns that it offers (and inspires) are more than slightly slimmer than those of finding someone to discuss the latest surprise disembowelment in *Game of Thrones*. But the difference I want to underscore isn't a matter of faddishness: the repeat viewer of such shows, the online gamer who gives up whole weekends to the quest, grow more authoritative, more certain in these imaginary worlds, and thus able to disregard the tedium or injustices of mere meatspace. The *Finnegans Wake* reader, it seems to me, instead becomes more doubtful and bewildered in both worlds in proportion to one another.

There might be perceptible stages of acclimatization—if that is the right word—to the *Wake*. Among the later stages, or at any rate not among the first, is a suspicion of words and phrases in the text that seem immediately sensible, that is, to all appearances syntactically sensible arrangements of readily identifiable words. In turn a reader may grow—as I, for one, have grown—suspicious of the *Wake* passages of which I seem (or seemed) to have some comprehension. We might think of this as one of those reversals of the unfamiliar, a sort of squaring of the uncanny, not unlike the moment in a foreboding narrative or dream when the recognizable friend who greets us in the terra incognita is revealed, precisely when it dawns on us how very out of place he is, as not our friend at all.

Thus a phrase such as "an equality of relations" (*FW* 283.11–12), which seems innocuous enough, not one of the verbal constructions in the text most likely to halt a reader conversant in English, and familiar as a slogan with no definite context, now gives great pause. Is "equality" able to be parceled into discreet units, "an equality"? Or do we hear in that phrase the sound of "inequality"? When is something equal and not? I propose to dig into this phrase as a way into the *Wake*, and as a way of understanding its politics—in other words, to try to understand why the *Wake* has these aforementioned social effects on its readers.

While literary history and cultural theory have adopted a now-familiar set of sociopolitical terms for understanding the power relations of representation as well as cultural and textual production (including, e.g., oppression, marginalization, authority, privilege, and sovereignty) conspicuously and perhaps unsettlingly absent is "equality." It understandably remains an elusive if not altogether opaque concept: what does it mean to say that one thing, person, or quantity is "equivalent" (of the same meaning or value) to another? Does it not seem that criticism—so much of it, if not by general definition—is a negation of equality, an establishing of different values?

More specifically, the words "Joyce" and "equality" might seem to have nothing to do with one another, despite the fact that the persistent and popular conception of Joyce's works (and, often as not, his views) as coldly elitist and inaccessible has in recent years faced some refutations, however measured. (It is interesting to note that, for example, while Declan Kiberd makes the case that *Ulysses* is a book of everyday life abducted by academics and kept hostage in an ivory tower, from which heights it must be rescued, no comparable appeal is offered for *Finnegans Wake*.[1]) These works, it is worth remembering, are in some cases many years apart from one another, and the name "Joyce" more aptly signifies an impressionable, highly sensitive, and adaptable man with a lifetime of international experiences than a stabilized set of aesthetic principles and social views. Much water has flown under the bridge between

---

[1] See Declan Kiberd, Ulysses *and Us: The Art of Everyday Life in Joyce's Masterpiece* (New York: Norton, 2009).

"The Day of the Rabblement" and the nights of a grandfather scribbling away in his "bellsybabble" (and if that is a mixed metaphor, it is Joyce's, not mine). One could argue that while the "chains" of *Exiles* and the "nets" of *A Portrait* display the rebellious young struggle for and affirmation of liberty, *Ulysses* is Joyce's study of fraternity, a sophisticated novelistic simulation, to borrow Roland Barthes's terms, of "how to live together."[2] The *Wake*, then, with all of its "clearobscure" (*FW* 247.34) confusion of identities, resembles that blank white space between the blue and red of the tricolor (or, in the Irish flag, between orange and green). I suggest that in writing his last book, a book that he conceived as being about everybody, for everybody, and in the sense that he was by degrees disavowing his own authorial centrality, *by* everybody, Joyce was exploring the meaning of "equality." Determining just what are the findings of these explorations may prove as elusive as the answer to the nagging question, "just what is this book about, anyway?"

Emer Nolan has written: "It is easy perhaps to grasp Joyce's later work as in many regards *prematurely* liberationist displaying the equality and interchangeability of all languages and cultures irrespective of the relations of power or domination which may currently obtain between them."[3] This thorny statement requires careful parsing. "Later work" seems to be an oddly roundabout way of referring to *Finnegans Wake*, given the reference to "all languages and cultures," but this is the least difficult part of the puzzle. The sentence appears to be a criticism of the *Wake*'s political idealism or naivete, or at any rate its remove from the contingencies and conditions of an immediate history. This might seem a muted sort of Caliban's rage at the mirror, but the stressed word "*prematurely*" complicates matters, as though the mirror dared to show Caliban his face as it *will* look, rather than how it does. But Nolan's assertion here is even more indirect than this, for her criticism (or is it a note of caution?) is directed at the reader, who ought to know better than to grasp anything that can be grasped easily—if, that is, it *can* be grasped easily, for that "perhaps" and the no less slippery "in many regards" make the whole problem harder to see as a problem at all. With its recurrent qualification of "not yet" (and of course, variants thereof) *Finnegans Wake* is explicitly "premature." Whether the book displays "the equality and interchangeability of all languages and cultures" is open to question, though it might be useful to ask whether "displays" is not a misleading verb choice. Instead it might be asked whether the *Wake* in some way posits or endorses some conception of an "equality of relations," or, in the more modest approach I am taking here,

---

[2] Roland Barthes, *How to Live Together: Novelistic Simulations of Some Everyday Spaces*, trans. Kate Briggs (New York: Columbia University Press, 2013).
[3] Emer Nolan, *James Joyce and Nationalism* (London: Routledge, 1995), 48.

whether it is a consideration of what "equality of relations" might mean to a reader, not "irrespective" of "relations of power or domination" but because of them.

The phrase "all things being equal" (ceteris paribus) is routinely used to deflate hopes that that which it qualifies has any validity or promise, and "equality of relations" is a phrase that likewise smacks of some utopian project. While there is a number of possible sources, either sociopolitical or mathematical, from which Joyce might have borrowed it, Herbert Spencer, whose work seeks to unite these different discourses and disciplines, is a compelling possibility. Outlining the advent and foundations of scientific thought, Spencer distinguishes between "equality of things" and "equality of relations":

> the notion of equality of relations is the basis of all exact reasoning. Already it has been shown that reasoning in general is a recognition of *likeness* of relations; and here we further find that while the notion of likeness of things ultimately evolves the idea of simple equality, the notion of likeness of relations evolves the idea of equality of relations: of which the one is the concrete germ of exact science, while the other is its abstract germ.[4]

We know from some of Joyce's earliest notebooks that he read and thought about Spencer, and his appropriation of the phrase "survival of the fittest" ("sowiveall of the prettiest" (*FW* 145.27); note Spencer's use of "evolves" here) demonstrates that Spencer was still in his mind to some degree during the composition of "Work in Progress," perhaps because he was thinking of his own writing as a form of evolution.

Let us pause and go back to the stages of getting to know (or, as I think it comes to the same thing, of getting lost in) *Finnegans Wake*, our evolution as readers of the *Wake*. The question of equality aside for the moment, it is a book of likenesses: twins and shapechangers and reflections on every page, and textual loops bring us back to things we feel we have read or seen or heard before:

> that's what makes lifework leaving (12.01–2)
> Was liffe worth leaving? (230.25)

---

[4] Herbert Spencer, "The Genesis of Science," in *Essays: Scientific, Political, and Speculative*, vol. 1 (London: Williams and Norgate, 1868), 154. Joyce's reading of Spencer is a subject deserving of greater critical examination than either has heretofore been done or I can offer here.

Is love worse living? (269F1)
harm's worth healing (246.31–32)

When we compare these variations, these "murmurrandoms of distend renations from ficsimilar phases" (358.03), or when we compare a *Wake* phrase such as, say, "as fenny as he is fulgar" (242.28–29) with a more familiar English "as funny as he is vulgar," what is it that we notice: the likeness, or the difference? Pattern recognition is much vaunted as the basis for intelligence, and in educational practice and psychological classification has made for some troubling norms and standards. Joyce challenges the clean causality and the self-centered bias of Spencer's recipe. A tricky distinction: is likeness like equality, or does likeness equal equality?

Joyce's guiding principle is "likeas equal to anequal" (17.35), in which we might hear a faint echo of Molly's "as well him as another." Whereas *Ulysses*, as Sam Slote has recently observed, "goes against the concept of *Sinn Féin*: we ourselves are never alone,"[5] *Finnegans Wake* goes even further: not only are we never alone, we aren't even ourselves. Marian Eide suggests that the *Wake* can instructively be read as "a model for an ethical relation between others that balances alterity with connection."[6] Joyce's "enduring ethical investment," Eide writes, "is an understanding of the subject as an unstable entity formed in relation to another from whom that subject is incommensurably different."[7] There is in the *Wake* a constant renegotiation of words and identities in relation to one another that effectively approaches at every point a kind of equality in that these relations are based on the precept that "the other cannot be wholly subsumed by the subject's conceptualization";[8] or, "likeas equal to anequal."

II

Mathematics was never Joyce's strong suit, a point that several commentators have found various occasions to reiterate, but he never seems to have lost interest in the subject. The *Wake* is replete with references to mathematicians (such as Lewis Carroll and the Irishman William Rowan Hamilton), formulae, and mathematical textbooks (such as James Hodder's delightfully titled *Arithmetick; or That Necessary Art Made Most Easy* (see *FW* 537.36)). Probably the densest concentration of these is found in the children's lessons of II.2, from

---

[5] Sam Slote, *Joyce's Nietzschean Ethics* (New York: Palgrave, 2013), 100.
[6] Marian Eide, *Ethical Joyce* (Cambridge: Cambridge University Press, 2002), 6.
[7] Eide, *Ethical Joyce*, 9.
[8] Eide, *Ethical Joyce*, 16.

which our key phrase "an equality of relations" comes, and also in which is found the most instances of Joyce playing with mathematical signs and notation. Here are a few (familiar) examples:

> either greater THaN or less ThaN the unitate we have in one (298.13)
> by cows ∵ man, in shirt, is how he is *più la gonna è mobile* and ∴ they wonet do ut (292.11–12)
> palls pell inhis heventh glike noughty times ∞, find, if you are not literally coefficient, how minney combinaisies and permutandies can be played (284.10–13)

II.2 is a protracted study of relations and proportions, in which students are instructed to either "construct ann aquilittoral dryankle" (286.19–20) or "Concoct an equoangular trilitter" (286.21–22). The chapter is a struggle for equality, with twins wrestling and changing places while their no less changeable sister looks on and makes wisecracks about various inequities of relations. She not only lends perspective but stresses perspective when she remarks (or coughs), "Ugol egal ogle" (297F2), which might be a way of saying equality is in the eye of the ogler. She is also helpful when it comes to wondering what "equals" means, for Issy is herself the best answer to Bill Clinton's dilemma about what the definition of "'is' is." The incest motif that surrounds Joyce's Isolde is also relevant, for according to the *Catholic Encyclopedia*'s entry on "Consanguinity (in Canon Law)":

> By the law of nature, it is universally conceded, marriage is prohibited between parent and child, for the reverential relation between them is recognized as incompatible with the equality of relations engendered by the bond of marriage.[9]

Be advised: the reason you do not marry your child is because doing so would irreverently make the two of you equals.

The word "equals" functions not just contradictorily, but as itself a contradiction. Here are a few examples that, all things being equal, I would gladly examine at length:

> An imposing everybody he always indeed looked, constantly the same as and equal to himself and magnificently well worthy of any and all such universalisation (32.19–21)

---

[9] "Consanguinity (in Canon Law)," *The Catholic Encyclopedia*. http://www.newadvent.org/cathen/04264a.htm (accessed April 20, 2020).

equals of opposites, evolved by a onesame power of nature or of spirit, *iste*, as the sole condition and means of its himundher manifestation and polarised for reunion by the symphysis of their antipathies. (92.08–11)

in the ersebest idiom I have done it equals I so shall do. (253.01–02)

Nola Bruno monopolises his egobruno most unwillingly seses by the mortal powers alionola equal and opposite brunoipso, *id est*, eternally provoking alio opposite equally as provoked as Bruno at being eternally opposed by Nola. Poor omniboose, singalow singelearum: so is he! (488.07–12)

in a more or less settled state of equonomic ecolube equalobe equilab equilibbrium (599.17–18)

Reading these passages together, we can observe how the very word "equal" is used as at once a doubtful assertion and a staggered transition. That is, equality is a markedly unlikely state of being ("equal to himself" is an extraordinary phrase with ordinary roots: "equal to another" and "he himself" are not thought redundant or unusual) and to equate is to change the subject. In the logic of the *Wake*, everything and everybody become equal, to the point that all distinction is provisional and short-lived.

Perhaps sufficient unto this day is the sign, which has its own history of mutability. Regiomontanus (the rather HCE-ish nom de nombres of Johannes Müller von Königsberg (1436–76)) used a long horizontal dash, while Xylander (Wilhelm Holzman (1532–76)) favored two vertical, parallel lines and Descartes (1596–1650) a backwards alpha, perhaps to signify the word *aequalis*.[10] Interestingly, the familiar pair of horizontal lines ("Gemowe lines") first introduced by Robert Recorde, a Welsh mathematician in his *Whetstone of Witte* (1557), came into popular usage when Leibniz (who himself preferred a kind of arch: ÿ)[11] and others adopted it for the revelations of calculus—in other words, just when mathematics became a matter of approximating equalities. Joyce uses the symbol twice in the *Wake*—

to = introdùce a notion of time (124.10–11)

Equal to=aosch. (286.02)

---

[10] Joseph Mazur, *Enlightening Symbols: A Short History of Mathematical Notation and Its Hidden Powers* (Princeton, NJ: Princeton University Press, 2014), xvii.

[11] Mazur, *Enlightening Symbols*, 166.

—but rather more often in the *Wake* notebooks:

audiometer = glasses (VI.B.1.061 (d))	not crossed out; no known *FW* use
ekumene = habitable O (VI.B.1.179 (j))	"let the whole ekumene universe belong to merry Hal" (*FW* 440.35–36)
ostrich = sparrow / — camel (VI.B.10.073 (a))	not crossed out; no known *FW* use
d = a (4th later letter) / Caesar's code (VI.B.16.078 (c))	not crossed out; no known *FW* use; taken from *Histoire de la poste aux lettres*
seamless robe = skin (VI.B.16.122 (j))	"The meteor pulp of him, the seamless rainbowpeel." (*FW* 475.12–13)
fog = cloud / in which / we are (VI.B.47.063 (c))	"the fog of the cloud in which we toil and the fog of the cloud under which we labour" (*FW* 599.30–31)

The random selection of these examples from an array of notebooks[12] from different points in the composition and evolution of the *Wake* demonstrates both the persistence of Joyce's use of the sign and, as with many features of the notebooks, how imperfectly we understand it. We can, however, by comparing such examples, risk a troubling assertion: Joyce appreciates different forms of equivalence. (Recall again our key phrase: "*an* equality of relations.") In Joyce's use of "=" there is what might be rather broadly and perhaps only provisionally understood to be a working synonymy between terms. The relationship between "audiometer" and "glasses," perhaps suggestive of the recurrent tropes of synaesthesia within the *Wake*, does not seem to be the same relationship between "d" and "a" (in a code reportedly favored by Caesar, in which each letter of a communicated text would be replaced with a later letter in the alphabet). And while "ekumene = habitable O" appears to be a shorthand definition, with the "O" representing the world, the "ostrich" note, which rather looks like an algorithm, is an instance of Joyce taking note of the historical roots of his methods, the compounding of names to stand as functional equivalent for the hitherto unnameable. Perhaps the ostrich and Caesar's code weren't ultimately brought into the *Wake* because these devices struck Joyce as, respectively, too much or too little like his own method: not equal to it. Such notes provide glimpses of *Wakes* that might have been.

Ciphers imply an act of substitution rather than observe an actual equivalence, though this fuzzy distinction highlights one of the central problems in

---

[12] In this instance I am drawing upon the published notebooks and the invaluable editorial insights they provide: *The* Finnegans Wake *Notebooks at Buffalo*, ed. Vincent Deane, Daniel Ferrer, and Geert Lernout (Turnhout: Belgium, 2001–4).

discussing equality: it cannot be separated from its implementation. Equality is something we make, just as we construct an equilateral triangle: we might even see it as work in progress. The grandiosity with which a mathematical or logical proposition begins ("let x = ") is that of the command of creation: "let there be light." To posit an equivalence is the artistic act at its most affirmative: "he was baby tuckoo." Yet the ever (but again, not yet) collapsing of opposites in *Finnegans Wake* warns against identifications—or at least fixed identifications. This is why it is misleading to think of the *Wake* as a code: because it is perpetually reassigning values and identities, it might be more usefully understood as a process of encoding, of ever-generated and ever-transitory meaning.

III

"But ein and twee were never worth three" (246.15). The question remains: why this preponderance of mathematics in the *Wake*? Surely one strong attraction for Joyce, suggested by his use of the notation and the similar "sigla" of the Doodles family, is its status as a universal language (both in its claims as the language of nature and more practically as a transnational vocabulary and grammar). One need not accept the views of Spencer to imagine, at least, how political initiatives to widen forms of social equality might not be so remote from mathematical thinking. As the political philosopher John Rawls writes:

> There is no reason to assume that our sense of justice can be adequately characterized by familiar common sense precepts, or derived from the more obvious learning principles. A correct account of moral capacities will certainly involve principles and theoretical constructions which go much beyond the norms and standards cited in everyday life; it may eventually require fairly sophisticated mathematics as well.[13]

The problem lies in how social mores are "characterized" and "derived," and Joyce derives his conception of the *Wake* from such problems as squaring the circle and, as we have seen, used mathematical characters to tackle, if not solve, those problems of unification and transformation. An equalization in communication—like that produced by the confounding of tongues among the builders of Babel, a universal and unexpectedly liberating incoherency—might represent an initial step in equalizing other relations, though this thought needs to be followed by the reminder that revolutions must continue, and thus

---

[13] John Rawls, *A Theory of Justice* (Cambridge, MA: Harvard University Press, 1971), 47.

the most equalizing form of language would have to be a language that constantly changes, constantly contradicts itself, constantly confuses. Joyce knocks down our incautious towers again and again.[14]

Moreover, we might deepen our understanding of the politics of *Finnegans Wake* if, in conjunction with considerations of its ethics of representation, we were to trace the "ethics of composition" (to borrow a suggestive phrase from Pablo Ruiz)[15] by which Joyce—as is evidenced in notebooks, drafts, and proofs—identifies, selects, and reconstructs equalities of relations. In trying to imagine a functional utopian society, Barthes posits "the idiorrhythmic group" that "sheds its worldliness," a project that "involves the impossible (superhuman) establishing of a group whose *Telos* would be perpetually to destroy itself as a group, that is to say, in Nietzschean terms: to enable the group (the Living-Together) to leap beyond ressentiment."[16] Joyce's gradual dismantling of mimesis and language, taken as (for it has often been accused of being) a shedding of worldliness, enables the aforementioned continuous, non-teleological process of encoding. *Finnegans Wake* is an algorithm that is always calculating itself, equating this with that and that and everything.

Questions of whether the son is (or might be) the equal of the father, the Irishman the equal of the Englishman, women the equal of men are, for Joyce, neither simple nor platitudinous, and certainly not just a matter of yes or no. Rather, these questions fold back upon themselves, as *Finnegans Wake* asks us: what does "equal" mean, what kind of action or transformation is implicit in the verb "to equate"? I have already suggested that these problems are connected with the determination of meaning. Is to make meaning, to make sense to equate, to make equal, or is it to differentiate, to assign varying and sometimes contrary values?

While online gamers and cult TV fans have their conspicuously active communities, I would suggest that the difference between such groups and that otherwise comparable gathering of oddballs, a *Finnegans Wake* reading group, is that on the whole the *Wake* group is more egalitarian. This is what this book has done to us: we wonder what it means to mean, and so we are humbled, confused, and equal. More or less.

---

[14] Strictly speaking, the destruction of the Tower of Babel is apocryphal: the book of Genesis makes no mention of the tower being destroyed.

[15] Pablo M. Ruiz, *Four Cold Chapters on the Possibility of Literature: Leading Mostly to Borges and Oulipo* (Champaign, IL: Dalkey Archive, 2014), 231.

[16] Barthes, *How to Live Together*, 48–49.

Chapter 7

SCATOLOGICAL

Mixplacing His Fauces

O Jamesy let me up out of this pooh
—U 18.1128–29

I

In late 2016, His Holiness Pope Francis rebuked the mass media in startling terms. In criticizing the proliferation of "fake news" and tawdry, sensationalist exploitation, he diagnosed "the disease of coprophilia: constantly looking to communicate scandal, communicate ugly things, even if they are true. [...] And since people have a tendency towards coprophagy, it can be very damaging." With their work cut out for them, Catholic apologists have hurriedly produced glosses such as this: "Our choice to read smut over real news is a major reason why media outlets continue to degrade and publish garbage instead of real news. We have an obligation to consume media intelligently, and to insist upon accurate news, not smut. Otherwise, we become consumers of our own excrement."[1] There are two aspects to this extraordinary papal statement worthy of serious consideration: the equation—or is it a comparison?—of the consumption of "fake news" with the consumption of bodily waste, and the strikingly broad and matter-of-fact assertion about "people" and their "tendency towards coprophagy."

Behind all of this is a very modern and ever more pressing question: what is to be done with our shit? The Pope's comments echo the common wisdom and all of the anxiety behind it: *we don't really know, but whatever you do, don't eat it!* If we can set taboos and reflexes aside, the reasonable rejoinder to this decree is to ask *why not? Especially if we don't know what else to do with it?* (And here one cannot help but think of the forbidden fruit of Eden: what was that fruit for, if not to be eaten?)

---

[1] Marshall Connolly, "What Is 'Coprophilia' and Why Is Pope Francis Talking about It?" *Catholic Online*, December 7, 2016.

In suggesting that Joyce is rather interested in these questions, I wish to revisit and revise the diagnosis of Joyce's "cloacal obsession," as H. G. Wells had it (and it is a little strange to recall that this observation was made about *A Portrait*, well before the more conspicuously stained and malodorous *Ulysses*).[2] Wells, in polite defense of artistic license, coined this phrase with a comparison to Swift. This is part of if perhaps not the beginning of a familiar theme, which occasionally expands this comparison to propose a connection with Irishness, with the fine details of causality and psychology left conveniently hazy.

Both of these links deserve to be examined and broken. Though we might generally suppose Swift to be a more practical-minded writer than Joyce, in this matter the contrary is the case. Disgust is the incontrovertible effect of excrement in Swift, and any comedy around it—or deep within it, as Gulliver finds himself—is noticeably nervous. For Swift, who in this respect is exemplary of the Enlightenment, bodily waste is repellent because it seems to directly oppose or even gainsay the noble and willful qualities of ourselves—and these qualities are precisely what make us both ourselves and of some significant purpose (in society, in God's creation).[3] The irrefutable, apparently traumatic, stammer-inducing fact that Celia, Celia, Celia shits is starkly conclusive: there is nothing more to say.[4] Joyce, unlike Swift, does not just recognize the problem of what to do with our waste but investigates it. Put another way, the horror for Swift is that by definition nothing is to be done with shit, while for Joyce, this essay hopes to show, in dung begin responsibilities. In particular, these responsibilities include a developed awareness of the difference(s) and, more significantly, the co-relation between the phenomena we conceive of as *subjectivity* and *environment*.[5]

---

[2] H. G. Wells, "James Joyce," in *Nation* (February 24, 1917; 710, 712) and *The New Republic* (March 10, 1917; 158–60), reprinted in *James Joyce: The Critical Heritage, Vol.1 1907–1927*, ed. Robert H. Deming (London: Routledge and Kegan Paul, 1970), 86–88.

[3] "Disgust," points out William Ian Miller in connection with Swift and the Enlightenment, "is more than just the motivator of good taste; it marks out moral matters for which we can have no compromise." He continues, invoking Hume: "The avowal of disgust expects concurrence" (*The Anatomy of Disgust* (Cambridge, MA: Harvard University Press, 1997), 194). Joyce's texts are, as a general rule, predicated on compromises of belief and question any prospect of "concurrence."

[4] Jonathan Swift, "The Lady's Dressing Room," in *Eighteenth-Century Poetry: An Annotated Anthology*, 2nd ed., ed. David Fairer and Christine Gerrard (Oxford: Blackwell, 2003), 81–85.

[5] While I will selectively draw upon the burgeoning body of ecocritical studies of Joyce, as one final note of difference here it can be observed that no comparable body of studies attends Swift's work. As the example of Mohammed Deyab's essay "An Ecocritical Reading of Jonathan Swift's *Gulliver's Travels*" (*Nature and Culture* 6.3 (2011): 285–304)

The repeated attribution of a "cloacal obsession" to the Irish is on the face of it more clearly problematic, but the question of the *use* of this disagreeable, useless stuff that we call bad names transports discussion beyond cultural stereotypes to a more historically specific, political ground (or "turf," perhaps I should say).[6] "In Ireland," testified George Bernard Shaw in his letter declining to buy a subscription to *Ulysses*, "they try to make a cat cleanly by rubbing its nose in its own filth. Mr. Joyce has tried the same treatment on the human subject. I hope it may prove useful."[7] Shaw's letter is at all points an assertion of his authority on the Irish, a group to which he belongs and at the same time of which he is something of an exception. He will not buy *Ulysses*, not simply because, as he tells Sylvia Beach, "you little know my countrymen" if it is believed that the Irish will fork out 150 francs for a book, but because he prescribes it for those who have not, as he has, "escaped" from "those streets" and "those shops" and "those conversations."

Shaw's original letter has a couple of intriguing differences from the much-quoted published versions, differences noted by neither Beach nor Richard Ellmann in their reproductions of the letter in their respective books.[8] Both texts present the memorable description of *Ulysses* as "all that foul mouthed, foul minded derision and obscenity," but Shaw writes "fouled mouthed," not "foul mouthed," and there surely is some distinction worth thinking about there. (Suggestive of more than mere profanity, "fouled mouthed" is rather reminiscent of that unequaled description of a hangover in *Lucky Jim*: "His mouth had been used as a latrine by some small creature of the night, and then as its mausoleum."[9]) The second typo—if that is what it is—is likewise silently deleted in publication: Shaw writes, "Mr. Joyce has tried the same treatment on the human subject subject." Is that second "subject" redundant, an instance of purposeless surplus (as shit itself so distressingly seems to be)? Or might the hint of a "subject subject" or "subject of the subject" not reveal exactly the crux of our dilemma: that while we can readily countenance,

---

demonstrates, "nature" as Swift considers it is manifestly animal; Gulliver focuses on inhabitants, not habitats. In his misadventures with excrement, Gulliver does not distinguish one sort from another, and the custom of revulsion at bodily excretions is presented as, effectively, the mark of universal reason. Joyce's more varied ecologies are also, we might say, more fecund.

[6] Here I am returning to questions explored more broadly in *Useless Joyce: Textual Functions, Cultural Appropriations* (Toronto: University of Toronto Press, 2017).

[7] Sylvia Beach, *Shakespeare and Company: The Story of an American Bookshop in Paris* (New York: Harcourt, Brace and World, 1965), 52.

[8] Stored in the British Library, the original typed letter can be seen online: https://www.bl.uk/collection-items/letter-from-george-bernard-shaw-responding-to-james-joyces-ulysses.

[9] Kingsley Amis, *Lucky Jim* (Hammodsworth: Penguin, 1968), 61.

in our economic imagination, a subject (i.e., someone recognized as having subjectivity) producing or possessing an object, we find it more difficult and disquieting to imagine a subject producing or possessing a subject—with the possible exceptional case of childbirth (though that one has its own unsettling qualities: "papa's little lump of dung, the wise child that knows her own father" (*U* 6.52–53)). Both the logic that holds that the child of a slave is a slave and the business policy that claims that any and all ideas or inventions of its employees belong to the company make the point: nonautonomous objects yield nonautonomous objects. To wonder whether one's excrement belongs to one's boss is no stranger than, and in fact quite like wondering whether a goddess defecates.

In his surprisingly brief *Histoire de la Merde* (*History of Shit*), Dominique Laporte traces an unexpected connection between subjectivity (and particularly the political subject of the modern state) and the handling of excrement. The modern city demands that the individual waive any claim to his or her feces and surrender it to official care, not at all unlike taxes. Dear dirty Dublin is dear and dirty because it is a colonial subject, in need of enlightened hygienic supervision. Invoking Professor MacHugh's blustery assertion in "Aeolus" that "the makers of waterclosets and the builders of sewers will never be Masters of our soul," Laporte observes that the contrary is the case: "the masters of waste and the wardens of souls are one and the same."[10] If power lies in the control of the means of production, the most common such means necessarily eludes centralized control, and so it follows that the most natural product of this most common means must be a priori without value; indeed, its value is entirely inverted, so that value is located exclusively in its disposal. Enter the Roman Empire, happy to be of service, and thereafter the monarchs and councils and privatized city services. ("The king was in his countinghouse," thinks Bloom when he is in the jakes (4.498–99).)[11]

Yet the foundation of Laporte's comments on *Ulysses* is not as solid as it might first appear. The statement about "the makers of waterclosets" attributed to MacHugh does not in fact appear in the novel at all. Instead, we find this:

---

[10] Dominique Laporte, *History of Shit*, trans. Nadia Benabid and Rodolphe el-Khoury (Cambridge, MA: MIT Press, 2000), 63.

[11] Joyce nicely captures the economic ironies of others laying claim to one's waste in "Eumaeus," a chapter all about unemployment and shiftlessness. Corley says, "I don't give a shite anyway so long as I get a job, even as a crossing sweeper" (16.202–03). "Not to give a shite" means not to care about, to have no concern for something, and thus to be impoverished, and by chapter's end we will see a sweeper, and a horse at the end of its tether (another metaphor for desperation) providing work.

—Wait a moment, professor MacHugh said, raising two quiet claws. We mustn't be led away by words, by sounds of words. We think of Rome, imperial, imperious, imperative.

He extended elocutionary arms from frayed stained shirtcuffs, pausing:

—What was their civilisation? Vast, I allow: but vile. Cloacae: sewers. The Jews in the wilderness and on the mountaintop said: *It is meet to be here. Let us build an altar to Jehovah*. The Roman, like the Englishman who follows in his footsteps, brought to every new shore on which he set his foot (on our shore he never set it) only his cloacal obsession. He gazed about him in his toga and he said: *It is meet to be here. Let us construct a watercloset*. (7.484–95)

The grandeur of the novel's Latin title is inextricably connected with this propensity for substituting a watercloset for an altar (house of gold, tower of ivory). This connection in turn maintains an ambiguous distance between the novel and this character's critique of empire, which leaves out consideration of the Irish, their buildings, and—Wells's phrase brought with a wink into service here—their own kind of "cloacal obsession." As usual with Joyce, any "obsession" is an ambitious synthesis, a matter of reconciling contraries. As Cheryl Temple Herr has observed, Joyce underscores "the impossibility of disentangling purity from pollution, humanity from excrement, post-colony from empire, and past from present."[12]

However eccentric or tongue-in-cheek (or even, given his manufactured *Ulysses* references, full of shit) Laporte's argument might have seemed 40 years ago, the questions it raises have assumed a new urgency today as the catastrophic effects of poor waste management loom. In this context we might recall that the fable of the ant and the grasshopper hinges on the fateful interrelation of climate and economy. The title of this essay is adapted from the song of the Gracehoper in the first chapter of Book III of *Finnegans Wake*:

He larved ond he larved on he merd such a nauses
The Gracehoper feared he would mixplace his fauces.

(*FW* 418.10–11)

---

[12] Cheryl Temple Herr, "Joyce and the Everynight," in *Eco-Joyce: The Environmental Imagination of James Joyce*, ed. Robert Brazeau and Derek Gladwin (Cork, Ireland: Cork University Press, 2014), 39.

Our jaunty insect laughs so hard and so loud that his face (or jaw: Latin *fauces*) might fall off—in a more recent idiom, to lose one's shit. One notable difference between the ant and the grasshopper is that the former manages its faeces, by constructing a kind of toilet chamber in its colony, and the latter does not. The ant, again in more recent idiom, has his shit together. "Fauces" also suggests "faces," and thus a connection between identity, one's sense of oneself (or, as the *Wake* would have us see, multiple selves), and what one excretes (note "merd" for "make"). "I" am responsible for "my" own shit if "I" am not to lose this sense of identity and of place.

II

The first delicate problem for responsible waste management is the separation of the excrescent matter from one's body, an everyday problem of which literature seldom stoops to take notice. In the earliest days of modernity, Rabelais recounts how Gargantua invented the "Arse-wipe" and, by experimenting with an astonishing variety of materials for the purpose, finally hit upon the ideal. His list of unsatisfactory wipes includes, among other things, a lady's velvet mask, cabbage, curtains, a pillow, straw, a basket, a chicken, a hare, a lawyer's bag, and an otter.[13] "But to conclude," Gargantua says, in J. M. Cohen's translation,

> I say and maintain that there is no arse-wiper like a well-downed goose, if you hold her neck between your legs. You must take my word for it, you really must. You get a miraculous sensation in your arse-hole, both from the softness of the down and from the temperate heat of the goose herself; and this is easily communicated to the bum-gut and the rest of the intestines, from which it reaches the heart and the brain. Do not imagine that the felicity of the heroes and demigods in the Elysian Fields arises from their asphodel, their ambrosia, or their nectar, as those ancients say. It comes, in my opinion, from their wiping their arses with the neck of a goose, and that is the opinion of Master Duns Scotus too.[14]

Rabelais, with whom Ezra Pound directly aligned Joyce after his death in 1941,[15] appears in *Ulysses* as the author of another one of those smutty books

---

[13] François Rabelais, *Gargantua and Pantagruel*, trans. J. M. Cohen (London: Penguin, 1955), 66–69.

[14] Rabelais, *Gargantua and Pantagruel*, 69.

[15] See "James Joyce: To His Memory," in *Pound/Joyce: The Letters of Ezra Pound to James Joyce*, ed. Forrest Read (New York: New Directions, 1967), 271.

that falls short of Molly Bloom's exacting standards: "some of those books he brings me the works of Master Francois Somebody supposed to be a priest about a child born out of her ear because her bumgut fell out a nice word for any priest to write" (18.487–90). Molly's literary criticism neatly dovetails—or perhaps goosenecks—with her husband's in "Calypso": "print anything now" (4.512). The aesthetic criticism is axiomatically somatic: you have to go with your bumgut feeling.[16] Judge Woolsey, who recognized *Ulysses* as an emetic, would surely agree.

Bloom's masterstroke, the first of many signs of his equanimity, even comfort, with his bodily functions, is as artful in its way as Shem's determination that "he would wipe alley english spooker, multaphniaksically spuking, off the face of the erse" (*FW* 178.06–07). That phrase "face of the erse" reverberates with "mixplaced his fauces," and the nod in "alley english spooker" to Ally Sloper, the vagrant hero of early comic strips who drifts in and out of the *Wake*, seems to confirm newsprint as a commendable wiping implement (for want of a goose). The *Wake* broadens this theme with the oft-recycled story of Buckley and the Russian General, the climax of which directly concerns the proper way to clean one's "beeoteetom." For the Irish soldier, a proverbial figure of fun, the use of Irish turf is an outrage: this is "how bulkily he shat the Ructions gunorrhal" (192.02–03). Exactly what happens is complicated by the various retellings. The explosive words "shoot" and "shot" get phonetically blended with sounds that they suggest. Shem is called—another instance of Joyce ahead of today's idioms—"the shit" (179.06) and "SHUT" is his "penname [...] sepiascraped on the doorplate" (182.32–33). Shem/Buckley is created by the very process of creation that he observes: not for nothing does "Buckley" sound like "Berkeley." We can observe how Joyce dizzyingly conflates tenuous subjectivity with minding the place of one's shit in the world.

Once the ordure has been satisfactorily removed from one's person, the obvious next question is what to do with it, and as I have been suggesting, the answer to that depends upon and reveals one's understanding of one's relation to this creation and to the environment. Joyce considers a few different possibilities, all of them utilitarian, in the sense that he imbues or at least tries to imagine human waste with a use value.

Collecting the stuff, hoarding and piling it up as a kind of treasure trove, is the possibility represented by the hen's midden. This option seems to the least apparent purpose, as many dismissals of *Finnegans Wake* likewise complain,

---

[16] Incidentally, Gargantua's absurd, high-handed invocation of the authority of Duns Scotus bears a surprising resemblance to Robert's extraordinary allusion in *Exiles*: "In the cab took place what the subtle Duns Scotus calls a death of the spirit" (*E* 155). The possible implications of this I leave to the reader.

until one considers the energy saved by composting. The *Wake* is a fascinatingly conservationist text, dedicated to perpetual self-mulching.[17] But corollary—or correspondent—to this energizing inertia is an active repurposing, seen in how Shem "made synthetic ink and sensitive paper for his own end out his wit's waste" (185.06–08). This procedure, outlined in a Latin that manages to be both discreet and ludicrously liturgical, has excited much commentary:[18]

> *Primum opifex, altus prosator, as terram viviparam et cunctipotentem sine ullo pudore nec venia, suscepto pluviali atque distinctis perizomatis, natibus nudis uti nati fuissent, sese adpropinquans, flens et gemens, in manum suam evacuavit* (highly prosy, crap in his hand, sorry!), *postea, animale nigro exoneratus, classicum pulsans, stercus proprium, quod appellavit deiectiones suas, in vas olim honorabile tristitiae posuit, eodem sub invocatione fratrorum geminorum Medardi et Godardi laete ac melliflue minxit, psalmum qui incipit: Lingua mea calamus scribae velociter scribentis: magna voce cantitans* (did a piss, says he was dejected, asks to be exonerated), *demum ex stercore turpi cum divi Orionis iucunditate mixto, cocto, frigorique exposito, encaustum sibi fecit indelibile* (faked O'Ryan's, the indelible ink). (185.14–26)

A phrase worth highlighting from this passage is "*stercus proprium*" (185.19): "his very own shit," and a proper shit at that. Both the hen's appropriations and Shem's acknowledgment of his own thing of darkness held in his hands void the need for "the makers of waterclosets and the builders of sewers." Shem's remarkable ink-making occurs "when the call comes" (185.28), a phrase that intermingles the call of nature, the patriotic jingoism of national service, and a 1921 speech to the American Association for the Recognition of the Irish Republic by de Valera's secretary, Harry J. Boland: "when the call comes from Ireland for a new loan you will be prepared to supply $100,000,000 should Ireland ask it in the name of liberty."[19] It remains an open question whether

---

[17] In this connection, see Alison Lacivita, *The Ecology of Finnegans Wake* (Gainesville: University Press of Florida, 2015), and Erin Walsh, "Word and World: The Ecology of the Pun in *Finnegans Wake*," in *Eco-Joyce: The Environmental Imagination of James Joyce*, ed. Robert Brazeau and Derek Gladwin (Cork, Ireland: Cork University Press, 2014), 70–90.

[18] The primary scatological survey is Vincent Cheng's "'Goddinpotty': James Joyce and the Language of Excrement," in *The Languages of Joyce: Selected Papers from the 11th International James Joyce Symposium, Venice, 12–18 June 1988*, ed. R. M. Bollettieri Bosinelli, C. Marengo Vaglio, and Chr. Van Boheemen (Philadelphia, PA: John Benjamins, 1992), 85–99.

[19] "Irish Leaders Greet Convention in Chicago," *New York Times*, April 19, 1921: see http://query.nytimes.com/gst/abstract.html?res=9907E1DD113FEE3ABC4152DFB26 6838A639EDE&legacy=true.

"crap in his hand" (185.17–18) is worth a hundred million in the bush, but that provision "in the name of liberty" does suggest that the loan need not be repaid. What goes into the midden stays in the midden.

A comparable strategy for conserving and using one's own waste (*sinn fein* of a different order) is glimpsed in "Ithaca." Bloom of Flowerville, dedicated to gardening and "inspection of sterile landscape" (17.1597–98), is to be seen "ameliorating the soil, multiplying wisdom, achieving longevity" (17.1586–87). I think that this dream is rich in manure. Whereas the hell described at diarrhetic length by Father Arnall sees the damned deluged with an endless stream of useless effluvium—perhaps as it were passed down from those "heroes and demigods in the Elysian Fields" blissfully goosing themselves on high— Bloom's rustic utopia appears to integrate the body within the land. This synthesis is in every sense the groundwork of *Finnegans Wake*.

III

And, finally, there is the coprophagic option. Why not simply eat one's own poop, and make that unpleasant remainder disappear, as the Pope suggests is a natural inclination? It is true that other animals (rabbits, dogs, insects) indulge where humans fear to tread. As a matter of fact and out of a sense of duty I ought to point out, before going any further, that feces can host many harmful bacteria. Of course there are any number of human indulgences, many of them dietary, that are ill-advised and still not avoided or even uncommon. So we might set aside reservations and qualms and inquire, as Joyce does, why one might partake, or why (apart from health reasons) one should not.

Recall this curious parenthesis in *A Portrait*:

—I speak of normal natures, said Stephen. You also told me that when you were a boy in that charming carmelite school you ate pieces of dried cowdung.

Lynch broke again into a whinny of laughter and again rubbed both his hands over his groins but without taking them from his pockets.

—O, I did! I did! he cried.

Stephen turned towards his companion and looked at him for a moment boldly in the eyes. Lynch, recovering from his laughter, answered his look from his humbled eyes. The long slender flattened skull beneath the long pointed cap brought before Stephen's mind the image of a hooded reptile. The eyes, too, were reptile-like in glint and gaze. Yet at that instant, humbled and alert in their look, they were lit by one tiny human point, the window of a shrivelled soul, poignant and self-embittered.

—As for that, Stephen said in polite parenthesis, we are all animals.
I also am an animal.
—You are, said Lynch. (*P* 172)

This description of Lynch—by any account a minor character—seems as unnecessary, as excessive as, well, the act of eating cowdung itself. (This is also the return and the legacy of the moocow, with whose entry the novel begins.) It is difficult to ascertain whether between Lynch's too-cheerful confession and the "one tiny human point" that Stephen discerns in him there is a connection or a contrast. When Lynch later laughs at Stephen's aesthetic puzzles and recognizes "the true scholastic stink" (180), we can be confident both that he knows what he is talking about and that he is at that moment displaying a shit-eating grin. Among those puzzles, of course, are questions about making a cow out of wood and, more to the issue at hand, "*Can excrement or a child or a louse be a work of art? If not, why not?*" (180). Here we have come back to the implications of seeing in excreta (broadly defined) an extension of our subjectivity, or even one distinct and sovereign from our own—that "subject subject," to repeat Shaw's phrase.

Taking up Stephen's question, Eugene O'Brien looks to the phenomenology of Merleau-Ponty, for whom a kind of "communion" is effected by the "synchronisation" of one's body with the world in which it is located. "This sense of unified perception," O'Brien observes, "unified in terms of mind and body and in terms of an 'already there' relationship with the world, is contiguous to what Joyce is attempting to set out as an aesthetic theory, or, to be more exact, an aesthetic process [in *A Portrait*]."[20] Yet this question has a broader context, and represents a broader concern, both within the novel and as it grows more complex in later works. That Stephen's asking about excrement's potential to be art directly follows the acknowledgment that his interlocutor has dined on it draws attention to the fact that what is called "aesthetics" is not merely a study of beauty (Lynch in passing and perhaps ironically says that it is all he admires) but the sensation of feeling (the opposite of "aesthetic" is not "ugly" but "anaesthetic"), which is inexorably connected to the definition of subjectivity, slippery though it is.

How readily we assume that the being who feels sensation is the subject, and that which provides or embodies these sensations is the environment; likewise,

---

[20] Eugene O'Brien, "'Can Excrement Be Art […] if Not, Why Not?': Joyce's Aesthetic Theory and the Flux of Consciousness," in *Eco-Joyce: The Environmental Imagination of James Joyce*, ed. Robert Brazeau and Derek Gladwin (Cork, Ireland: Cork University Press, 2014), 201.

the user is the subject, and that which is used the object. The apparent uselessness of both art and shit casts suspicion on these tidy, comforting formulas. In *The Usefulness of the Useless*, Nuccio Ordine observes that "a work of art does not ask to come into the world. Or to borrow [...] from Ionesco, the work of art 'asks to be born' in the same way 'as a child asks to be born.'"[21] From this perspective, we can see how Swift's *Modest Proposal* is in fact his most scatological work: the children to be consumed as gross national product are creations with no other plausible economic future, and thus without purpose.[22] The question of whether and to what degree we might recognize some form of subjectivity in such disparate-seeming phenomena as art, children, lice, and excrement is surprisingly proximate to the question of what use we can conceive for or attribute to each or all of them.

Stephen's wisecrack about "normal natures," undone by the admission that "we are all animals," is worth comparing with the pontiff's claims about human tendencies, though as ever it becomes both important and difficult to look to distinguish Stephen's thinking from Joyce's. Try to imagine Stephen writing this, as Joyce did to Nora on December 20, 1909:

> Do you come in the act of shitting or do you frig yourself off first and then shit? It must be a fearfully lecherous thing to see a girl with her clothes up frigging furiously at her cunt, to see her pretty white drawers pulled open behind and her bum sticking out and a fat brown thing stuck half-way out of her hole. You say you will shit your drawers, dear, and let me fuck you then. I would like to hear you shit them, dear, first and then fuck you. Some night when we are somewhere in the dark and talking dirty and you feel your shite ready to fall put your arms round my neck in shame and shit it down softly. (*SL* 191–92)

Though I blush to admit it, that last sentence strikes my ear as tender and lyrical; and what's more, its cadences faintly echo those of the end of "The Dead," written only two years before ("the snow falling faintly" is now "shit it down softly"), and that susurrating of "shite" and "shame" and "shit" anticipates *Finnegans Wake*. But my main point in recalling this letter is to note how uncertain, how questioning, how probing it is: "Do you ... it must be

---

[21] Nuccio Ordine, *The Usefulness of the Useless*, trans. Alastair McEwen (Philadelphia, PA: Paul Dry Books, 2017), 12; ellipsis added.

[22] Jonathan Swift, *A Modest Proposal for Preventing the Children of Poor People in Ireland from Being a Burden to Their Parents or Country, and for Making Them Beneficial to the Publick*, in *Gulliver's Travels and Other Writings*, ed. Louis A. Landa (Boston, MA: Houghton Mifflin, 1960), 439–46.

... you will ... I would ..." Worry about "normal natures" aside, Joyce is exploring the limits of his own subjectivity and those of his relationship with Nora, the same kind of exploration that Molly does in wanting to "shout out all sorts of things fuck or shit or anything at all" (18.588–89) or "let out a few smutty words smellrump or lick my shit or the first mad thing comes into my head" (18.1531–32).

Perhaps, contra Pope Francis, coprophagy offers a form of transcendence, especially if it is not a matter of to each his own but a shared partaking of one another's. Laporte cites this passage from O'Donovan's *Irish Annales*:

> *Once when he [Aedh], not yet King, came through Othna Muru, he washed his hands in the river that goes through the middle of the town. (Othna is the name of the river, and from it the town —i.e., Othna—is named.) He took a handful of water to put on his face but one of his men stopped him.*
> *"O King," he said, "do not put that water on your face."*
> *"Why?" asked the King.*
> *"I am ashamed to say," he said.*
> *"What shame can there be in speaking the truth?" asked the King.*
> *"This is it," he replied: "the clergy's privy is over that water."*
> *"Is it there," asked the King, "that the cleric himself goes to defecate?"*
> *"It is indeed," said the youth.*
> *"Not only," said the King, "shall I put it upon my face, but I shall also put it upon my mouth, and I shall drink it (drinking three mouthfuls of it), for the water into which his feces go is a sacrament to me.*[23]

Holy shit, indeed. Laporte notes that because this incident immediately precedes Aedh's becoming king of Ireland, "the legitimacy of power has its foundations in the shit of the clergy. The mouth of power swallows the shit of God himself."[24] Yet power need not be hierarchical, if no one's droppings are superior to anyone else's. For a lover to say, as Molly at least thinks of doing, "smellrump or lick my shit," is to make a profound submission, to enter into an economy of shared creation with another.

Clive Hart many years ago judged Joyce's scatology in *Finnegans Wake* "in the main quite successful"—a puzzling verdict.[25] That "success" is a term seldom used in conjunction with either scatology as such or *Finnegans Wake* points to the fact that neither of them has a self-evident end or teleology as such, and

---

[23] Qtd. in Laporte, *History of Shit*, 109.
[24] Laporte, *History of Shit*, 110.
[25] Clive Hart, *Structure and Motif in* Finnegans Wake (Evanston, IL: Northwestern University Press, 1962), 208.

we find no vantage point from which to take such a confident measure. As always, we find Joyce's work is itself an incomplete, ongoing process, as are our determinations of what we do with Joyce (what use to make of him) and what we do with our waste (what use to make of it). Joyce's awakening conception of scatology as ecology—with all of the problems of ethics, desire, and memory that triangulate subjectivity—might teach us to stop worrying about "fake news" and get our shit better organized before we have no other choice but to eat it. The *Wake* extends this invitation: "*Shite!* will you have a plateful?" (*FW* 142.07).

Chapter 8

THANATOLOGICAL

"Don't You Know He's Dead?": Postmortem Uncertainties

In a Yale University laboratory in April 2019, a team of scientists was able to restore functions to the brains of pigs that had been dead (without oxygen) for four hours, far longer than anyone had previously supposed any form of resuscitation possible.[1] Though its results have yet to reproduced elsewhere, this experiment poses significant challenges to the accepted definition of "dead," a definition troublingly mired in the negative. The *OED* offers "deprived of life," "insensible," and "no longer in use or existence," while in medical practice everything depends on expected reactions; the understanding inherited from the Enlightenment is summed up by Xavier Bichat: life is "the sum of all functions by which death is resisted."[2] The Irish saying "dead, but he won't lie down"[3] thus assumes new force today, and points us back to Joyce, in whose works the definition of death remains persistently uncertain. This essay ventures the argument that this particular, pervasive form of uncertainty in Joyce, while not infrequently vexing for readers, suggests a conception of fiction as a suspended animation, a state without dead certainties.

"Good idea a postmortem for doctors," thinks Leopold Bloom, who is not above posing as a medical man: "Find out what they imagine they know" (6.86–87). There are so many things that readers of Joyce do not know—and perhaps even things that we only imagine we know—even after much rereading and the insights of decades of criticism, research, and discussion, but it can be fairly said that the very word "know" in Joyce's texts often presents a slippery problem for readers. An extraordinary phrase such as "Do

---

[1] See Zvonimir Vrselja et al., "Restoration of Brain Circulation and Cellular Functions Hours Post-Mortem." *Nature* 568 (2019): 336–43.
[2] Cited in Thomas W. Laqueur, *The Work of the Dead: A Cultural History of Mortal Remains* (Princeton, NJ: Princeton University Press, 2015), 185.
[3] Roger Shattuck, *The Banquet Years: The Origins of the Avant-Garde in France, 1885 to World War I*, rev. ed. (New York: Vintage, 1968), 152.

you know what I'm going to tell you?" (4.115–16) is simply common speech in Joyce's Dublin, and the words "don't you know" do not necessarily constitute a question that can be answered. (For some, like Richard Best in the library chapter, it is a verbal tic.) The question which I've taken as my title, "Don't you know he's dead?" comes, don't you know, from "Cyclops," a chapter stocked with highly questionable kinds of knowledge, misperceptions, and leading questions. The question compounds problems of ontology and epistemology: it asks not just for confirmation that someone is dead—something our society designates a "pronouncement" by a licensed expert—but whether I "know" him to be dead.

Though there are of course many dead in *Ulysses*, there are no deaths. Leaving aside the mass suicide of Bloom-smitten women in and the sightseers crushed in urban demolition in "Circe" (which fantasies are such outsized exceptions as to underscore the rule), nobody dies in the course of the novel—and to realize how extraordinary that is, one need only try to name an earlier novel of comparable length of which this may be said. Buck Mulligan's claim to "see them pop off every day" (1.205) does not seem to hold for June 16, 1904, a day which is often thought to be just like any other day, but in this respect it isn't.[4] That the novel was written during a period of unparalleled European catastrophe makes this fact all the more singular.

Still more generally it can be observed that Joyce, eschewing the dramatic force of any direct representation of death, prefers the offstage death, with all of its attendant ambiguities and uncertainties. There are reports of death in *Dubliners*: the young boy in "The Sisters" is only "persuaded" that Father Flynn is dead by the posted notice (4), which is not quite the same thing as his "knowing" it, and Mr Duffy is surprised by a newspaper account of Emily Sinico's grim death, but only after rereading it and later drinking two glasses of hot punch in a pub does he "[realise] that she was dead" (112)—again, not quite "know"—and by his story's end he is consumed by doubt of "the reality of what memory told him" (113–14). There are, in *A Portrait*, deaths muted, fallen into the background, such as that of Uncle Charles, and remembered deaths: Michael Furey, "a person long ago" (220), and the interstitial death of May Dedalus, who dies between books. And there are deaths fabled, foretold, and "retaled" in *Finnegans Wake*, a book whose title refers to a ritual of setting watch over someone, in effect to make sure they're properly dead.

---

[4] By contrast, the long day of *Ulysses* does feature a birth, and despite the long shadow of the nineteenth-century fiction's conventions and the moral conundrums drunkenly aired in "Oxen of the Sun," nobody perishes in the operation. The "dead sea" in the child's name, Mortimer, intertwines with the novel's various themes of water, drowning, birth, and death.

The wonderful exchange between Alf Bergan, Joe Hynes, Bob Doran, and the narrator in "Cyclops" concerning Dignam's vitality deserves to be read as a kind of Wittgensteinian exercise. "Just to make talk" (12.312)—a variation on "passing the time of day" (12.01), a defining sort of minimal sign of life—the narrator asks after Willy Murray, to which Alf replies, "I don't know," even though he says he has just seen him. This is already puzzling, because the reader doesn't know, and won't find out, who Willy Murray might be, though she recognizes the name Paddy Dignam. The reader may well say at this moment, but isn't he the one they just had a funeral for? But the reader, and especially the first-time reader, may have doubts, because this crazy book has already messed her about by turning back the clock, representing scenes and encounters that are only taking place in characters' minds, and having people seem to know things that they could not know. Who is she, this beleaguered reader, to say for sure that Dignam could not have been in Capel Street with Bergan, since ghosts and panthers and even the ace of spades have been reported in this fantastical Dublin?

Bob Doran's interrupting efforts to understand who the "he" is add another layer to the uncertainty. These were not in the original manuscript: Joyce's various revisions and additions to the chapter, never simplifying matters, so changed the cast of characters as to render the determination of who is talking about whom the stuff of farce. The reader's laughter at this scene, while partly a tribute to Joe Hynes's witty "took the liberty" remark (originally credited to Ned Lambert (*JJA* 13.91)), is at least partly the product of anxiety. Some comfort may be found in seeing Joyce's characters as unsure about the distinctions between what's true and what's being said as we are.

But the reader's respite is brief and the confusion continues as more conversational lines, all of them attempts to ascertain something different, become crossed:

—There he is again, says the citizen, staring out.
—Who? says I.
—Bloom, says he. He's on point duty up and down there for the last ten minutes.
And, begob, I saw his physog do a peep in and then slidder off again. Little Alf was knocked bawways. Faith, he was.
—Good Christ! says he. I could have sworn it was him. (12.377–83)

This collision of mistaken identities, recurrent visions, death, and "Good Christ!" harkens back to the story of Mulcahy's grave: "*Not a bloody bit like the man*" (6.730); and the blend of recognizing Bloom as Christ, the dead man seen again, anticipates the ascent of ben Bloom Elijah to heaven at the end of the chapter.

Dignam (whose name might conceivably be translated as "stately") is himself a most uncertain phenomenon. The reader of *Ulysses* learns rather little about him: his (at least one-time) employer (if not exactly what work he does), the numbers of his family (wife plus five children), and the repeated suggestion that he was somehow "little." He seems to have enjoyed alcohol, which is no truly distinguishing mark, though it may have played a part in his death, which took place on the unlucky thirteenth. The cause of death changes with each iteration, from "breakdown" (6.305) to his ghost's testimony that "the wall of the heart hypertrophied" (15.1232) and in "Ithaca" comes the clinical term "apoplexy" (17.1255). (It's interesting, incidentally, how each of these diagnoses is itself representative and descriptive of the episode in which it is found.)

Yet stranger than the reader's ignorance is that characters who do "know" him seem no better informed, and frequently confused. Even by the novel's end, exactly how Bloom knows Dignam is no clearer than how he knows Emily Sinico, whose funeral he also attended. (Is Bloom just one of those people who habitually attend funerals?) C. P. M'Coy, who claims to be "just keeping alive" (5.88), has a long and involved story to tell about how he came to hear about Dignam's death, a man he calls "one of the best" (5.137), but has clearly forgotten the day of the funeral, and does not go, though he wants to be recorded as having attended.[5] M'Coy's story, though mercifully fragmented by Bloom's divided attention, seems to suggest that he got the news either from Bob Doran or while in Doran's company, yet a few hours later Bob Doran is not only apparently staggered to hear that Dignam is dead, but mixes up his name with Willy Murray's. And Alf Bergan, also a "little" man (12.249), is "what you might call flabbergasted" (12.337) to hear that he could not have seen Dignam moments before in Capel Street. When Long John Fanning is unsure who Dignam was, Martin Cunningham says, "I don't think you knew

---

[5] Although we never find out whether M'Coy has some ulterior motive for wanting to be officially recorded as being somewhere where he was not, the recurrent "alibi" theme in *Ulysses* is worth considering in this context. Stephen recalls how he "used to carry punched tickets to prove an alibi if they arrested you for murder somewhere. Justice. On the night of the seventeenth of February 1904 the prisoner was seen by two witnesses. Other fellow did it: other me" (3.179–82). In "Circe," the second Watch ambiguously says to Bloom, "An alibi. You are cautioned" (15.736): it may be an accusation, or is it a request? Or—this seems likely—has he confused the word with "alias" ("other me")? The etymological *al- root of alibi, meaning "beyond" (where the dead are often said to have gone, and those long dead days are precisely beyond recall) is also found in such *Ulysses* keywords as adultery, alias, and parallax.

him or perhaps you did, though" (10.1023–24), which nicely sums up the whole business.

Although his obituary, such as it is, calls him "*a most popular and genial personality in city life*" (16.1250–51), in practice Dignam seems neither recognizable nor memorable. His fullest eulogies come from Simon Dedalus, who calls Dignam "As decent a little man as ever wore a hat" (6.03), and his young son, whose flat averral "Never see him again" (10.1169) is a simplified echo of Hamlet's "He was a man, take him for all in all. / I shall not look upon his like again" (1.2.394–95). Young Patrick Dignam's being his father's namesake can be as confusing as the shared names of the former king and the prince of Denmark, but Hamlet is premature in his judgment and is about to again see and hear the "like" of his father. Little surprise, then, that Dignam's spirit beseeches "List, list, O list!" in "Circe."[6]

The last and perhaps the most astute word on Dignam is Molly Bloom's, who remembers him as a "comical little teetotum always stuck up in some pub corner" (18.1281–82). A teetotum is a spinning top used in gambling, an early relative of the dreidel and, in Mexico, the perinola. It is precisely an instrument of uncertainty, offering a procedure by which to attain a provisional determination by means of a brief suspension of determinacy. The word teetotum seems to come from the mark on one of its sides, signifying the best result, a total win (just what readers never get in *Ulysses*—and say, did *anybody* in Dublin collect on Throwaway's victory?); it is also, as Joyce's beloved Skeat notes, a plausible origin for the coinage teetotaller,[7] exactly the wrong word for somebody "always stuck up in some pub corner." This same contradiction reoccurs in *Finnegans Wake*: "a teetotum abstainer" (*FW* 489.17).

Dignam is himself more a device than a character,[8] one of those apparently simple facts that readers may seize upon as a guiding star ("he is dead") before discovering how unfixed that star is (who is he? How do I "know" that he is dead?). While we "know" him as a kind of Elpenor, whose death by drunkenly falling from Circe's roof marks him as exceptionally stupid among Odysseus's

---

[6] A very brief note on ghosts, themselves a somewhat different, larger, and much discussed subject, is necessary here. A ghost might seem a clear and decisive indication of death, but, remarkably, this is not so in "Circe," whose spectres include the animate, the inanimate, and the downright abstract.

[7] Walter W. Skeat, *An Etymological Dictionary of the English Language* (Mineola, NY: Dover, 2005), 633.

[8] The same has been said of Homer's Elpenor. Daniel Mendelsohn, for example, writes that "Elpenor functions as a kind of emotional and narrative human sacrifice: he is a figure whose death, which can mean nothing to the audience since we never really got to know him, nonetheless serves as a bridge between the worlds of the living and the dead" (*An Odyssey: A Father, a Son, and an Epic* (New York: Vintage, 2017), 169).

crew (no small feat, that), his role as "teetotum" may also remind us of another rather curious rewriting of Homer's character: Eutychus, whose name means "good fortune." My text here is Acts 20:7–12:

> And upon the first day of the week, when the disciples came together to break bread, Paul preached unto them, ready to depart on the morrow; and continued his speech until midnight.
>
> And there were many lights in the upper chamber, where they were gathered together.
>
> And there sat in a window a certain young man named Eutychus, being fallen into a deep sleep: and as Paul was long preaching, he sunk down with sleep, and fell down from the third loft, and was taken up dead.
>
> And Paul went down, and fell on him, and embracing him said, Trouble not yourselves; for his life is in him.
>
> When he therefore was come up again, and had broken bread, and eaten, and talked a long while, even till break of day, so he departed.
>
> And they brought the young man alive, and were not a little comforted.
>
> (Acts 20:7–12)

Dignam, Elpenor, Eutychus: these tossed dice and dead tossers are precursors of Tim Finnegan, variations on a theme of uncertainty. And to these might be added Jesus, Lazarus, Parnell ("Some say he is not in that grave at all" (6.923)),[9] HCE and ALP—which is to say, everybody. Only the Marvel Cinematic Universe rivals Joyce's for vacillating mortality.[10] Eutychus is only "a certain young man," sitting in a window as he just as might be stuck up in some pub corner: a name and a precarious situation, a fall and an uncertain death. Is Humpty Dumpty, of the same lineage, dead? No—the nursery rhyme concludes that it was impossible to "put him together again"; though other versions say things like "Four-score Men and Four-score more, / Could not make Humpty Dumpty where he was before." The die is cast [...] until it is cast again.

---

[9] How ironic that the negation of this suggestion—"Parnell will never come again, he said. He's there, all that was mortal of him" (6.926–27)—comes from Hynes, who is hardly an authority on matters of *who* is *where*.

[10] In his review of the blockbuster *Avengers: Endgame*, Michael Wood delightfully quotes Adorno's characterization of Samuel Beckett's *Endgame* as "a parody of the philosophy of the remainder" (*London Review of Books*, June 6, 2019, 28). Something similar might perhaps be said of Joyce—indeed, perhaps the critical attention to "surplus" and "exhaustion" in his writing ought to be shifted to the terms of "remainder" and even "remains."

Cleo Hanaway-Oakley points out how "Hades" is a kind of exploration of "the difference between the lived body (the body-subject who experiences the haptic and visual experience of a carriage journey) and the inert, dead body who takes up space in the world but does not *engage* with it (Paddy Dignam's corpse)."[11] Here we hit upon what is fundamentally a problem of perspective: it would be fairer to say that we do not and perhaps cannot *know* whether the corpse engages with the world, but it might also be objected that the unstated definition of "engage" favors the living. Even if we grant that fidgeting in discomfort because of the soap in one's pocket is a sign of life, it would clearly be fallacious to conclude that anyone not currently fidgeting is dead.

As for being inert or insensate, consider Mr Duffy, who disengages more and more from the world until

> He halted under a tree and allowed the rhythm to die away. He could not feel her near him in the darkness nor her voice touch his ear. He waited for some moments listening. He could hear nothing: the night was perfectly silent. He listened again: perfectly silent. He felt that he was alone. (*D* 114)

This is, I think, the closest thing we get to a death scene in Joyce's published works. (Here am I leaving out the death of Isabel in *Stephen Hero*, a glaringly flat scene whose attempts to tramp out all uncertainty may well be one reason why no such character appears in *A Portrait*.) Mr Duffy does not move, does not feel, does not hear. With what certainty can I say that, at the end of the story, he is *not* dead?

As a thought experiment, consider the differing degrees to which and ways in which the following statements seem "wrong":

Hamlet is dead.
May Dedalus is dead.
Leopold Bloom is dead.
Paddy Dignam is dead.

Two immediate problems need to be acknowledged and, if possible, set aside: (1) the open question of whether a fictional person can die (is this what happens when we stop believing in our imaginary friends?) and (2) the critical convention of discussing fictional events in the continuous present tense (never mind habits of loftily referring to "the immortal Hamlet" and the like).

---

[11] Cleo Hanaway-Oakley, *James Joyce and the Phenomenology of Film* (Oxford: Oxford University Press, 2017), 105.

Yet I wager that most readers will find at least one of these four statements unsettling or untenable.

Hamlet is dead at the end of the play because the stage directions tell us he dies, he is eulogized onstage, and the curtain falls. Never fear, though—he'll be up and about when the curtain rises on the next evening's performance. May Dedalus is dead in *Ulysses* but alive in *A Portrait*, and if it seems strange simply to say "May Dedalus is dead," it is perhaps a different kind of strange than the strangeness of saying "Hamlet is dead" but not quite as strange as the urge to qualify, "but she was alive before she was dead," as we might say to a student of *Ulysses* who has not read *A Portrait*. And Leopold Bloom, in his late 30s in 1904, must be dead in 2020, though who would dare declare it so? Imagine for a moment if we spoke of "the late Mr. Bloom": on what basis would we be corrected? "Paddy Dignam is dead" is in a sense the premise of *Ulysses*: in more than one sense, he is dead before the novel begins, though the same can't be said for May Dedalus, exactly, since the episode we know as "Telemachus" was at one point imagined by Joyce as a sixth chapter to *A Portrait*.

The death of Finnegan is not so much the premise of *Finnegans Wake* as its question, or at any rate one of its many questions. *Ulysses* asks, "don't you know he's dead?" and Tim Finnegan asks, "do you think I'm dead?" There seems no reasonable way to answer no to the first or yes to the second. H. G. Wells's 1928 judgment of "Work in Progress" as "a dead end" (*Letters I* 275) is both exactly wrong and exactly right: Wells could not appreciate that phenomena beyond our intelligible experience (including death) might demand a language somewhat removed from both experience and intelligibility, nor could he see that a "dead end" might not be so definitive a conclusion.

"Death," says Wittgenstein in one of the most enigmatic statements in the *Tractatus*, "is not an event in life: we do not live to experience death."[12] This assertion seems at once obvious and inscrutable, but Joyce reminds us that we nevertheless imagine being dead, trying to figure out what it means, and so if death is not an "event in life," it is at the very least a kind of preoccupation: an *eventuality*. And the eventual is the province and purview of fiction, which includes imagining, if not "experiencing" in Wittgenstein's sense of the word, not just other lives but our own deaths, interchangeably with those lives. The *Wake* (ever obliging in this regard) has a nice word for this: "eventualising" (51.22).

---

[12] Ludwig Wittgenstein, *Tractatus Logico-Philosophicus*, trans. D. F. Pears and B. F. McGuinness (London: Routledge, 2008), 6.4311.

After Stephen has been pushed into the slimy ditch in *A Portrait*—how regularly Joyce likes to connect falls with death—he thinks of the consciousness of rats:

> They could understand how to jump. But the minds of rats could not understand trigonometry. When they were dead they lay on their sides. Their coats dried then. They were only dead things. (*P* 18)

Sent shortly thereafter to the infirmary, Stephen

> wondered if he could die. You could die just the same on a sunny day. He might die before his mother came. Then he would have a dead mass in the chapel like the way the fellows had told him it was when Little had died. (19)

The sequence of these eventualising thoughts is fascinating: first comes the question of whether he *could* die, which might mean laying on one's side, apparently unable to understand trigonometry. This is followed by the answer of someone talking to himself, "You could die," before reverting to the third person and "might," stretched even to the inconceivability of "before his mother came." Having accepted the possibility, Stephen ventures to "Then," and imagines his own funeral service, which requires his thinking about what others perceive and think. These shifts of pronouns and fine shades of subjunctive represent a struggle of the imagination, to think oneself dead, to dissolve selfhood. Years later he recalls this time when he "dreamed of being dead" and realizes that his younger self "had been lost or had wandered out of existence for he no longer existed. How strange to think of him passing out of existence in such a way, not by death but by fading out in the sun or by being lost and forgotten somewhere in the universe!" (78).

In "Oxen of the Sun," Bloom pictures his younger self in a manner worth comparing with these thoughts of Stephen's. The active voice abruptly switches to the passive: "There, as in a retrospective arrangement, a mirror within a mirror (hey, presto!), he beholdeth himself. That young figure of then is seen" (14.1044–45). However, this vision is short-lived: "But hey, presto, the mirror is breathed on and the young knighterrant recedes, shrivels, dwindles to a tiny speck within the mist" (14.1060–62). Bloom's breath on the mirror—one of those classic signs by which one is determined not to be dead—prevents him from seeing his past self, his lost and "dead" self.

In a work written long after his *Tractatus*, *On Certainty*, a more skeptical Wittgenstein meditates on what it means to say that one "knows" something. To say "I know" is in a sense already a problem because it brings together the subjective "I" with the objectivity implied by knowledge.[13] Writes Wittgenstein, "The *truth* of my statements is the test of my *understanding* of these statements,"[14] but to say "I know he's dead" or simply "he's dead" thus seems to require that I "understand" what it is to be dead. More agreeably Joycean is the assertion, "My *life* consists in my being content to accept many things" (Wittgenstein's emphasis, and his word is *zufrieden*, "satisfied").[15] Yet imagination's eventualising always turns over the possibilities—never exactly or entirely "content" or "satisfied." Here is Bloom, a secular man with no belief in the afterlife, nonetheless struck by the thought that the funeral's guest of honor might not be quite dead:

> And if he was alive all the time? Whew! By jingo, that would be awful! No, no: he is dead, of course. Of course he is dead. Monday he died. They ought to have some law to pierce the heart and make sure or an electric clock or a telephone in the coffin and some kind of a canvas airhole. Flag of distress. (6.865–69)

That repetition of "of course" and the subsequent rambling list of expedient means to decide the question bespeak a nervous effort to reassure himself on the point. This prevarication or nagging doubt is called by *Finnegans Wake* the "heaviest corpsus exemption" (362.17) and is in operation in passages like this one:

> bunged to inglorious, healed cured and embalsemate, pending a rouseruction of his bogey, most highly astounded, as it turned up, after his life overlasting, at thus being reduced to nothing. (*FW* 498.36–499.03)

The "threadbare phrases" so despised by Mr Duffy (*D* 111) are disentangled and reknotted here, as the blissful promises of "bound to glory" and "life everlasting" are paired with the grim mortuary procedures of embalming and "bunging" the orifices, just as the logic and sequentiality of life, death, and afterlife are muddled (the body isn't resurrected, according to Catholic doctrine; only a "bogey" or ghost "turns up" after death; and so on). The phrase "most highly astounded" implies both sensation and, turned to stone, insensate being—stone-cold dead.

---

[13] Ludwig Wittgenstein, *On Certainty*, trans. Denis Paul and G. E. M. Anscombe (New York: Harper & Row, 1972), 10e.

[14] Wittgenstein, *On Certainty*, 12e; italics in original.

[15] Wittgenstein, *On Certainty*, 44e.

In the final chapter of the novel *Mr. Palomar*, Italo Calvino's meditative hero decides to act as though he were dead, and see the world, as it were, without him. He determines that "the most difficult step in learning how to be dead" is "to become convinced that your own life is a closed whole, all in the past, to which you can add nothing and can alter none of the relationships among the various elements."[16] Perceiving life *in summa* is, as the second essay in this volume has sought to show, an illusion in Joyce, and an illusion that Joyce encourages us to discover. Too, the notion of any sort of existence "to which you can add nothing" is perhaps the only sort of notion that might rightly be called distinctly *un*Joycean: the writer of constant revisions accordingly does not blithely "kill off" his characters, but lets the dead endure as a doubtful category.

Thomas Laqueur, in his engrossing book *The Work of the Dead: A Cultural History of Mortal Remains*, calls the dead "a powerful category of the imagination."[17] The dead, he says, "matter because we cannot bear to give them up,"[18] and by putting these two statements together we can syllogize an understanding of how indispensable are the dead to the imagination, and by extension, how Joyce's continuous pivots and turns on the question of how we "know" someone is dead are a central part of his fiction, where the negation of subjectivity (living, knowing) intersects with its affirmation. If philosophy is a means of preparing to die and historiography is a labor of and against death—to invoke the formulations of two Michels, Montaigne and de Certeau[19]—then fiction, Joyce suggests, is an effort to cleave open the distinction between life and death, between events and eventualising. Just as *The Odyssey* is a story of man who must prove that he is not dead, *Ulysses* might be described as the sum of all functions by which the *certainty of death* is resisted. And just as the latest production of *Hamlet* at which we bid the prince and other dead to rise and speak again—a performance rightly called a "revival"—so too when we read *Ulysses*, we set Paddy Dignam, that teetotum, spinning in his grave. Round and round he goes, and where he stops, nobody knows.

---

[16] Italo Calvino, *Mr. Palomar*, trans. William Weaver (New York: Harcourt Brace, 1985), 125.
[17] Laqueur, *The Work of the Dead*, 79.
[18] Laqueur, *The Work of the Dead*, 54.
[19] Michel de Montaigne, "That to Philosophize Is to Learn to Die," in *The Complete Works*, trans. Donald M. Frame (New York: Knopf, 2003), 67–82; Michel de Certeau, *The Writing of History*, trans. Tom Conley (New York: Columbia University Press, 1988), 5.

Chapter 9

METEOROLOGICAL

Weathering the *Wake*: Barometric Readings of I.3

"Atmosphere" as a literary or aesthetic term appears to have by and large fallen out of usage. It is much less likely to be employed now in, say, a serious discussion of poetry than it is in a restaurant review. Yet the term still has a home in the ninth edition of *A Glossary of Literary Terms* (2009), though its definition is brief: "the emotional tone pervading a section or whole of a literary work, which fosters in the reader expectations as to the course of events." If this begs the question of what distinction there might be between "atmosphere" and "tone," synonymy further obscures, dilutes, and perhaps even empties the term's value when "mood" and "ambiance" are proffered as "alternative terms frequently used."[1] The *OED* categorizes such usage as merely "figurative," not specific to any particular discourse: "Mental or moral environment; a pervading tone or mood; associations, effects, sounds, etc. evoking a characteristic mood."

The apparent obsolescence of "atmosphere" has, I think, a network of interconnected causes. In part, it is the term's ineluctable uncertainty, imprecision, and slipperiness that make it weak and impractical: in addition to the variety of synonyms clustered around it, "atmosphere" is so often combined or connected with other formal elements—setting, theme, character—as to make it almost inseparable from them. This is most dramatically the case with genre, some kinds of which are wholly enveloped by an "atmosphere" because those genres are themselves committed to establishing and strictly maintaining a particular "mental or moral environment." Such popular genres extend from the Gothic to *World of Warcraft*. The tough guy poise of a Sam Spade or Philip Marlow's acumen requires just the right admixture of cigarette smoke and perfume, and would be abruptly snuffed out by the introduction of fluorescent office lighting, or a few choice notes from a harpsichord: the saturation

---

[1] M. H. Abrams and Geoffrey Galt Harpham, *A Glossary of Literary Terms*, 9th ed. (Boston, MA: Wadsworth Cengage Learning, 2009), 17–18.

is total but precarious, and must be carefully preserved as atmosphere and style become one. The paradox is that "atmosphere" is essential to more or less fixed genres that try to limit the variability or, in Umberto Eco's vision of the "open work,"[2] close a given text (it is uphill work to read *The Monk* as not horrific, or demonstrate that Sherlock Holmes has, at a story's end, sent a guiltless party to prison), but the term's usefulness seems to have diminished for discussions that try to resist absolute, oppressive interpretations.

There is, too, something rather mawkish about "atmosphere." Not only is it technically imprecise or at any rate vague, it implies an emotional response within the reader, one which can more or less safely be generalized. Again, critical trends have moved away from what are seen as unnecessarily constraining interpretations; yet for all that, the purposes of "atmosphere" have in some respects been usurped by the now *de rigueur* (though perhaps no less slippery) term "affect." Whatever the comparative strengths or weaknesses of "affect," it most distinctly lacks the environmental connotations of "atmosphere." While this takes a step away from the pitfalls of pathetic fallacy often inherent if perhaps not unavoidable in the use of "atmosphere," the preference for "affect" may represent a most literal displacement, a removal of the contingencies of place from considerations of readerly response.

After Derrida, the containment of the text implied by a differentiation of an "atmosphere" within a work from an indistinct other or even a vacuum without lacks feasibility: literature without air locks. Thus talk of "atmosphere" may well seem to smack of a fogeyish criticism, hermetically sealing off the world of the text from the world of the reader, with all the attendant depoliticizing effects such a gesture has by design.

Yet these tangled problems with talking about the "atmosphere" of a literary work—its unquantifiable and affective vagueness and its implied hermeneutics of separation and closure—make it tantalizing to reassess for studies of *Finnegans Wake*, a book that infamously troubles the very tools and terminology on which literary criticism so often relies. As readers have over the decades had cause to marvel and moan, the *Wake*'s counter-teleological distortions of time and space prohibit a delineation of causality integral to "plot" as such; these same distortions as well as those to language make "setting" an effectively indeterminable variable; and the ways in which speakers and subjects keep collapsing into one another reduce "character" to a cluster of attributes that occasionally align into a recognizable pattern, such as the initials HCE and ALP. Given the book's volatile, persistent mutability (of character, language, and so on), might not the nebulous concept of "atmosphere," with a refreshed

---

[2] Umberto Eco, *The Open Work*, trans. Anna Cancogni (Cambridge, MA: Harvard University Press, 1989).

understanding of the world's atmosphere as itself a mutable phenomenon, turn out to be more useful in considerations of the *Wake* than these other, typically more stable ones have been?

Finnegans Wake is a very cloudy book, but this essay will concentrate its meteorological survey on the third chapter, which, as Roland McHugh has observed, begins with a fog ("you spoof of visibility in a freakfog" (48.01–02)) and ends with rain (though it's ambiguous whether the rain has begun or is abating: "Rain. When we sleep. Drops. But wait until our sleeping. Drain. Sdops" (74.18–19)). McHugh remarks that the whole of the chapter "is embraced by the Irish climate" (and I'll return to this rather odd phrasing later).[3] This strategy of focusing on this one chapter in order to test a kind of reading approach for the book, it probably needs to be pointed out, does not imply or suggest that the *Wake* is neatly or usefully divisible into coherent, independent parts; and yet, as I have discussed in an earlier essay in this volume, neither is Joyce's book a cohesive, syncretic whole that can be safely summarized. This paradox also highlights how serviceable the contemplation of "atmosphere" is to our appreciation of the *Wake*, for the discussion of— indeed the very concept of—climate and environment necessitates both an understanding of the phenomenon as local and relative and an acceptance of the provisionality and the erroneousness of its study.

The weather is the universal subject of conversation par excellence. It allows for amicable oscillation between the particular and the general, and everyone is entitled to and usually has an opinion. It is also, for these reasons, often viewed as a harmless, even pacifying subject. The newspaper's phrase "Snow is general all over Ireland" that haunts Gabriel Conroy (and the reader) at the conclusion of "The Dead" is first voiced by Mary Jane as a polite way of moving the conversation away from the rudeness of Bartell D'Arcy. It is a means of moving from the uncomfortably specific to what seems an inoffensively general scale of things:

—It's the weather, said Aunt Julia, after a pause.
—Yes, everybody has colds, said Aunt Kate readily, everybody.
—They say, said Mary Jane, that we haven't had snow like this for thirty years; and I read this morning in the newspapers that the snow is general all over Ireland. (*D* 212)

Watch the pronouns here, for Joyce neatly captures the irregular way that they tend to be employed in what seem like banal, innocuous conversations. "It"

---

[3] Roland McHugh, "Recipis for the Price of the Coffin," in *A Conceptual Guide to* Finnegans Wake, ed. Michael H. Begnal and Fritz Senn (University Park: Pennsylvania State University Press, 1974), 30.

would seem, if very indirectly, to refer to the cause of D'Arcy's hoarseness (if not his coarseness), but "it" could mean just about anything, just as the "it" habitually used in an utterance like Lily's "Is it snowing again, Mr Conroy?" (*D* 177) has no definite referent. (What snows? It.) "Everybody" is repeated to remove all doubt, but the assertion is factually incorrect, an exaggeration. "They" is the abstract authority behind every weather report.

All of this becomes valuable for readers of *Finnegans Wake* when we recall that it is a book composed, as Finn Fordham has it, of "unravelling universals."[4] After the snow that "is general all over Ireland" has fallen, "by now one hears turtlings all over Doveland" (61.02). Unique wordflakes everywhere, and every possible weather system is likewise lexicalized. The *Wake*'s various voices are an indistinct "they" full of contradictory reports, dubious prophecies of a future hopelessly jumbled with the past, all "falsetissues, antilibellous and nonactionable" (48.18), none of which inspire confidence: "Thus the unfacts, did we possess them, are too imprecisely few to warrant our certitude" (57.16–17). Similar pronoun trouble, of course, plagues the reader on every page, if not in every sentence. In this chapter, it is variants of "he" and "his" that make for an unfixed subject, and "he" begins as a singer, "quite a musical genius in a small way and the owner of an exceedingly niced ear, with tenorist voice to match" (48.20–21) like Bartell D'Arcy or the other legendary singers reverentially recalled in "The Dead." Whatever he is—for he is or may also be (or was or may have been) in the course of this chapter, an actor, a fisherman, a dustman, a tailor, a photographer, and a giant, among other things, and at the chapter's end is a list of "abusive names he was called" (71.05–06)—he emerges from "a poisoning volume of cloud barrage indeed" (48.05). He materializes from the air itself.

The connections between character and atmosphere discernible in the *Wake* are radical versions of the notions that Bloom entertains in *Ulysses* about how climate shapes temperament, how one can see more clearly after a rainfall, and so on. (Joyce himself expresses such sentiments from time to time in his correspondence, complaining of the adverse effect a "bad climate" has on him and his work (*Letters I* 116).) In a book whose characters are topographies (e.g., a masculine mountain and a feminine river), the properties of a geographical region and the qualities of a person are so effectively indistinguishable as to efface the neat causality of such ideas as Bloom's about the Cinghalese made lethargic and lazy by the "sleeping sickness in the air" (*U* 5.36) and the Mediterranean's heating of its people's blood and passion. Here is one of the countless versions of the creation of the world given in the *Wake*:

---

[4] Finn Fordham, *Lots of Fun at* Finnegans Wake*: Unravelling Universals* (Oxford: Oxford University Press, 2007).

Before he fell hill he filled heaven: a stream, alplapping streamlet, coyly coiled um, cool of her curls: We were but thermites then, wee, wee. Our antheap we sensed as a Hill of Allen, the Barrow for an People, one Jotnursfjaell: and it was a grummelung amung the porktroop that wonderstruck us a thunder, yunder. (57.10–15)

Some exegetical notes are due here, scattered as they must be. God created heaven before He fell ill, or before Jack fell down the hill, and some time just before Satan had his fall, God opened an empty hell to catch him. Eve was made of Adam, and was herself a kind of improvement of paradise. The emergence of mountains shapes the paths of rivers, which can then be said to be lapping the Alps. The German word *um* is "of," in the sense that here is being spoken what things are made "of," and is incidentally the prefix for *Umwelt*, "environment." Termites, "wee" as they are, build tall mounds, just as ants build antheaps and humans misguided towers, meant to unify. To speak of when we were "but ... wee" is a remembrance of childhood, and termites predate human beings on the earth by many millions of years. In physics, a therm is a specific measure of heat or energy; in antiquity, it is a public bath or hot spring. To thermalize is to bring something into or to attain equilibrium with the surrounding environment, and the formation of the earth's landscapes was a gradual cooling process. And then of course there is thunder, never long unheard in the *Wake*, the sound of a god, in Vico's thinking the inspiration for human speech, wondrous grumbling, which changed isolated hermits (also in "thermites") into communities. Those communities in turn tell the story of how the world and they were formed.

The creator is his creation; character is not only place but the formation of place. Joyce does not fetishize "nature" as an object but instead conceives of it, like his own writing, as a process. This significantly disrupts the conditions for pathetic fallacy. When, say, the name of Count Dracula is uttered, or the detective announces to the gathered suspects that the murderer is among them, the lightning flashes, the thunder crashes—these atmospheric phenomena are symbols, which is to say that they possess an equivalence with something other than themselves.[5] With its functional, changeable language

---

[5] There is an interesting exercise to be had in comparing the effects of the infamous opening "It was a dark and stormy night" with those of the concluding sentences of "The Dead." Gabriel's egotism loses its site as central focus (the story does not begin with it and it is under threat from the moment it appears) and the inversion of deixis points away from the individual human self, to everywhere, nowhere in particular. A similar displacement of the subject by the very concept of atmosphere occurs in Bloom's fumbled advice to Stephen in "Eumaeus": "—It will (the air) do you good, Bloom said, meaning also the walk, in a moment" (*U* 16.1718–19).

of rain, wind, and thunder, the *Wake* presents the reader with the unsettling possibility that, in addition to the dissolution of such reliable traits and bellwethers as plot, character, and setting, the concept of "symbols" may have little value for the study of this book, that there is no symbolization as such in *Finnegans Wake*.[6] The climate may be connected with or comparable to many different and disparate things, but there is no definite equivalence. The "everintermutuomergent" principle of *Finnegans Wake* (55.11–12), according to which all twains are always meeting (or always about to meet), depends upon a priori difference, just as there can be no reconciliation if there has not been a sundering: "the coincidence of their contraries reamalgamerge in that identity of indiscernibles" (49.36–50.01)

Why does McHugh say that "the whole of I.3 is embraced by the Irish climate" rather than that the Irish climate is embraced by the text? Both are quite abstract assertions, but one does not seem more probable than the other. "I have called the weather 'uncaring,'" writes McHugh, "but at some levels it is obviously personified."[7] That "obviously" is undone by the phrase preceding it, which is another way of saying that at some levels McHugh is obviously incorrect, for the problem with personification is that it puts the man-made cart before the natural horse. For some reason, we do not speak of Earwicker the publican as an instance of "mountainfication." It is understood that the "natural world" is a projection screen; but as I have said, the *Wake* does not operate under this assumption. Much of I.3 is concerned with how to identify the multiform "he" who emerges from its opening miasma, and the problem is that, to borrow the terms of Marshall McLuhan, the figure cannot be made out from the ground, nor portrait from landscape:

> It is nebuless an autodidact fact of the commonest that the shape of the average human cloudyphiz, whereas sallow has long daze faded, frequently altered its ego with the posshing of the showers (Not original!). Whence it is a slopperish matter, given the wet and low visibility (since this scherzarade of one's thousand one nightinesses that sword of certainty which would identifide the body never falls) to indendifine the individuone. (*FW* 50.35–51.06)

What does "he" look like? Like the "commonest" and "average" man: "Come on, ordinary man with that large big nonobli head, and that blanko berbecked

---

[6] Whether or not he was the first to have his idea, Clive Hart's expression of it is probably the most forceful and succinct: "Our lives are full of fucking symbols: we don't need them in our reading matter as well" (see Roland McHugh, *The* Finnegans Wake *Experience*, 46).
[7] McHugh, "Recipis for the Price of the Coffin," 30.

fischial ekksprezzion" (64.30–31). To make matters worse, his appearance changes with the weather: not only can he not be absolutely identified for the "wet and low visibility" of a downpour (the Irish regularity of which occasions is why he carries "the state slate umbrella" (52.26–27)), he assumes new identities, alter egos, with each precipitation, and there may be no "original" or bonafide (in "identifide") identity for him anywhere.

Our indeterminable hero is also the cause of the weather that causes him. The dainty fog or "little cloud" of "nebuless" presages the vision of "Nuvoletta in her nightdress" in I.6 (157.08–159.18) and the "little cloud, a nibulissa" alternately weeping and laughing in II.2 (256.33–57.02). At the end of I.3, she mourns him, dissolves into rain; but she also looks forward to the day when he returns, gathering "nubilettes to cumule" (73.35) and flashing his "lightning lancer" (73.36). The cloud will become the river, the daughter will become her mother when her father awakes after the one thousand and one nights. This parent-child confusion, part of the understanding of nature as a process of transition and recurrence, is why the questions "what formal cause made a smile of *that* tothink? Who was he to whom? [...] Whose are the placewheres?" (56.31–33) remain unanswerable. The phrase "windy Nous blowing [...] through the hat" (56.29–30) blends *nous* (thought) with *pneu* (air) to make a perverse sort of reference to the inspiration celebrated by Shelley: "the mind in creation is as a fading coal, which some invisible influence, like an inconstant wind, awakens to transitory brightness."[8] Joyce unites the consciousness of character and/or narrative with the wind, so that mood and setting and character all "reamalgamerge" to form what might well be called "atmosphere." This effect is significantly more complex than personification.[9]

Written while "Work in Progress" was just a few years away from becoming *Finnegans Wake*, William Empson's *Seven Types of Ambiguity* wrestles with the problem of "atmospheres." "Interest in 'atmospheres' is a critical attitude designed for, and particularly suited to, the poets of the nineteenth century,"[10] Empson observes, but he also conjectures that "the belief in Atmosphere"—notably capitalized—may be a product of "the belief in Pure Sound":

---

[8] Percy Bysshe Shelley, "A Defence of Poetry," in *The Selected Poetry and Prose of Percy Bysshe Shelley*, ed. Carlos Baker (New York: Modern Library, 1951), 517.

[9] HCE is also undone by the atmosphere, or (at least in one incarnation, like Mohammed lifted into heaven) vanishes into it: he "disappeared [...] from the sourface of this earth, that austral plain he had transmaried himself to, so entirely spoorlessly (the mother of the book with a dustwhisk tabularasing his obliteration done upon her involucrum) as to tickle the speculative to all but opine [...] that the hobo [...] had transtuled his funster's latitat to its finsterest interrimost" (50.08–17).

[10] William Empson, *Seven Types of Ambiguity* (New York: New Directions, 1966), 20.

> Critics often say or imply casually that some poetic effect conveys a direct "physical" quality, something mysteriously intimate, something which it is strange that a poet could convey, something like a sensation that is not attached to any of the senses [...] It can be either felt or thought; the two are similar but different; and it requires practice to do both at once. Or the statement might, one cannot deny, mean that there has been some confusion of the senses. But it may mean something more important, involving a distinction between "sensation" and "feeling"; that what the poet has conveyed is no assembly of grammatical meanings, capable of analysis, but a "mood," an "atmosphere," a "personality," an attitude to life, an undifferentiated mode of being.[11]

The apparent strangeness of Empson's declining even to mention Joyce in *Seven Types*, though he does discuss Proust and T. S. Eliot (we can hear the influence of Eliot in the word "personality" and what follows it) might be explained by the apprehension shown about this potential "confusion of the senses." Empson's last sentence quoted above could be applied to the *Wake*, which certainly "is no assembly of grammatical meanings" as such, may or may not be "capable of analysis" (Empson surely means "capable of being analyzed," but the ambiguity is entertaining), and does seem to enjoy "an undifferentiated mode of being." Discomfited by the notion that the sound of words are themselves the meaning of poetry—which discomfort allows the critic to ignore Joyce and the entire body of avant-garde poetry produced in the 20 years prior to his book—Empson is resigned to the position that "atmosphere is conveyed in some unknown and fundamental way as a by-product of meaning" and "is the consciousness of what is implied by the meaning."[12]

Finnegans Wake revels in this "confusion of the senses," which Empson sees as an effect of atmosphere (or Atmosphere), which is itself linked to the conception of a language that can mean what it says, if not say what it means. Examples of synaesthesia in I.3 are not hard to find: there is "the touching seene" (52.36), conflating touch and sight, or "some seem on some dimb Arras, dumb as Mum's mutyness [...] is odable to os across the wineless Ere" (53.02–04), a parody of Joyce's own earlier prose that muddles together at least three and perhaps four of the senses (sight, hearing, smell, and taste). The deprivation of the senses, and the alleged augmentation of compensations of others, is a paradoxically apocalyptic theme: "The mouth that tells not will ever attract the unthinking tongue and so long as the obseen draws theirs

---

[11] Empson, *Seven Types of Ambiguity*, 16–17.
[12] Empson, *Seven Types of Ambiguity*, 17, 18.

which hear not so long till allearth's dumbnation shall the blind lead the deaf" (68.32–34). In the *Wake*, the primary revelation is also the ultimate revelation: that we cannot comprehend what is revealed.

Take this confusing cataclysm, for example:

> he dreamed that he'd wealthes in mormon halls when wokenp by a fourth loud snore out of his land in byelo while hickstrey's maws was grazing in the moonlight by hearing hammering on the paddywhank scale emanating from the blind pig and anything like it (oonagh! oonagh!) in the whole history of the Mullingcan Inn he never. This battering babel allower the door and sideposts, he always said, was not in the very remotest like the belzey babble of a bottle of boose which would not rouse him out o' slumber deep but reminded him loads more of the martiallawsey marses of foreign musikants' instrumongs or the overthrewer to the third last days of Pompery, if anything. And that after this most nooningless knockturn the young reine came down […] ruinating all the bouchers' shurtes and the backers' wischaundtugs so that be the chandleure of the Rejaneyjailey they were all night wasching the walters of, the weltering walters off. Whyte. (64.04–21, ellipsis added)

The dreamer wakes to a "hammering" and "battering" reminiscent of a volcanic explosion (the last days of Pompeii), followed by a drenching rain, or perhaps the queenly wife of the man who "dreamt that he dwelt in marble halls" angrily comes downstairs and lets fly with all her devastating wrath. On the one hand, this all seems the stuff of fable, tall tale, and nursery rhyme, with the proverbial blind pig, references to the tower of Babel and the fantasia of a nocturne, and even, for good measure, the butcher, the baker, and the candlestick maker. Yet there is a real account of a store's caretaker, the very Maurice Behan named in the text (63.35), startled from his bed one night by the sound of three men trying to break into the store or, in their version of events given at their trial, "only trying to open a bottle of stout by hammering it against the gate."[13] The end of this passage anticipates the last lines of I.8 (216.04–05), which recurrence might signal an operatic sort of leitmotif, though the ruinously bleaching "Whyte" becomes "Night!" leaving readers unable to establish a definite, revelatory last word or note to this repeated but varied apocalyptic scenario and rhythm. This passage's comparison of this tempest to "foreign

---

[13] Bill Cadbury, "'The March of a Maker': Chapters I.2–4," in *How Joyce Wrote Finnegans Wake: A Chapter-by-Chapter Genetic Guide*, ed. Luca Crispi and Sam Slote (Madison: University of Wisconsin Press, 2007), 92n14.

musikants' instrumongs," prompting the reader to consider that what seems like incomprehensible babble might be music produced by an uncommon means, can be juxtaposed with a 1928 letter that Joyce wrote to Harriet Shaw Weaver:

> We had some dreadful wind storms here [in Paris], one when we were out in the clinic which threw my wife back a little, accompanied by some unseemly remarks by the Reverend Mr Thor [...] The groaning of the lift mingling with the howling of the blast and shrieking of the trees and the cannonading of the hailstorms making anti-music with the frenzied shouts of the French staff, causing the rubber carpeting sound proofed edifice to form a pandemoniacal box for the wren-like twittering of my nerves. (*Letters I* 277–78)

Joyce's "anti-music," an arresting concatenation of independent noises (emulated by the string of gerunds, a frequent device in the *Wake*), is an ambient effect. Whereas music proper is produced by musicians, "anti-music"—here heard in, of all places, an elevator—is produced by the environment. Perhaps Empson's worried characterization of a belief in "Pure Sound" is a little off the mark here, for it might be more apt to call the *Wake*'s ambient soundscape of noise that is reminiscent of but not synonymous with music as such "Impure Sound," in keeping with the text's mongrel hybridizations of languages and cultures, figure and ground.

Useful insights are to be discovered in more recent "ecocritical" debates. Timothy Morton argues for the production and appreciation of an "ambient poetics" which

> interferes with attempts to set up a unified, transcendent nature that could become a symptomatic fantasy thing. Critical close reading elicits the inconsistent properties of this ambient poetics. Ambience compromises ecomimesis because the very processes that try to convey the illusion of immediacy and naturalness keep dispelling it from within.[14]

I have already pointed out that *Finnegans Wake* resists conceiving of or representing nature as an object, and in I.3 the fog, wind, rain, and thunder are subjects in the fullest possible sense—articulate, doubtful, and self-doubting subjects—but subjects always in progress (the weather is never certain at any given moment). Since honest readers of the *Wake* can attest that the more

---

[14] Timothy Morton, *Ecology without Nature: Rethinking Environmental Aesthetics* (Cambridge, MA: Harvard University Press, 2007), 77.

they read of the book, the less rather than more certain they become about how to read it, such "inconsistent properties" that simultaneously frustrate and enliven close readings might persuade us to think of the *Wake*'s ambient poetics. "Ambient poetics," Morton writes, "is about making the imperceptible perceptible, while retaining the form of its imperceptibility—to make the invisible visible, the inaudible audible."[15] This formulation accepts the *Wake*'s synaesthesia as a means for developing a sensorial matrix (in the most primal connotation, an *aesthetic*) with which to perceive the elements of the world otherwise unknown to us, though all around us.

Again, take the world's atmosphere. What is it that we are breathing?

> We might leave that nitricence of oxagiants to take its free of the air and just analectralyse that very chymerical combination, the gasbag where the warderworks. And try to pour somour heiterscene up thealmostfere. (67.07–10)

Here the invisible elements are literally elements: the nitrogen, oxygen, and hydrogen of which air is made (helium appears in the next sentence). Moreover, the thunderstorm, the ur-signifier, is itself being submitted to analysis, so as to better understand how wind ("gasbag" recalls Aeolus), rain ("warderworks" as waterworks), and lightning (the electrical in "analectralyse") combine to make the ineffable, "Him Which Thundereth From On High" (62.14). Between the sublime and the banality of chemistry lies "thealmostfere" (almost fear, or fear of the almost).

The natural and the supernatural are not distinct categories in the *Wake*'s ambient poetics because both nitrogen atoms and Zeus elude the deadened or habituated senses (those possessed by that "ordinary man" (64.30) or "the common or ere-in-garden castaway" (62.19)). This is not entirely surprising, for where else would one expect to find the ethereal but in the ether? Marina Warner notes: "Air, clouds, vapour, smoke, foam, froth, steam, and their spiritous, sublimed counterparts among airy and even gaseous substances (as Joyce noticed) have served to make manifest the invisible, supernatural, imponderable, and ineffable according to the promptings of belief and fantasy."[16] The legend of the "humphriad" (53.09) variously recounted and recanted in I.3 depends upon a nebulous conjoining of the air of plausible history and the mist of myth; a constant production, in other words, of an "aerily perennious" atmosphere (57.22).

---

[15] Morton, *Ecology without Nature*, 96.
[16] Marina Warner, *Phantasmagoria: Spirit Visions, Metaphors, and Media into the Twenty-First Century* (Oxford: Oxford University Press, 2006), 79–80.

A number of abrupt transitions between paragraphs in this chapter smack of an ostentatiously procedural performance, such as that of an investigation, a legal case (either a contract or a hearing), or a lecture: "But resuming inquiries" (66.10); "To proceed" (67.07); "Now to the obverse" (67.28). Such rhetoric so smacks of officialdom that it seems to constitute what would typically be called an atmosphere, such as that of a boardroom or courtroom. Accordingly, there is "Sylvia Silence, the girl detective" (61.01) leaning back "in her really truly easy chair" (61.05), puzzling over the clues in the obscure mystery, and with such Holmesian deductions as "by the siege of his trousers there was something else behind it" (61.25–26). But such overtones are overrules, the classic atmosphere of detective fiction permitted to be sensed only to be contradicted—for example, when Sylvia breaks her silence (just as the "cloudletlitter silent" (73.29) will later burst) to speak with the voice of Elmer Fudd, the reader is told, "Your machelar's mutton leg's getting musclebound from being too pulled" (64.32–33), and sylvan mystery is supplanted by floral factuality:

> There are 29 reasons why blossomtime's the best. Elders fall for green almonds when they're raised on bruised stone root ginger though it winters on their heads as if auctumned round their waistbands. (64.35–65.02)

Gardening tips, fashion notes, or courtship advice? The heady fragrance of the romance novelette is also scented in I.3: tales of "rushy hollow heroines in their skirtsleeves" (67.04) either ruining their reputations or doing away with themselves. Genres and their respective atmospheres clash and commingle, allowing the reader to perceive how those genres function, just as spectroscopic study of gaseous interactions divulge the constituent properties of the respective elements.

Recall the inevitable precariousness of a unified (essentially noncontradictory) atmosphere, and how easily the (actually aberrant) consistency of that atmosphere can be sabotaged by the introduction of an uncalled-for element, or the wrong proportion of necessary elements. This observation makes for an entertaining thought experiment: calculate with what minimal change to a recognizably "atmospheric" work one can wreak the maximum damage to that atmosphere (and thus to the affect) of a work. The languorous ache of a scene in a soap opera could be devastated with one strategic dialogue change, or even a slight change in tempo. Now try to imagine sabotaging the "atmosphere" of *Finnegans Wake*—and despair. The utter inconsistency of tone, idiom, mood, temporality, and so on give the text an impressive integrity. Yet this integrity is not a form of purity, not the effect of a profound circumscription, a containment that readers cannot spoil because they cannot penetrate. On the contrary, the impurity of the *Wake* contaminates and is in turn willingly permeated by the corrupting "atmosphere" in which the reader reads. The reader cannot but bring his or her idioms, moods, and setting into play trying to read a text whose often alien-seeming but tantalizingly familiar language invites and passively accepts the reader's impressions and projections. If "atmosphere" is imagined to be a pure and undiluted phenomenon, the way that Mikel Dufrenne does in contending that "the unity of an atmosphere is thus the unity of a *Weltanschauung*; its coherence is the coherence of a characteristic or quality,"[17] then it might be said that the slasher film *Saw IV* has an atmosphere but *Finnegans Wake* does not; but if "atmosphere" is acknowledged to be composite and changeable, then the *Wake* is a dynamic ecosystem and *Saw IV* is a bottled, inert sample on some laboratory shelf.

Responding to the work of Gernot Böhme,[18] Morton points out that atmosphere is "inevitably not only spatial but also temporal":

> A shower of rain is atmospherically different if you stand in it for two hours, as opposed to five minutes. The "same" atmosphere is never the "same" as itself.
>
> This is a matter not of ontological nicety, but of political urgency. The notion of atmosphere needs to expand to include temporality. *Climate* (as in climate change) is a vector field that describes the momentum of the atmosphere—the rate at which the atmosphere keeps changing. A map of atmospheric momentum would exist in a phase space with many dimensions. The neglect of temporality in thinking about the weather is why it is practically impossible to explain to people that global warming might result in pockets of cool weather.[19]

This neglect also happens to be why "maps" and "outlines" of *Finnegans Wake* founder: they are the equivalent of the chain of curly lines meant to represent clouds, which serve well enough for the most rudimentary sort of abstraction but offer little insight into the composition and none into the motion and effects of gaseous phenomena. Such schemes make stable and timeless what is—conceptually, at any rate—continuously in flux, and I wonder how much more satisfyingly the cartographic problem of the *Wake* might be dealt with using animated maps, something akin to the satellite imaging seen in televised

---

[17] Mikel Dufrenne, *The Phenomenology of Aesthetic Experience*, trans. Edward S. Casey et al. (Evanston, IL: Northwestern University Press, 1973), 177.
[18] Gernot Böhme, *Atmosphäre: Essays zur neuen Ästhetik* (Frankfurt am Main: Suhrkamp, 1995).
[19] Morton, *Ecology without Nature*, 166.

and online weather reports, that allow a representation of, say, the transformation of a Kevin into a Shaun and then into an Ondt, or one version of a phrase into another over the course of the book —the very "everintermutuomergent" principle I underscored earlier in this essay. As Morton instructively writes, "atmosphere is subject to the same paradox as identity—it does for the weather what identity does for idea of self."[20]

In a condemnation of Heidegger (made all the more caustic by the omission of Heidegger's name), Adorno declares, "Wherever philosophy imagines that by borrowing from literature it can abolish objectified thought and its history—what is commonly termed the antithesis of subject and object—and even hopes that Being itself will speak, in a poésie concocted out of Parmenides and Jungnickel, it starts to turn into a washed-out cultural babble."[21] If we leave aside the proscription regarding philosophy and recognize the scornful final phrase ("ausgelaugten Kulturgeschwätz") as a plausibly fair assessment of *Finnegans Wake*, we can tunnel backward through Adorno's statement and acknowledge that Joyce's book is an effort both to coax "Being itself" to "speak" and to elide "the antithesis of subject and object." This we have seen in the foregoing, localized meteorological survey of the *Wake*'s ambient poetics (which could readily be extended beyond the environs of I.3). Thus the *Wake* might be philosophy turning into literature, or in Adorno's stricter terms, philosophy imagining itself as literature—and given how the *Wake*'s mutations are always reversible, also literature imagining itself as philosophy. Against Adorno on this score is Arthur C. Danto: "When art internalizes its own history, when it becomes self-conscious of its history as it has come to be in our time, so that its consciousness of its history forms a part of its nature, it is perhaps unavoidable that it should turn into philosophy at last."[22] Given the interesting (and unusual) juxtaposition of the terms "history" and "nature" here, I think we might draw upon this suggestion to shape a new definition of atmosphere: the degree or tendency to which (or even, in the most interesting cases, the fluctuations with which) a literary text's or work of art's consciousness of its history threatens to make it "philosophy at last."

Words, Joyce reminds us in *Finnegans Wake*, are air, the seemingly insubstantial stuff without which there would be no sound, no philosophy, no life. "Words weigh no more to him than raindrops to Rethfernhim," the text boasts, adding: "Which we all like. Rain" (74.16–18). The book is raining words: we

---

[20] Morton, *Ecology without Nature*, 166.
[21] Theodor W. Adorno, *Notes to Literature*, vol. 1, trans. Shierry Weber Nicholsen (New York: Columbia University Press, 1991), 6.
[22] Arthur C. Danto, *The Philosophical Disenfranchisement of Art* (New York: Columbia University Press, 1986), 16.

see, hear, and feel them falling. Besides being a ritual for the dead, a *wake* is a disturbance of water, a phenomenon of air turbulence, even an open hole in ice. "Finnegan's wake" is his movement through the elements, his figuration of and within the environment. Reading *Finnegans Wake*, in which we move through the obscurity and precipitation, shaping the ambient "anti-music" as much as we hear it, makes for unique disruptions of atmosphere, wakes of our own.

Chapter 10

HYSTERICAL-EXEGETICAL

Petitions Full of Pieces of Pottery

> They know how they believe that they believe that they know. Wherefore they wail.
> —*FW* 470.11–12

I

At the Budapest Joyce symposium in 2006, in the same building in which the proceedings took place, another conference was being held at the same time, a gathering of industrial paint manufacturers. At the time I wondered, as I still do, what would happen if a delegate from each event were by mistake to sit down for a talk at the other conference. Which of them, the Joycean or the paintmaker, would be the first to realize the mistake or else simply have enough of the presentation and discreetly leave? Surely the odds are on the paintmaker; it is all too easy to imagine the Joycean patiently listening on and on with the quiet assurance that eventually all of what was being said would come back to *Ulysses* or, even more likely, *Finnegans Wake*.

That assurance can become reckless, even breathtaking. Though all writing is—as if by definition—susceptible to confused interpretations, there are certain texts and cultural artefacts that have historically, repeatedly attracted more than their share of monomaniacal readers with elaborate and bizarre theories. Holy writ, most conspicuously and consistently, inspires fiercely eccentric interpretations, the result of such texts' combination of claims to universal, unassailable truth and the various nonliteral registers in which they are written. And while their uncertain authorship, too, contributes to the license with which their readers may cultivate their ideas free from worry about intention and textual history, the canonical brand of Shakespeare yields an opposite reaction, with complex conspiracies of plagiarism, pseudonymous authorship, or worse. (By contrast, even the most far-out readings of Joyce salute him as their genius spirit, but it's curious to observe that it is textual genetics, the hermeneutics most pledged to material evidence, that most assiduously dislocates

Joyce's authorship of "his" texts.) And then there are records that have to be played backward or paired with films made generations before or after, iconography deviously concealed in currency: these texts and objects await their undiscovered functions as maps, spells, prophecies.

We might posit a kind of textual or more broadly hermeneutical equivalent or correlative to the phenomenon known as Jerusalem Syndrome. Victims of this reported but contested affliction are people, even those without any apparent religious background or inclination, who shortly after their arrival in the Holy City are possessed by the conviction that they are messiahs or prophets. And just as it seems vaguely, if only potentially logical that Jerusalem of all cities might have this effect, and yet it is just as clear that it is not *evident* why it should—why there should be an observable Jerusalem Syndrome and not, say, a Boca Raton Syndrome—*Finnegans Wake* seems, on the face of it, as eminently capable as any book of overthrowing noble minds, but exactly how it might do this is not immediately easy to pinpoint.

Constructing taxonomies of misreading can be as difficult, as messy, and perhaps as pointless as building a tower of eggs, and yet there is an unshakeable sense that some interpretations are more *systematically* wrong than others. Yet we must be cautious about labels and summary dismissals, and both give every argument its fair hearing and acknowledge how subjective are the shades of differences along the unmeasured spectrum between the incontestable and the inconceivable. A given reading can be challenged for its basis either on incorrect information or on ambiguities or uncertain points, or else for its value, its larger import, its relevance. The kinds of reading to be considered here do not, almost as a general rule, readily allow their basis and value to be challenged because they are, in their authors' view, self-evident, and are sometimes by implication one and the same. (God told me to do it, and I did it because God wanted me to do it.) The astronomer Carl Sagan kept a box of the many letters he received detailing reports of alien activities and he labeled this box "Broken Ceramics"—an ironically polite translation of "crackpots." The *Wake*, of course, beat him to the joke, and provides my title: "I have been reciping om omominous letters and widelysigned petitions full of pieces of pottery about my monumentalness" (543.06–08). This essay offers a series of cautionary tales, presented to enable an exploration of what it is about Joyce, and *Finnegans Wake* in particular, that attracts, inspires, or even encourages the most specious, pathological, and even lunatic readings.[1]

---

[1] It needs to be made clear and even emphasized that it is a class of interpretations that is being discussed here and not a class of readers or people. Moreover, the examples selected for examination here all come from published writings, whether that publication be by university or vanity press, by print or online. Student work, for example, is

To explain his absence from Stephen's *Hamlet* lecture in the library, Haines tells Mulligan, "Shakespeare is the happy huntingground of all minds who have lose their balance" (*U* 10.1061–62). In this, as in other respects, Joyce competes with Shakespeare, and at this moment in history may seem to have outdone him, for if reading Shakespeare is generally considered respectable cultural work, reading Joyce is a more suspect activity: one need not look long among the counsels and bromides of the Internet to find it condemned as a sign of intellectual pretension, a waste of time, a perversion, insanity.[2]

Right after Stephen denies that he believes his own theory,

John Eclecticon doubly smiled.

—Well, in that case, he said, I don't see why you should expect payment for it since you don't believe it yourself. Dowden believes there is some mystery in Hamlet but will say no more. Herr Bleibtreu, the man Piper met in Berlin, who is working up that Rutland theory, believes that the secret is hidden in the Stratford monument. He is going to visit the present duke, Piper says, and prove to him that his ancestor wrote the plays. It will come as a surprise to his grace. But he believes his theory. (*U* 9.1070–77)

Eglinton at this moment becomes "Eclecticon" as he suggests that the degree to which an interpretation is "eclectic"—the word comes from the Greek *eklektikos*, "selective"—such as theories about Rutland's authorship of Shakespeare's work, discredits them less than Stephen's declining to "believe" does his own.

The importance of being earnest! To Wilde's painfully just remark about how "genuine feeling" underwrites all bad poetry can be added a corollary: the more dubious a given critical interpretation is, the more likely it is most sincerely believed and cherished.[3] There is more than a faint tang of irony in the word "naturally" as it is deployed in Fritz Senn's statement that "Scholars, and

---

therefore excluded from such a survey, and rightly so, since student work is by definition the work of learners and so distinct from any of the classifications of misinterpretation outlined in what follows.

[2] Joyce himself is often probed for signs of mental illness, in ways that may say more about the physicians' inattendance than about the patient. Among the gravest assessments are Joseph Collins's *The Doctor Looks at Literature: Psychological Studies of Life and Letters* (New York: George H. Doran, 1923), a book which so amused Joyce that it was admitted into the *Wake*, and N. J. C. Andreasen's "James Joyce: A Portrait of the Artist as a Schizoid," *Journal of the American Medical Association* 224 (1973): 67–71.

[3] Oscar Wilde, "The Critic as Artist," in *The Complete Works of Oscar Wilde* (London: Collins, 1991), 1052.

that includes Joyceans, naturally believe their own theories" (98). Joyce called himself "misbeliever" (*Letters I* 53)—and yet, what but some form of strong belief could propel someone to work at a book for seventeen years despite all of the adversities and the misgivings of others? It is precisely here that we must find our first note of caution: many of the qualities observed in or projected onto Joyce are those that readers and critics may themselves possess, even dormantly, or envy: obsessiveness, for example, that "meticulosity bordering on the insane" (173.34); or else a capacity to synthesize disparate information; or unfettered ambition.

II

Though it may well be a form of pathology, the perpetually frustrated but renewed need to find patterns, discern order, and locate possible meanings is not at all exclusive to those readings that we might judge unhinged—it is what brings all readers to the *Wake*, and what keeps us under its spell. Nor is the perceived need for explication itself the cause or defining feature, but it might be the *degree of urgency* to that explication that can so distort judgment. My paradigmatic example of what I've called a theocratic reading[4]—that is, the treatment of a given text as inescapably true and requiring an immediate transformative action—lies in the series of letters and telegrams sent by George Andrews to Sylvia Beach in the 1950s. From *Finnegans Wake* he had learned not only of the imminent threat of atomic war but the exact date of its outbreak. "Howday you doom? [...] The uneven day of the unleventh month of the unevented year" (517.33–34) clearly meant that doomsday was to fall on the eleventh of November.[5] Andrews's letter-writing campaign called for the evacuation of major cities. In a telegram on November 8, 1954 (see Figure 2), the young American poet's typos seem to enhance the desperation of his message:

> I HAD HOPED THAT AT LEWST YOU WOULD BELIEVE ME DONIT YOU UNDERSTAND THAT JOYCE WAS [A] PROPMET [?] THE STORM WILL BREAK NOVEMBER ELEBENTH GIVE THE BOOK TO ANYONE WHO WILL PUBLISH IT IMMEDIATELY
> LOVE, GEORGE

---

[4] See Conley, *Useless Joyce*, 20–22.
[5] See Noel Riley Fitch, *Sylvia Beach and the Lost Generation: A History of Literary Paris in the Twenties and Thirties* (New York: Norton, 1983), 394.

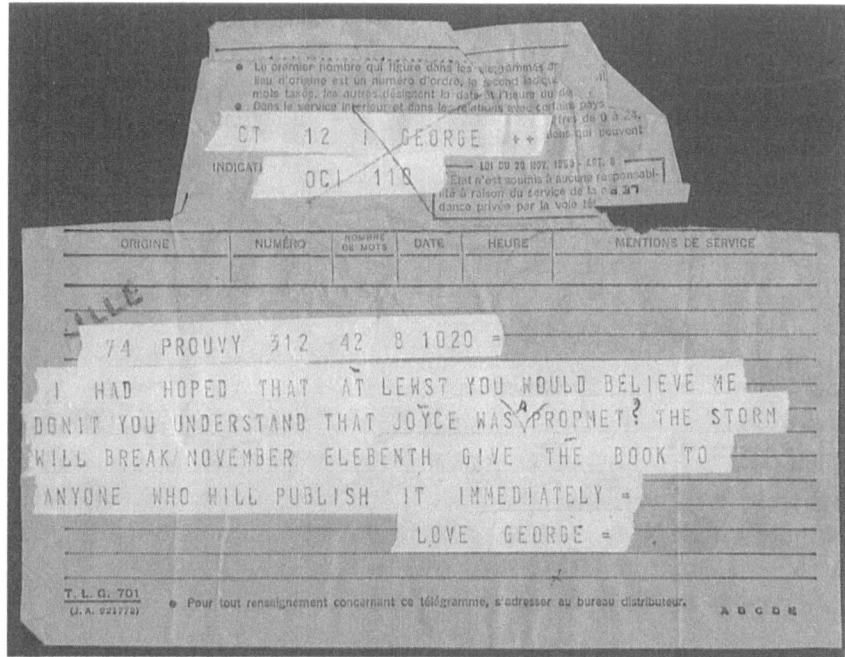

Figure 2 A desperate telegram sent to Sylvia Beach in 1954

The book in question was his own manuscript, a muddled blend of poetry and prophecy. Beach's note on the back of the telegram envelope indicates, among other things, her own admirable calm in the face of armageddon: "replied / was working / DO NOT DISTURB." When the catastrophe did not come to pass, Andrews wrote Beach again in October 1956: perhaps she remembered his earlier predictions, found in *Finnegans Wake*, that "the last world war would start with an alliance between Moscow and Mecca, that Russia (Willingdone) would attack England, France, and America (Lipoleum) without warning"? Well, he had the year wrong then, and 1956 was it for sure. But on November 13, 1956, he admitted, "My interpretation of Finnegans Wake has once again been proven incorrect."[6] Few readers can make that assertion with such certainty.

If the apparent clarity of its message(s) can spark such drastic reactions, by the same token, the inscrutability of the *Wake* can likewise prompt urgent action: in his memoirs, Anthony Burgess recalls how, when a soldier stationed

---

[6] All correspondence quoted here comes from the Sylvia Beach papers at Princeton University Library.

at Gibraltar, his copy of the book was "generally supposed to be a code book" and thus he became a figure of suspicion, unlike the "harmless" Christian missionary's distributed pamphlets whose exhortations, one can infer, were so unthreatening in that military milieu that they could be simply ignored.[7]

These commitments of belief and urgency are two key ingredients for the crackpot, but alone, however heated, do not constitute a meal. For that is needed what the *Wake* calls "sensationseeking an idea" (121.03; see *JJA* 46.333), a phrase that potently combines an implied reversal of sensory data leading to an intellectual observation with the craving of strong stimulation or desperation for thrills. Added to a typescript probably in early 1925, it might also suggest Joyce's own uncertain pursuit of the indefinite, the book that possessed him. Which of these madnesses is the greater?

The "idea" can become "just that fixed idea" as Haines puts it, without taking note of his own manias. A drive to find or else impose consistency can produce a key, a singular key that opens all the doors, answers all the questions; one key to rule them all. This recognizable, resilient trope is found most recently in Grace Eckley's *The Encryption of* Finnegans Wake *Resolved* (2018), the very title of which is symptomatic: just what does it mean to "resolve an encryption"? The phrase sounds like a bad translation of other metaphors already taken by other village explainers: *A Skeleton Key to* Finnegans Wake or *The Wake Lock Picked*.[8] The predication of a code itself predicates a decoding, but the notion that there is a "key" to the code—there's the rub.

It is Eckley's conviction that Joyce is obsessed with British journalist and editor William T. Stead. "Obsessed" is not her word, but she herself appears to have trouble characterizing Joyce's attitude, apart from its being tangible everywhere in his work. (Think of the final word of *A Portrait of the Artist as a Young Man*, and you might begin to see the light.) "One may ask," she writes, "is W. T. Stead a motif [of *Finnegans Wake*]? Probably not. He is an injection of intellectual energy whose activism supports an uncountable number of motifs."[9] While I dare not presume to gloss that last assertion, it seems fair to say that for Eckley, *Finnegans Wake* is "about something," and that something is Stead.

---

[7] Anthony Burgess, *Little Wilson and Big God* (New York: Grove Weidenfeld, 1987), 255. In a 1920 letter to Stanislaus, Joyce refers to a British war censor's claiming that "*Ulysses* was a prearranged pro-German code" (*Letters III* 22).

[8] Joseph Campbell and Henry Morton Robinson, *A Skeleton Key to* Finnegans Wake (New York: Viking, 1961); Harry Burrell, *Narrative Design in* Finnegans Wake: *The Wake Lock Picked* (Gainesville: University Press of Florida, 1996).

[9] Grace Eckley, *The Encryption of* Finnegans Wake *Resolved* (Lanham, MD: Hamilton Books, 2018), 21.

Perhaps what is most disarming about Eckley's book is its stated solidarity with the principles (though conspicuously not the methods) of genetic research. She invokes and praises such scholars as Geert Lernout, Dirk Van Hulle, and Luca Crispi,[10] and applauds and echoes their works' constitutive demands for evidence, even as she provides none of her own, at least none that is verifiable. Instead—that's one word, not two—she repeatedly refers to what she calls "the Stead information" in assertions like this one: "Nurturing the Stead information solves the puzzles and transplants the 'unknown' from the encrypted to the unencrypted column that matures in a consuming respect for Joyce's organizational powers."[11] "Nurturing" information is a curious expression that may itself reveal a certain fading of disinterested or measured judgement, especially when it is that very act of "nurturing" that "solves the puzzles." Imagining a column that matures in respect does test one's powers a little more, though it is the term "information" that remains most conspicuously elusive. When Eckley sums up her intertextual navigations with the statement that "Multitextual signage serves as a type of shorthand that is easily penetrated," even more worrying than the significance of "penetrated" is the sureness of "easily."[12]

The logic at work in Eckley's book, if not truly circular, does tend to arrive where it begins, right before heading out for another loop. She claims that "Joyce penetrates the maze of facts of life to build a case for Stead as Campbell's hero of a thousand faces,"[13] expressing an understanding that the *Wake* is some sort of "case for Stead"—perhaps primarily so—and seemingly implying that Joyce read and was inspired by Joseph Campbell. Because Stead used the word "thunderbolt" to describe one of his journalistic exposés, Eckley promptly identifies that as "the thunderbolt of which Joyce constructed ten variants composed of 100 letters each, except the last, which totals 101 letters to signal the ongoing pattern."[14] And yet earlier in the book she locates the central meaning of that thunder in Joyce's psychology. According to Eckley, Joyce's "fear of thunderstorms may be traced" to a case of "desperate disciplinary tactics": "May Joyce 'is said sometimes to have pushed Jim's head down the lavatory and flushed.' [...] This could incite fear of thunder and sensitivity to excrement, which before the advent of the horseless carriage was commonly visible and adhesive to the point of desperation."[15]

---

[10] Eckley, *The Encryption of* Finnegans Wake *Resolved*, 26, 3, 21.
[11] Eckley, *The Encryption of* Finnegans Wake *Resolved*, 22.
[12] Eckley, *The Encryption of* Finnegans Wake *Resolved*, 353.
[13] Eckley, *The Encryption of* Finnegans Wake *Resolved*, 353.
[14] Eckley, *The Encryption of* Finnegans Wake *Resolved*, 117.
[15] Eckley, *The Encryption of* Finnegans Wake *Resolved*, 66. That passive phrasing "is said" is a tacit acceptance of unattributed information found in John Wyse Jackson and Peter

Stead, too, proves adhesive to the point of desperation. Eckley's exegeses of chosen passages are all of a piece. For instance, to the question "Who'll brighten Brayhowth and bait the Bull Bailey and never despair of Lorcansby?" (448.18–19), Eckley steadily answers: Stead.

> Stead's first name William and his trial at the London Central Criminal Court called "the Old Bailey' [*sic*] and his incarceration made him suitable for "bait/beat the Bull Bailey" (448.19), who was the icon John Bull caricature of the British empire; and the song "Bill Bailey, Won't You Please Come Home?" indicative of his pending release from jail. (2)

That phrase "made him suitable" allows Eckley to imply intention without having to demonstrate it and is also suggestive of the kind of forced reading that is possibly at work here. Fixation does not necessarily entail consistency, as we see when Eckley returns to a portion of text that she has already analyzed, and though the details of interpretation may change, the meaning remains, well, steadfast. Here's a passage from I.3 with Eckley's glosses in square brackets:

> His Thing Mod [Viking parliament; Stead's jury] have undone him: and his madthing [Maiden Tribute] has done him man. His beneficiaries [of the C. L. A. Act] are legion in the part he created [as "Secret Commissioner" of MT]: they number up his years. Greatwheel [superintendent and cycles of progressions] Dunlop was the name was on him: behung [descended], all we are his bissacles [beneficiaries, bicycle tires make the system go]. (58.01–04)[16]

And here is another, somewhat different exegesis of the same passage made in the very next chapter:

> His Thing Mod [Stead's law; the Old Bailey] have undone him [disgraced him with criminal conviction]: and his madthing [reform zeal] has done him man [made a leading man of him]. His beneficiaries [women] are legion in the part he created; they number up his years [he worked for the cause all his life]. Greatwheel Dunlop [the universe] was the name was on him: behung [descended], all we are his bissacles/bicycles. As hollyday in his house [Stead's Sunday worship] so was he priest and

---

Costello's biography of John Joyce (*John Stanislaus Joyce: The Voluminous Life and Genius of James Joyce's Father* (New York: St. Martin's Press, 1997), 143).

[16] Eckley, *The Encryption of Finnegans Wake Resolved*, 339.

king to that; ulvy came, envy saw, ivy conquered. Lou! Lou! [female plus "loo," the "filth" of the MT]. They have waved his green boughs [healthy growth of the nation] o'er him as they have torn him limb from limb [hounded like Actaeon for publishing "filth"]. (58.01–08)[17]

If we look back to Eckley's 1985 book, *Children's Lore in* Finnegans Wake—among the courageous first monographs on the *Wake*, published a year before John Bishop's *Joyce's Book of the Dark*—we find the obsession is already in place. There, too, she writes of how because of "the Stead information […]" much of speculative criticism will have to be rewritten" and asserts that "it is doubtful that Joyce could have invented any human perversion that Stead had not uncovered."[18] The same anew.

Debatably less monomaniacal than Eckley's book but worthy of comparison in this regard is Martha Fodaski Black's *Shaw and Joyce: "The Last Word in Stolentelling,"* an extensive argument that Joyce took nearly everything from George Bernard Shaw. Black's claims about a "secret struggle with his literary progenitor,"[19] as even that word "secret" might indicate, sometimes hit notes of evangelism, and intimate a sense of being suppressed by intellectual fashion.

> Because of Shaw, this book is not just an exercise in literary criticism […] [It] may reveal relevant messages (an unpopular word, but one that studying Shaw has given me the courage to use) from Shaw translated into Joyce's fiction […] Although sophisticated Joyceans may not want to admit Shaw's presence in Joyce, my book illustrates his ubiquity in the younger Dubliner, in whose fictions the irrepressible, waggish laughter of G. B. S. turns into parodic tributes that reveal the lessons of the *"Immensipater."*[20]

Note first the force implied in that opening phrase, "Because of Shaw"; then compare it with the scorn in the designation "sophisticated Joyceans." One might suppose that this last *Wake* word (342.26) might be more readily or plausibly associated with Daniel O'Connell (known as "the Emancipator")

---

[17] Eckley, *The Encryption of* Finnegans Wake *Resolved*, 353. This second iteration of the passage mistakenly has a semicolon rather than a colon after "created."
[18] Grace Eckley, *Children's Lore in* Finnegans Wake (Syracuse, NY: Syracuse University Press, 1985), 211.
[19] Martha Fodaski Black, *Shaw and Joyce: "The Last Word in Storytelling,"* (Gainesville: University Press of Florida, 1995), 22.
[20] Black, *Shaw and Joyce: "The Last Word in Storytelling,"* 23.

or Walter Pater, never mind the name of the racehorse Emancipator, who appears to be running in this section of Joyce's book, than with Shaw. But perhaps such guesses are those of "sophisticated Joyceans." In any event, the hagiographic treatment (if not exaltation) of "G. B. S.", together with the emphasis on transmitted (but concealed and/or disregarded) "messages" and "lessons," give cause for concern.

Influences are of course both a ripe and proper topic, now enriched and substantiated by genetic criticism, and we have come to recognize that no "source," however unlikely or obscure, can be discounted out of hand. Yet how total, how all-encompassing is the influence in the respective theses of Eckley and Black, and how unsurprising, then, that when Black came to review Eckley's earlier (1994) book about Stead's dominant role in *Finnegans Wake*, the quarrel is over chosen heroes. Writes Black, "Grace Eckley is like the blind man who felt the elephant's tail and concluded that the world's largest mammal was a reptile." Clearly rankled by Eckley's assertion that Shaw "scarcely qualifies" as a Nobel Prize winner, Black underscores that "HCE, unlike Stead has won" "Noblett's surprize" (*FW* 306.04).[21] Rather than question the notion of a key, she vigorously polishes her own, and concludes: "Even though Eckley continues to back Stead, placing her money on him instead of more likely winners, in the HCE sweepstakes, Stead is an also-ran."[22] Isn't that Black the pot calling Eckley the kettle black?

The pivotal "key" or "keys" need not be so localized or discreet as those of Eckley and Black. Joyce's remark to Beckett that he "may have oversystematized *Ulysses*" (*JJ II* 702) notwithstanding, the perception of systems underpinning this or that compositional, thematic, or formal principle of the *Wake* has not infrequently prompted readers to apply entire systems which themselves are no less complex and arcane than anything Joyce wrote—and here I mean "apply" in precisely the way I warn students against in their engagements with theory, in the way that one applies paint to a prone surface. Inevitably these systems are found to resonate in perfect harmony with Joyce's text, and may thus be said to be a conscious part (if not the whole!) of his design. In other words, the systems are doctrinal, or, to use the apposite *Wake* term, "dogmad" (158.03), and the *Wake* is understood as not simply in agreement with but a manifest confirmation of the doctrine.

In her 1968 book *Hermes to His Son Thoth*, Frances Boldereff determines the *Wake* to be "perfect Bruno doctrine" (129). She explains,

---

[21] Martha Fodaski Black, review of *The Steadfast "Finnegans Wake": A Textbook*, by Grace Eckley, *James Joyce Quarterly* 32.2 (1995): 444.

[22] Black, review of *The Steadfast "Finnegans Wake": A Textbook*, 446.

> What he [Joyce] is [...] trying to do [in *Finnegans Wake*] is to give a new physical model of the universe—one that will satisfy all the known characteristics, and unlike those presented to us by modern science—one which will project onto the retina of our consciousness an actual impulse of the reality.[23]

It is worth dwelling a moment on that phrasing "trying to do": though this points the way to a whole other argument for another day, these kinds of statements, these particular gestures treat texts as disabled, forever "trying" to do something that by implication they are unable to do. Fortunately there are ably eloquent people willing to do and speak for them: in disability studies this habit is sometimes referred to as "ablesplaining"; by others it is called literary criticism. In extreme cases it assumes the tones of the faith healer who rescues the afflicted object from its troubled (i.e., meaningless) existence.

Boldereff's "actual impulse of the reality" promises just such a transfiguration. Its blend of hermetics and poetics flatters the reader who subscribes to it and leans conspicuously into theocratic reading. The book "is not handed out for casual perusal; it is put in the hand to get one places—it tells how far, how much, what's there": this is the closest we get to a stated thesis, and emphasizes an instrumental quality, nebulous though that is, even as it hints at a rite of initiation.[24] Her book also possesses a fairly common feature among the lunatic readings: gradually longer and longer passages from Joyce's texts with less and less commentary, evidence of a tacit understanding that the crucial connection is by that point so readily discerned so as to need no elaboration, context, or discussion.

Astrological schema and numerological fancies, because they are spotted at play in the *Wake*, sometimes serve as license to make sweeping claims, in the same way that observing the penguins in the Dublin Zoo might allow the assumption that they are not only general all over Ireland but the dominant species. Michael Harding, for example, has plotted trajectories according to something called "Astro*Carto*Geography"—one wonders how to pronounce those asterisks—and finds remarkable determinations of important sites to the subject:

> [Joyce's] Pluto line runs exactly through Zurich, where he died, while Neptune runs straight through Detroit. Detroit? This was the birthplace of Professor Richard Ellmann, who made Joyce his life's work and,

---

[23] Frances M. Boldereff, *Hermes to His Son Thoth: Being Joyce's Use of Giordano Bruno in Finnegans Wake* (Woodward, PA: Classic Non-Fiction Library, 1968), 100.

[24] Boldereff, *Hermes to His Son Thoth*, 21.

until his death in 1987, was the world's foremost authority on the writer. Another exact contact in America is Jupiter running through Buffalo, New York. This is the home of the State University of New York's collection of Joyce papers, making this one of the world centres for Joyce studies.[25]

All very neat. Systems like these have terrific hindsight.

Numbers, too, sing a siren song that lures readers into treacherous waters. Numerology is predicated on a concept of number (or, given its own variety, a range of such concepts) that differs from that upon which mathematics is based, and here again arises the sometimes hazy problem of the degree to which similar concepts may be found at work in Joyce's texts or else are imposed upon them. Making matters that much more complicated is the fact that Joyce *does* sometimes use number schemes for various thematic and symbolic purposes (and not a few of those are inflected with parody or irony)—not all of which are especially clear. The story "Grace" offers a straightforward and uncomplicated example: following Dante's trinities, the story has three parts (an *inferno*, the not entirely accidental fall of Tom Kernan downstairs; a *purgatorio*, a lethargic recovery accompanied by tedious conversation; and a *paradiso*, a retreat, featuring a sermon designed for "men of the world") and each of those three parts includes one use of the word "grace," though each has a different meaning. On the other hand, there are the more convoluted calculations found in *Finnegans Wake*, such as this one: "how the hen is not mirely a tick or two after the first fourth fifth of the second eighth twelfth—siangchang hongkong sansheneul—but yirely the other and thirtieth of the ninth from the twentieth, our own vulgar 432 and 1132 irrespectively" (*FW* 119.23–27).

In considering whether Joyce may "have relied, at least minimally, upon the so-called unofficial knowledge of Numerology and the Hermetic but Christian cabalistic tradition" in arranging the poems of *Chamber Music*, José Maria Tejedor Cabrera admits that this hypothesis "belongs to the realm of sheer speculation—and yet the sedulous reader is always suspicious of Joyce's ways—but it looks like Stanislaus kept it in mind when he came to provide a pattern for the sequence in *Chamber Music*."[26] Prevarications and

---

[25] Michael Harding, "James Joyce," in *Working with Astrology: The Psychology of Harmonics, Midpoints and Astro*Carto*Graphy*, by Michael Harding and Charles Harvey (London: Penguin, 1990), 340–41.

[26] José Maria Tejedor Cabrera, "The Numbers of *Chamber Music*," *Papers on Joyce* 17/18 (2011–12): 125.

qualifications too often serve as prelude to a vigorous leap into that realm of sheer speculation.

Altogether less diffident about numerological exegesis is John Kidd, who in 1981 assembled a prospectus for a book entitled *Ulysses Unveiled: James Joyce's Secret Numerology* (a book presumably never written, certainly never published). The title's echo of *Isis Unveiled*, H. P. Blavatsky's 1877 book, hints at a theosophical bent stirs the imagination—what might this book have been like?—but the prospectus provides a sense of the logic and tone it would probably employ:

> Any text of *Ulysses* will automatically if unknowingly retain the 1111 sections of Circe simply by printing all the words. Bu[t] the page and line must conform to the format of the first edition of Paris so that the first eighteen chapter-sections in Wandering Rocks will have 1111 plus one lines; the nineteenth section was designed to have the 101 plus 1 lines of the first edition. The presence of the extra "1" is clear from the number of sections in Wandering Rocks, 19, that is, 18 plus 1, making, a microcosm of the books [*sic*] total 18 chapters, with one thrown in as an extra factor of unification. This is seen in the Eastern practice of adding 1 to the 4 and 10 to get 5 and 11, numbers of the Tao; in the West the 4 and 10 stand alone as the chief numbers of wholeness. But Joyce's use of the extra one is not only unifying in the Eastern sense, he also uses the notion of the extra as an ominous portent of excess. The nameless extra one appears first in the Hades chapter, where there are 1001 and 1 extra lines; I call the addition or subtraction of the extra one the Mackintosh Factor after a name mistakenly given to this Nameless One in Hades.[27]

Kidd further notes that it is "imperative" that the Gabler edition, then in progress and in time to become the object of his well-publicized scorn, "incorporate these intended structures. Fortunately, my discovery came soon enough for the typesetting to be designed to restore these harmonic forms to the text as designed by Joyce." The urgency behind this statement also serves as warning, and of course that "fortunately" hits a false note, intentional or otherwise, before Kidd's subsequent all-out siege on Gabler's work.

How to reconcile this fascination with numerological patterns with the fact that Kidd's many and various points of textual correction, were they to be implemented, would inevitably disrupt such patterns? For his part, Kidd does not seem to observe any inconsistency between these concerns, and never lost

---

[27] This typed prospectus I found among a cache of Kidd documents in the Zurich James Joyce Foundation in the spring of 2017.

this number-fixation.[28] In a "proof" of the "Editor's Preface" (dated August 21, 1994) to his then-allegedly-forthcoming edition of *Ulysses*[29] (with Lilliput Press):

> Some number-play was reserved for late additions to the proofs when Joyce could tell how many lines of print a passage would consume. After extensive elaborations, Joyce topped off the 33rd and final line of a section of Aeolus: "Three bob I loaned him in Meager's. Three weeks. Third hint" [...] And three threes in the 33rd line.[30]

It is one thing to distinguish and ascertain a pattern (and it is certainly contestable whether Kidd manages that in this instance) and another to identify that pattern's meaning (which here Kidd does not even attempt). Interpretations devoted to their "keys" as a rule disavow the possibility of coincidence, which is all the odder in connection with Joyce, whose works (especially *Ulysses* and the *Wake*) thrive on different forms of coincidence.

The patterns (numerological or otherwise) need not be confined to the text at issue but, *mirabile dictu*, may be readily linked to similar patterns elsewhere. And what greater excitement than to find confirming echoes of one's

---

[28] John Kidd, "Editor's Preface," Proof for Lilliput Press, August 21, 1994 (unpublished). This perseverance is visible in Kidd's review of Danis Rose's "Reader's Edition" of *Ulysses*:

> "Oxen of the Sun," the fourteenth chapter, is now broken into fourteen sections. Whether this is Joyce's numerology or Mr. Rose's, the editor never says. In "Circe" Joyce's personal style of centering the names of each speaker with ample white space above and below is dispensed with, shortening the chapter by forty pages. (Just enough to make room for the second, redundant "Penelope.") Mr. Rose's bold type, moved to the left, leaps off the page in "Circe," contrasting with the excessively diminutive type used for Joyce's once-blaring headings in "Aeolus." Separating Joycean compounds into two or three words breaks up the page and Mr. Rose's new hyphens and swarming capitals give the Reader's Edition a counter-Joycean granularity. (Kidd, "Making the Wrong Joyce," *New York Review of Books* 25 September 1997, 54–56.)

> The called-for distinction between "Joyce's numerology or Mr. Rose's" is exactly the kind of distinction that Kidd does not ask of his own interpretations, and that notion of "granularity" seems to imply that better editing would involve a kind of "smoothing out" of the text.

[29] Norton listed Kidd's *Ulysses* as forthcoming in June in its spring 1992 catalogue. Kidd next moved to publish with Lilliput, which project likewise failed to materialize. Just how far he may have progressed with his editing of the novel remains unknown.

[30] Kidd, "Editor's Preface," 51. This text is likewise available in the Zurich Joyce Foundation.

discovery in another text redolent of comparable or greater complexity, mystery, and cultural esteem? Kidd leaps to scripture:

> Stately, plump Buck Mulligan is introduced in three sentences of 43 words stopped with a colon. Then follow the first four words spoken in *Ulysses*, themselves from the opening of the Mass: "*Introibo ad altare Dei.*" Turning to that fount of English letters, the Protestant King James Bible, which Joyce drew on more often than the Catholic Douay version, we find at Psalms 43:4, "then will I go to the altar of God." Even the first fruits of *Ulysses* are counted and apportioned according to Joyce's private numerology.[31]

Well, why Psalms? There are 321 instances of the word "altar" in the King James Bible, so why should Joyce direct readers—very select readers, to be sure—to this one in particular and not some other? And if the verse number (4) comes from the number of words taken from the Mass, what is the significance of the *three* sentences about Mulligan, or is that three for some reason not as important as the four?

"Joyce's private numerology" is, like "my personal option," a puzzling formula: one struggles to conceive of an impersonal opinion or distinguish a public numerology from the private one. But thanks to the Internet, I now have Joyce's number. A website called *Celebrities Galore* claims that James Joyce has a personality number of 8. Among other things, this means that

> James Joyce appears strong and powerful. He has an impressive personality and can influence and even intimidate through sheer force. He has natural authority. James' competence and enthusiasm attract people with resources [...] Although most eights have a strong constitution, they can be prone to indigestion, ulcers, and heart disease due to their reckless eating and drinking habits and their propensity to be workaholics.[32]

Upon entering my own name, gender, and date of birth to the site's engine for calculating my "compatibility" with Joyce, I was told that we have a "relationship that presents frequent challenges and requires much compromise," which is certainly accurate. More than this, I learned that

---

[31] Kidd, "Editor's Preface," 52–53.
[32] See https://www.celebrities-galore.com/celebrities/james-joyce/personality-number/ (accessed May 16, 2018).

Tim Conley can become a source of frustration and jealousy for James because Tim Conley gives love freely and generously. In order to keep harmony, James needs to understand that this is simply Tim Conley's nature. James is quick with hugs and shows of care and love to other people, but this should not be a reason for James not to trust Tim Conley, or to be jealous.[33]

Note that the applied systems need not themselves be wholly untenable, any more than the algorithms that measured this special relationship are not mathematically solid. That is, "scientific" readings of the *Wake* can get as weird as those reliant upon mysticism. There are claims about Joyce divining the existence of quarks, or of how "he came to regard microbes as a vital key within evolutionary cosmology" (to quote Clara Mason's enigmatic 2015 book on that previously unexamined subject).[34]

III

So far we have three not quite unmistakable marks of the Snarks we are hunting: conviction, urgency, and a key. But of course there are two more, and the proviso—to anticipate my conclusion—not every Snark is a Boojum.

One of the more eccentric participants on Joyce listservs in the 1990s was Peter Nigel Best, who contributed enthusiastic if rambling and often unpunctuated notes to discussions of *Finnegans Wake*. He habitually referred to his own two self-published books on the *Wake*: *Dawn: A Study of the Present Age and* Finnegans Wake *through a Close Look at FW Page 594, One Page Sufficient for Our Time* (1979) and *Again! The Mighty Maze of Human Being and the Freeing of Conscience: James Joyce's Whirling Mandala, or the Great* Finnegans Wake *Game* (1998).[35] His posts gave no room for doubt about his complete devotion to the book, but room enough to question his judgment. *Again!*—perhaps appropriately, with that title—gives the same impression, at greater length.

On first reading the book he abbreviates as "Fw," Best recounts that he felt "as if a door was opening for humankind."[36] This language of revelation,

---

[33] See https://www.celebrities-galore.com/celebrities/james-joyce/tim-conley.919746/compatibility-01C8/ (accessed May 16, 2018).

[34] Clara Mason, *Mister Germ's Choice* (Singapore: James Joyce Press, 2015), 13.

[35] Peter Nigel Best, *Dawn: A Study of the Present Age and* Finnegans Wake *through a Close Look at FW Page 594, One Page Sufficient for Our Time* (New Plymouth, New Zealand: Dawn, 1979), and *Again! The Mighty Maze of Human Being and the Freeing of Conscience: James Joyce's Whirling Mandala, or the Great* Finnegans Wake *Game* (New Shore City, New Zealand: Dawn, 1998).

[36] This and all subsequent quotations from Best come from *Again!* (which is unpaginated).

echoed by claims that the book "is an organising principle for the world" and that Joyce found "the universal principle," demonstrates that Best is another instance of a theocratic reader, someone who "see[s] the text before them as an invasion into the world at large, a new reality that expands or irrevocably alters their own."[37] On details of particular passages of the *Wake*, Best now and again offers some rich and interesting insights and suggestions, yet it is the ready reversion to broad, breathless statements about "the world" and "modern man" and the "unity" and "liberation of consciousness" that Joyce's book brings that illustrates how slippery is the slope from zeal to zealotry. Especially striking (and unsettling) are those moments when Best momentarily calls into question his own balance of mind, usually while offering caveats to potential initiates. For example:

> A warning: the 'toomuchness, the fartoomanyness', Fw122, of the information may get to you. It gets to me, every time, even after thirteen years. It is meant to. It is part of Joyce's diabolically cunning plan to make us suffer the whirlpool of mental death by abundance. Our ego-self comes under attack as our idea of how much can—and how much ought to—go into a passage is confronted with the facts. Concentration, abundance like this has never been seen before [...] Joyce wants to do something to us. He wants us to suffer death by drowning in marriage to the world.

Commentary might seem superfluous, but it is worth observing the strong cast of fear in this, as well as the call for readers to submit to the convoluted but dread "something" that "Joyce wants to do" to "us."

Clearly the density of multiple and contradictory possible meanings in *Finnegans Wake* stretch the limits of "equivalence." The book slyly admits as much: a familiar formula from *Ulysses*, "God becomes man becomes fish becomes barnacle goose becomes featherbed mountain" (3.477–79), becomes in *Finnegans Wake* "Nummers that is summus that is toptip that is bottombay that is Twomeys that is Digges that is Heres" (*FW* 313.25–27). Top is bottom, greatest is least. Best offers a plum example of how sequential equivalences, or what we might call a chain reaction of self-sustaining metonymy, can get out of hand:

> What then is Fw? It is a synthesis of all meaning and a trial of all spirit. It is a mountain, a pyramid. It is every facet of life organised in a grand incontrovertible original pattern. But this is a false truth. For this pattern

---

[37] Conley, *Useless Joyce*, 21.

is the light at the end of the tunnel. More truly it is a dark place, a special environment of mystery, of hell, in which a person may choose—for unlike the world, it is optional—to find themselves lost, so that, being found—by one's self—it is a dazzling experience.

One thing is another thing, and another, and another, and then, unexpectedly: "But this is a false truth." Why? Because the last something is really something else, and "more truly" it is something else again. And so on. Whatever one may think of the various characterizations above ("mountain," "pyramid," "dark place," etc.), it is in the *syntax* that the real trouble lies. Let's replace all of the nouns in the above quotation with either random nouns or simply letters of the alphabet (like variables in a mathematical formula), to see how little they matter compared to the force of the chain reaction:

It is a bubble of all tomatoes and a doorknob of all perplexity. It is a dessert, a radiator. It is every jot of glue organised in a grand incontrovertible original cabbage. But this is a false sound. For this cabbage is the banquet at the top of the skyscraper. More truly it is a dark residue, a special whirligig of bullion, of rainwater, in which a mountaineer may choose—for unlike the spatula, it is optional—to find luggage lost, so that, being found—by one's cousin—it is a dazzling porcupine.

This isn't circular logic, because that would suggest a closed circuit that comes around to where it began, though as we have seen, we can find that kind of thinking behind other, no less embellished and no less deranged readings of Joyce. Rather, it is so entirely open in its trajectory that it traces no recognizable shape at all: connecting dots without the need for an image to thereby come into focus.

Though Best was not, so far as I am aware, an academic or professional scholar, such credentials in no way guarantee against this sort of associative mania. This is no minor point to this discussion: if there is a category of madness to certain interpretations of Joyce, it is not limited to "amateurs"— as bizarrely right *and* wrong a designation as one can imagine—and in fact there may be more tenured members among its ranks than any others. And I might as well add that "theocratic reading" in itself is no absolute indicator of such interpretations, nor does it have any exclusive claim to them. Aristocratic readings, for example, the default mode of scholars, can both indulge theocratic sensibilities and by their own merits fit neatly into a broken ceramics file.

In his strange book *The Language of the Devil: Texture and Archetype in* Finnegans Wake, C. George Sandulescu proposes that in addition to what he calls "the

Heterogeneity Constraint, which takes the dissimilar as similar," and "the so-called [and, I would add, less comprehensible] '*Imponderability*' Constraint," without an understanding of which no one can achieve an "understanding" of the *Wake*, there is a third, "*super-constraint*." This "can be formulated as the Constraint of the *Willing Suspension of Logical Constraints*" and "its nearest approximation" is the line I have just quoted from "Proteus": "God becomes man becomes fish becomes barnacle goose becomes featherbed mountain" (*U* 3.477–79).[38] Although he adds, rather more obscurely, that it "also operate[s] at meta-level in a way that should perhaps be better elucidated elsewhere," Sandulescu appears to offer another term for the phenomenon when he later refers to a "Protean Postulate of semantic fluidity."[39] I wonder whether the "meta-level" of this "*Willing Suspension of Logical Constraints*" isn't precisely the deranging effect that Joyce's texts, at least *Ulysses* and *Finnegans Wake*, is evidently capable of having on some readers. Just as readers of fiction risk such immersion in alternative worlds and, at least in discussing that fiction, lose sight of its place within the larger world, context, or reality—whatever one wants to call it—in which that fiction is produced and lives, so might the unusual, intriguing forms of narrative logic at work in books such as Joyce's threaten to subsume the logics of the wider world.[40]

How far, then, can or should a reader observe this "*super-constraint*" and suspend his or her sense of logic while allowing "semantic fluidity" or open semiosis? "The danger," Beckett pointed out, "is in the neatness of identifications" (3), but unfortunately he offered no subsequent practical points of advice about how to shut off this natural propensity to recognize, recognize, recognize. What legitimates those identifications is the conceived relationship between the world of the text and the world of the reader. If the openness of the *Wake* seems to offer new, expanded horizons for the otherwise confining, unilluminated world of the poor reader, a perceived hermeneutic closedness to *Ulysses* seems to allow the notion that mysteries and points of uncertainty can all be solved with materials provided within the text (the predication of the mystery genre). Hence the colorful variety of theories about the man in the mackintosh, who in different accounts is Joyce himself, Parnell, the devil, the ghost of Hamlet's father, the ghost of Bloom's father, Mr Duffy from "A Painful Case," the Nameless One from "Cyclops" (as John Kidd at least once believed, as we have seen) and so on.

---

[38] C. George Sandulescu, *The Language of the Devil: Texture and Archetype in* Finnegans Wake (Gerrards Cross, UK: Colin Smythe, 1987), 4–5.

[39] Sandulescu, *The Language of the Devil*, 5, 30.

[40] Incidentally, this idea cues the question of whether a book can be judged insane, or only a reader; whether calling a book mad is akin to calling a virus sick.

That this is a game that may be taken too seriously is suggested more than once by the novel itself. In "Nausicaa," Bloom appears to wonder momentarily whether the young woman with whom he has just shared fireworks could perhaps be his erotic correspondent, Martha Clifford: "Then I will tell you all. Still it was a kind of language between us. It couldn't be? No, Gerty they called her. Might be false name however like my name and the address Dolphin's barn a blind" (*U* 13.943–45). Just another projection in a chapter or projections, produced by a sequence of glancing associations—though of course the reader can't with absolute certainty say that Gerty *isn't* Martha, and that limitation may be the trickiest, since it requires readers not to simply assume that Bloom is wrong, and that because Bloom is wrong, their own theories are right.

The shortest answer in "Ithaca" (barring the "point bien visible" at the end) is one of the most ridiculous moments in the whole novel and is another such caveat for readers:

What rendered problematic for Bloom the realisation of these mutually selfexcluding propositions?

The irreparability of the past: once at a performance of Albert Hengler's circus in the Rotunda, Rutland square, Dublin, an intuitive particoloured clown in quest of paternity had penetrated from the ring to a place in the auditorium where Bloom, solitary, was seated and had publicly declared to an exhilarated audience that he (Bloom) was his (the clown's) papa. The imprevidibility of the future: once in the summer of 1898 he (Bloom) had marked a florin (2/-) with three notches on the milled edge and tendered it in payment of an account due to and received by J. and T. Davy, family grocers, 1 Charlemont Mall, Grand Canal, for circulation on the waters of civic finance, for possible, circuitous or direct, return.

Was the clown Bloom's son?

No. (*U* 17.973–86)

For this decisiveness much thanks. Joyce repeatedly depicts an imagination running away with itself and it might be said that a constituent element of Bloom's low-key and humane heroism is his ability, demonstrated above, to bring it to a halt.

My casual description of Sandulescu's book as "strange" deserves further comment. After all, any book devoted to *Finnegans Wake* can be reckoned "strange," as might any book of literary criticism *tout court*: the discussion of events that never actually happened makes for a suspect and often ontologically unsettling occupation. But there's a distinction that needs to be made more explicit in order to test its integrity: I am not suggesting that Sandulescu's book is unhinged in the way that Best's and other "petitions full of pieces of pottery" considered here are, though we might say that it is on the spectrum, as it were. In many respects, appropriately enough, it is a matter of language when it comes to why we find a given critical discussion alien or unsympathetic. A pronouncement like "[i]t all boils down to the fact that genuine Science, Art, and Culture does *not* advance by either consensus or majority vote, but rather by rape,"[41] for example, can shock or puzzle as much by its sentiment as by its terms: so much is exposed by that "rape" and so much concealed in that "genuine." But sentiments that are unshared do not in themselves constitute crackpottery. A little closer to that end of the spectrum is a denial of a widely held view or fairly evident point without clear evidence and without clear purpose. A case in point:

> It is a myth to say that the last sentence of the book [*Finnegans Wake*] runs into the first. It was said once inadvertently and then endlessly repeated by researchers, teachers, and students alike. It might also have been said by an imp of an author, only too prone to mislead. But there is no textual evidence whatever that the last partial whole forms a more complete whole if it is conjoined with the very first subwhole. It is primarily contradicted by narrative data, for how can part of a monologue be simultaneously part of something else which, though most certainly not a monologue, seems not to be part of an omniscient sentence either. As a sample of textual evidence, I do not think that the *us* of (003.02:4) is in any way compatible with the female *I* of (628.01 to 16) repeated 18 times.[42]

Here Sandulescu seems to forget all about his "Constraints" and demands things that anyone reading just a few pages of the *Wake* quickly learns to do without: a consistency of pronouns, a tangible distinction between "monologue" and some other form of expression ("omniscient" or otherwise), and a sense of textual divisibility into "partial wholes" and "subwholes" (which particular subject was discussed in an earlier essay in this volume). Note the last sentence: what is offered as "textual evidence" is simply what the author "thinks." Sandulescu so overwhelms himself with his mapping of semantic principles, maxims, and rules that he loses his own bearings. Again, this is not the farthest shore of the happy huntingground, but very much on the way there.

---

[41] Sandulescu, *The Language of the Devil*, 273.
[42] Sandulescu, *The Language of the Devil*, 210.

That path takes readers away from irony to, ultimately, the attribution of fantastical properties to the *Wake*. In its least feverish form, this approach—an oddly literal take on Ellmann's statement about our still learning to be Joyce's contemporaries (*JJ II* 3)—finds the book foretelling concepts, idioms, and memes with its neologisms such as "quarks," "emailia," and "hogwarts." More alarming is the earnest acceptance of the *Wake*'s tongue-in-cheek posture as "secret stripture" (*FW* 293F2). According to Best, Joyce is "the first prophet who has offered to give the basis for his prophecies. The prophet simply has more data, more perception, more judgement and more digestion than others"; for he found "the universal principle in the world and the language technique appropriate to it and capable of containing it." It might be surprising—if you can be surprised any longer—to hear that Best thinks that

> Joyce was by nature Platonic, and had the very deep wisdom to avoid being himself, as Platonic, and deliberately to embrace Aristotle and Aquinas as an opposite of his inclination, so that he, dying to self, would be resurrected a more universal man.

But we do well to recall Senn's remark that "we might well admit that most of us dabblers at the *Wake* are still haunted by some Platonic ideal to capture its quintessential core—the ideal of the Ultimate Reduction."[43] Thus our ideals can betray us.

Another such "grand incontrovertible original pattern" and "special environment of mystery" is to be found, for example, in Rolf Loehrich's *The Secret of Ulysses: An Analysis of James Joyce's* Ulysses (1955), an early psychoanalytic study of the novel. Perhaps not all that surprisingly, Loehrich's attentions are especially fixed on "Circe":

> *Cissy sings she gave the leg of the duck to Molly.*
>
> The leg is the third leg, part of Bloom's phallic powers representing his emotional, mental, and spiritual powers which are no longer available to him; they were lost to the QUEEN. It now belongs to Molly, hence Bloom's fascination. Bloom in his relation to Molly has acted and acts like a duck, a coward; he is subjected by her, she functions for him as QUEEN—Queen Victoria, Empress of the United Kingdom which represents the *lex eterna*.[44]

---

[43] Senn, *Joyce's Dislocutions*, 99.

[44] Rolf Loehrich, *The Secret of Ulysses: An Analysis of James Joyce's* Ulysses (London: Peter Owen Limited, 1955), 27.

Molly is an archetypal queen, the queen is Queen of the United Kingdom, the United Kingdom is *lex eterna* [...] and one can't help wondering: why stop there? The associations, weaving from concrete particularity to symbolic abstraction and back again, are another example of the chain reaction of self-sustaining metonymy, just like Best's commentary on the *Wake*, and they show that the *Wake* isn't the only text that can trigger it. (On the other hand, one doesn't see much of this sort of response to, say, *Dubliners* or *Exiles*, and while this may seem intuitively obvious, it is a little tricky to say comprehensively *why* this should be so.)

For Loehrich, what is amazing about the novel is its discovery of what he holds as psychological truths. "Did Joyce know about the meaning of dream-occurrences presented by him?" he wonders. "Or, formulated in technical language: Did Joyce know the sign-values of dream-figures in accordance with the system of factual sign-relations [?] [...] The rather baffling answer is that he did."[45] Loehrich uses the example of the kidney and lists its various "correlations" in the novel, before finally affirming that "'to urinate' is equal to 'to kill' or 'to eliminate'. Joyce either intuited these facts, or he knew about them."[46] That last sentence's distinction between intuiting and knowing would give Wittgenstein great pause, and many might beg leave to doubt whether the equation of urination with killing ought to be called a "fact." The "secret" knowledge that Loehrich discerns in *Ulysses* is no less luminous a guiding light than "Joyce's private numerology" is for Kidd. Joyce's "insights," as he calls them, "were years ahead of his time; he presented them in artistic form rather than as a scientific document. If he [Joyce] would have acted as a scientist, he would have presented the new theory of psychosomatics."[47]

While it may be that one delights in a book (or any work of art) because it affirms or substantiates one's own prior beliefs or what one holds as "truth"—though this seems to me far from axiomatic—at least there are different kinds or degrees of truth-claims that a reader can plausibly make. When Loehrich praises Joyce as a scientist discerning "facts," he is claiming a certain sort of truth-value for *Ulysses* that many if not most readers would find untenable. When Senn identifies "the paradogmatic nature" of *Finnegans Wake* as its "method to express incontrovertible truth—to enact the process of controversion itself,"[48] even so canny a reader as he may be too idealistic, for the readings of Best, Kidd, Loehrich, and others who find prophecy, secret

---

[45] Loehrich. *The Secret of Ulysses*, 162.
[46] Loehrich, *The Secret of Ulysses*, 164.
[47] Loehrich, *The Secret of Ulysses*, 165.
[48] Senn, *Joyce's Dislocutions*, 112, 116.

knowledge, and vaunted truth in Joyce's texts suggest that for every controvert there may be a true believer.

IV

For sheer industry it is hard to beat the work of John P. Anderson (arguably the most unrabbinical name imaginable). His multivolume work, *Joyce's* Finnegans Wake*: The Curse of Kabbalah* (2008–14), finds in Joyce's book a highly coded admonition to reject a false god, which he calls "the TZTZ [*Tzimtzum*: Hebrew for "constriction"] god," and recognize a true one that is in some sense within our individual selves. But industry certainly isn't the fifth mark I've promised, however indefatigable some of these bizarre readings can seem.

Only "a select few" readers will care for the "spiritual balance and harmony" of the *Wake*, says Anderson; "I believe that the more of an independent individual you are, the greater is the chance that you will cherish this work."[49] In agreement with Best, Anderson singles Joyce out as a visionary, "the only author to have seen face to face the full human condition."[50] The very first words of the book are "I am not an academic," which Anderson then explains means that he does not "scour all of the literature to see if someone else has already said the same thing I am saying."[51] While this does not apparently mean that he will not refer to other works on the *Wake* or Kabbalism (because he sometimes does), it does signal that he feels no need to do so. This might seem, depending on one's point of view, somewhat naive or arrogant, but it turns out to be the opening notes of a swelling theme. Why a Kabbalistic reading of the book? Anderson explains:

> Kabbalah is a Jewish gnostic and mystical tradition that presents a strange but compelling view of the human experience. So compelling that even someone like Madonna has been reported seeking meaning through Kabbalah. Kabbalah also worked for Joyce to create meaning. It worked for both of them, different though they may [!] be.
>
> Madonna's T shirt said, "Kabbalists do it better." Joyce's T shirt would have read, "Kabbalists do it independently."[52]

---

[49] John P. Anderson, *Joyce's* Finnegans Wake*: The Curse of Kabbalah*, vol. 1 (Boca Raton, FL: Universal, 2008), 13.

[50] Anderson, *Joyce's* Finnegans Wake*: The Curse of Kabbalah*, vol. 1, 138.

[51] Anderson, *Joyce's* Finnegans Wake*: The Curse of Kabbalah*, vol. 1, 11.

[52] Anderson, *Joyce's* Finnegans Wake*: The Curse of Kabbalah*, vol. 1, 14–15.

One might suppose that everything depends on what "it" refers to, but in fact "it" really is beside the point, and that point is "independently." He emphasizes how "subjective" and thus "alone" the *Wake* reader is:

> This personal, individual and subjective creation of the reader requires active participation. There is no manna for the lazy reader with a dependent "feed it to me" attitude. The children of television will not make it. With Finnegans Wake, you have to feed yourself. You have to feed independently.[53]

I lack the time to show how he unpacks specific passages, but the idiosyncrasy of the approach is illustrated, I think, by his commentary on the passage from Edgar Quinet reproduced on page 281 of the *Wake* (often misreported to be a verbatim quotation) and elsewhere in the book. "The point of all this," Anderson sums up, "is that flowers don't fight with each other even though they are competing for reproduction."[54] There is a strong whiff of the Ayn Rand school of thinking here, but also something very sad, a loneliness that, as *Finnegans Wake* reading groups all over the world attest, need not go unshared. Anderson's framing of both his venture and the reading of the *Wake* as the individual's struggle as a revelation that would benefit all, even those ungrateful children of television, weaves together themes of messianism, romantic isolation, egotism, and even persecution. It is this quest of the loner, this self-identification as the maverick or voice in the wilderness, that is the fifth common trait of crazed readings. Eckley's invocation of a "person desiring to serve but maligned and misunderstood"[55] all too likely points not only to William T. Stead or HCE, but also to the author herself.

Here are the final two paragraphs of *The Encryption of* Finnegans Wake *Resolved*:

> The defense rests.
>
> It has been a privilege to work with this master.[56]

This mic drop leaves open the question: which master, Joyce or Stead? It is hard to say which one Eckley admires more, though in some respects, these fuse into the same being. And defense of whom or what, on what charge? Such aggressively defensive and sometimes passive aggressive posture is an

---

[53] Anderson, *Joyce's* Finnegans Wake*: The Curse of Kabbalah*, vol. 1, 66.
[54] Anderson, *Joyce's* Finnegans Wake*: The Curse of Kabbalah*, vol. 1, 140.
[55] Eckley, *The Encryption of* Finnegans Wake *Resolved*, 60.
[56] Eckley, *The Encryption of* Finnegans Wake *Resolved*, 377.

all too typical tic of academic writing, which often feels compelled to declare the lands in its purview untilled if not virtually undiscovered, but by degree it can also be symptomatic of the raving crank, though again that degree of difference can prove difficult to calculate exactly. The very last sentence of Anderson's 10-volume epic exegesis defies characterization and response alike. After more than four thousand pages, Anderson writes, "Thank you for your attention."[57] However earnest the gratitude might be, the gesture is primarily a cue for applause, or a bid for redemption.

Perhaps the greatest send-up of deranged readings of Joyce is Robert Anton Wilson's 1987 essay, "Coincidance," which weaves connections between, among other things, numerology, Osiris, the Phoenix Park murders, Alice Liddell, the *I Ching*, quantum physics, Beethoven, killer rabbits, Swift, DNA, heraldry, the bombing of Nagasaki, international banking, Orson Welles, the CIA, and, it might go without saying, Freemasonry. The really striking thing about that list of disparate subjects is that the distinction between those might seem readily or plausibly related to Joyce's work and those that seem, let us say, far-fetched proves difficult to articulate succinctly. Replete with diagrams, charts, and illustrations, Wilson captures the mannerisms and growing sense of urgency typical of that slide from critical analysis into manifesto: "The serious scholar will investigate, in this connection ..."[58]

Yet what starts out as a pseudo-scholarly joke can, given enough runway, take full flight into mania, as Umberto Eco dramatizes in his novel *Foucault's Pendulum*. The Internet is flush with examples. Take the July 20, 2014, entry from the blog *Groupname for Grapejuice*, entitled "A Blooming Buzzing Infusion." After beginning with some numerological finger exercises, the author declares, "Both *Ulysses* and *Finnegans Wake* are bottomless kabbalistic enigmas."[59] It is one thing to advance this as an open question (e.g., what is a bad interpretation of the *Wake*, how would we recognize one?), and another to embrace it as an endorsement, a sort of imprimatur for one's own arcane exegesis. This blogger, known as znore, acknowledges that "crackpot bloggers like myself are in no way subject to" scholarly rigor or restraint, and so is off to the races. The Hermetic Society, solstices, Bavarian Illuminati, Rosicrucians, fascism—it's all grist for this busy mill. Even Eco's novel is consulted as a source and praised as "incredible" (*le mot trop juste*) though znore notes in passing that "it takes a skeptical tone towards the existence a such occult plots." The blogger reminds

---

[57] John P. Anderson, *Joyce's* Finnegans Wake: *The Curse of Kabbalah*, vol. 10 (Boca Raton, FL: Universal, 2014), 303.

[58] Robert Anton Wilson, "Coincidance," *Semiotext(e)* 13 (1987): 166.

[59] See http://groupnameforgrapejuice.blogspot.com/2014/07/a-blooming-buzzing-infusion.html (accessed June 4, 2018).

us of the curious fact that Aleister Crowley wrote an enthusiastic review of *Ulysses* in 1923, and wonders

> Was he reading it in *The Little Review* during the months of the Amalantrah Working? A tantalizing thought. And did *Ulysses* have anything to do with the working's completion on June 16th? Or was this date chosen for its earlier significance? Or is this all coincidence?

These are not questions whose answers matter, for the blogger simply hurries onward:

> But the Amalantrah Working was not just any magical working. It was not even just any Crowley working. From 1918 on this series of rituals and visualisations has taken on more and more significance. This is all the result of the manifestation of an entity who is not even directly mentioned in Liber XCVII. This intelligence is called "Lam," and it is still an open debate as to whether Lam is the Wizard Amalantrah or not. Lam only became famous through a sketch by Crowley published in 1919. As is now well known, the figure of the sketch bears an uncanny resemblance to the archetypal Gray Alien.

This, quite naturally, raises the question of whether Bloom is the alien "Lam," and, just as naturally, the question is left to linger. I confess that I am haunted by it still.

And it is right to be haunted by rather than simply disregard such strange, highly schematized, outlier interpretations. Jonathan P. Eburne, writing of "outsider theory" and unorthodox or heretical contributions to scientific and cultural debates, cautions that

> unless contemporary thinkers recognize such efforts as part of our intellectual "heritage," we end up inventing arbitrary starting points for the systems of knowledge we claim to study and adapt as our own. Unless we take into consideration the evolution of any set of "starting points," that is, we render knowledge homogeneous and thus ultimately tautological.[60]

Such a tautological inclination would in effect trouble any distinction between readings that seem plausible and those that, however "gethobbyhorsical"

---

[60] Jonathan P. Eburne, *Outsider Theory: Intellectual Histories of Unorthodox Ideas* (Minneapolis: University of Minnesota Press, 2018), 17.

(*FW* 434.08) they are, are unshakable, impervious to criticism. Thus it might be said that the minimal (maybe even the only) distinction between what William James, contemplating the allure of mysticism, calls "irrational doorways,"[61] and "portals of discovery" is the acknowledgment that one might always be mistaken—though no point of entry ought to be dismissed out of hand.

Arnold Bennett, reviewing *Our Exagmination* in the *Evening Standard* in August 1929, declared that "Work in Progress" "will not be read, because it cannot be read by any individual normally constituted." By this same logic he diagnoses Joyce as abnormal and the *Exagmination* authors "a dozen other bizarre human beings."[62] At the very least it can be said that Bennett grossly underestimated the variation of readerly constitutions, and in this he too, with all of the others I have cited here, provides an object lesson for all of us bizarre human beings gathered here. Let us not dismiss or ignore those readings that strike us as aberrant or perverse, or for that matter handily assume that our readings are (more) normally constituted. The ongoing histories of reading *Ulysses* and *Finnegans Wake* has and will have chapters more startling and more byzantine than Joyce's texts themselves, but if the meaning of a book is its social history, these pieces of pottery are a significant part of the uncertain work in progress.

---

[61] James, *The Varieties of Religious Experience*, 417.
[62] Arnold Bennett, "Books and Persons: The Oddest Novel Ever Written," *Evening Standard* (August 8, 1929), 7.

BIBLIOGRAPHY

Abrams, M. H., and Geoffrey Galt Harpham. *A Glossary of Literary Terms*. 9th ed. Boston: Wadsworth Cengage Learning, 2009.
Adorno, Theodor W. *Negative Dialectics*. Trans. E. B. Ashton. New York: Continuum Books, 1973.
———. *Notes to Literature*. Vol. 1. Trans. Shierry Weber Nicholsen. New York: Columbia University Press, 1991.
Airplane! Dir. Jim Abrahams, David Zucker, and Jerry Zucker. Los Angeles, CA: Paramount Pictures, 1980.
Amis, Kingsley. *Lucky Jim*. Hammodsworth: Penguin, 1968.
Anderson, John P. *Joyce's* Finnegans Wake*: The Curse of Kabbalah*. 10 vols. Boca Raton, FL: Universal, 2008–14.
Andreasen, N. J. C. "James Joyce: A Portrait of the Artist as a Schizoid." *Journal of the American Medical Association* 224 (1973): 67–71.
Anyfanti, Alexandra. "Time, Space, and Consciousness in Joyce's *Ulysses*." *Hypermedia Joyce Studies* 4.2 (2003–4), online.
Aquinas, Thomas. *Summa Theologicæ*. Trans. Thomas Gilby. London: Eyre and Spottiswoode, 1964.
Ayto, John. *Dictionary of Word Origins*. New York: Arcade, 1990.
Barthes, Roland. *How to Live Together: Novelistic Simulations of Some Everyday Spaces*. Trans. Kate Briggs. New York: Columbia University Press, 2013.
———. *Le plaisir du texte*. Paris: Éditions du Seuil, 1973.
Beach, Sylvia. *Shakespeare and Company: The Story of an American Bookshop in Paris*. New York: Harcourt, Brace and World, 1965.
Beckett, Samuel. "Dante … Bruno. Vico. Joyce." In *Our Exagmination Round His Factification for the Incamination of Work in Progress*. New York: New Directions, 1972. 1–22.
Belluc, Sylvain, and Valérie Bénéjam, eds. *Cognitive Joyce*. Cham, Switzerland: Palgrave, 2018.
Bennett, Arnold. "Books and Persons: The Oddest Novel Ever Written." *Evening Standard*, August 8, 1929. 7.
Bergvall, Caroline. *Goan Atom*. San Francisco: Krupskaya, 2001.
Best, Peter Nigel. *Again! The Mighty Maze of Human Being and the Freeing of Conscience: James Joyce's Whirling Mandala, or the Great* Finnegans Wake *Game*. New Shore City, New Zealand: Dawn, 1998. Online, viewed via waybackmachine. Accessed May 30, 2018.
Best, Peter Nigel. *Dawn: A Study of the Present Age and* Finnegans Wake *through a Close Look at FW Page 594, One Page Sufficient for Our Time*. New Plymouth, New Zealand: Dawn, 1979.
Bishop, John. *Joyce's Book of the Dark: "Finnegans Wake."* Madison: University of Wisconsin Press, 1986.

Black, Martha Fodaski. Review of *The Steadfast "Finnegans Wake": A Textbook*, by Grace Eckley. *James Joyce Quarterly* 32.2 (1995): 441–46.

———. *Shaw and Joyce: "The Last Word in Stolentelling."* Gainesville: University Press of Florida, 1995.

Blanchot, Maurice. *The Space of Literature*. Trans. Ann Smock. Lincoln: University of Nebraska Press, 1989.

Böhme, Gernot. *Atmosphäre: Essays zur neuen Ästhetik*. Frankfurt am Main: Suhrkamp, 1995.

Boldereff, Frances M. *Hermes to His Son Thoth: Being Joyce's Use of Giordano Bruno in* Finnegans Wake. Woodward, PA: Classic Non-Fiction Library, 1968.

Borat!: Cultural Learnings of America for Make Benefit Glorious Nation of Kazakhstan. Dir. Larry Charles. Los Angeles, CA: 20th Century Studios, 2006.

Borges, Jorge Luis. "The First Wells." In *Other Inquisitions, 1937–1952*. Trans. Ruth L. C. Simms. Austin: University of Texas Press, 2000. 86–88.

———. "John Wilkins' Analytical Language." In *Selected Non-Fictions*. Trans. Eliot Weinberger. New York: Viking, 1999. 229–32.

Boyd, Brian. *On the Origin of Stories*. Cambridge: Harvard University Press, 2009.

Bradstreet, Anne. "In Reference to Her Children, 23 June, 1659." In *The Works of Anne Bradstreet*. Ed. Jeannine Hensley. Cambridge, MA: Harvard University Press, 1967. 232–34.

———. "A Letter to Her Husband, Absent upon Public Employment." In *The Works of Anne Bradstreet*. Ed. Jeannine Hensley. Cambridge, MA: Harvard University Press, 1967. 226.

Broch, Hermann. "Hugo von Hoffmansthal and His Time: Art and Its Non-Style at the End of the Twentieth Century." In *Geist und Zeitgeist: The Spirit in an Unspiritual Age*. Trans. Michael P. Steinberg, ed. John Hargreaves. New York: Counterpoint, 2002. 141–210.

———. "Joyce and the Present Age." In *Geist und Zeitgeist: The Spirit in an Unspiritual Age*. Trans. Maria Jolas, ed. John Hargreaves. New York: Counterpoint, 2002. 65–95.

Bürger, Peter. *Theory of the Avant-Garde*. Trans. Michael Shaw. Minneapolis: University of Minnesota Press, 1984.

Burgess, Anthony. *Little Wilson and Big God*. New York: Grove Weidenfeld, 1987.

Burrell, Harry. *Narrative Design in* Finnegans Wake*: The Wake Lock Picked*. Gainesville: University Press of Florida, 1996.

Cabrera, José Maria Tejedor. "The Numbers of *Chamber Music*." *Papers on Joyce* 17/18 (2011–12): 117–44.

Cadbury, Bill. "'The March of a Maker': Chapters I.2–4." In *How Joyce Wrote* Finnegans Wake: *A Chapter-by-chapter Genetic Guide*. Ed. Luca Crispi and Sam Slote. Madison: University of Wisconsin Press, 2007. 66–97.

Calvino, Italo. *Mr. Palomar*. Trans. William Weaver. New York: Harcourt Brace, 1985.

Campbell, Joseph, and Henry Morton Robinson. *A Skeleton Key to* Finnegans Wake. New York: Viking, 1961.

Certeau, Michel de. *The Writing of History*. Trans. Tom Conley. New York: Columbia University Press, 1988.

Cervantes, Miguel de. *Don Quixote*. Ed. E. C. Riley. Trans. Charles Jarvis. Oxford: Oxford University Press, 1998.

Cheng, Vincent. "'Goddinpotty': James Joyce and the Language of Excrement." In *The Languages of Joyce: Selected Papers from the 11th International James Joyce Symposium, Venice, 12–18 June 1988*. Ed. R. M. Bollettieri Bosinelli, C. Marengo Vaglio, and Chr. Van Boheemen. Philadelphia, PA: John Benjamins, 1992. 85–99.

Coleridge, Samuel Taylor. *The Collected Works of Samuel Taylor Coleridge.* Ed. James Engell and W. Jackson Bate. Princeton, NJ: Princeton University Press, 1983.

Collins, Joseph. *The Doctor Looks at Literature: Psychological Studies of Life and Letters.* New York: George H. Doran, 1923.

Conley, Tim. "'Are You to Have All the Pleasure Quizzing on Me?' *Finnegans Wake* and Literary Cognition." *James Joyce Quarterly* 40.4 (2003): 711–27.

———. "Auguries: The Stuff of Modernism," *Hyperion* 8.2 (2014): 71–81.

———, ed. *Joyce's Disciples Disciplined: A Re-Exagmination of the 'Exagmination' of 'Work in Progress.'* Dublin: University College Dublin Press, 2010.

———. *Joyces Mistakes: Problems of Intention, Irony, and Interpretation.* Toronto: University of Toronto Press, 2003.

———. "'Oh Me None Onsens!': *Finnegans Wake* and the Negation of Meaning." *James Joyce Quarterly* 39 (2002): 233–49.

———. *Useless Joyce: Textual Functions, Cultural Appropriations.* Toronto: University of Toronto Press, 2017.

Conn, Andrew Lewis. *P.* Brooklyn: Soft Skull Press, 2003.

Connolly, Marshall. "What is 'Coprophilia' and Why Is Pope Francis Talking about It?." *Catholic Online,* December 7, 2016.

"Consanguinity (in Canon Law)." *Catholic Encyclopedia.* http://www.newadvent.org/cathen/04264a.htm. Accessed 15 June 2017.

Corballis, Michael C. *The Recursive Mind: The Origins of Human Language, Thought, and Civilization.* Princeton, NJ: Princeton University Press, 2011.

Crispi, Luca, and Sam Slote, eds. *How James Joyce Wrote* Finnegans Wake: *A Chapter-by-Chapter Genetic Guide.* Madison: University of Wisconsin Press, 2007.

Danto, Arthur C. *The Philosophical Disenfranchisement of Art.* New York: Columbia University Press, 1986.

Deane, Vincent, Daniel Ferrer, and Geert Lernout, eds. *The* Finnegans Wake *Notebooks at Buffalo.* Turnhout, Belgium: Brepols, 2001–4.

Dennett, Daniel C. *Consciousness Explained.* Boston, MA: Little, Brown, 1991.

———. *Sweet Dreams: Philosophical Obstacles to a Science of Consciousness.* Cambridge: MIT Press, 2006.

Deppman, Jed. "Joyce and the Case for Genetic Criticism." *Genetic Joyce Studies* 6 (2006).

Deppman, Jed, Daniel Ferrer, and Michael Groden, eds. *Genetic Criticism: Texts and Avant-Textes.* Philadelphia: University of Pennsylvania Press, 2004.

Derrida, Jacques. *Of Grammatology.* Trans. Gayatri Chakravorty Spivak. Baltimore, MD: Johns Hopkins University Press, 1967.

Deyab, Mohammed. "An Ecocritical Reading of Jonathan Swift's *Gulliver's Travels,*" *Nature and Culture* 6.3 (2011): 285–304.

Dufrenne, Mikel. *The Phenomenology of Aesthetic Experience.* Trans. Edward S. Casey et al. Evanston, IL: Northwestern University Press, 1973.

Eburne, Jonathan P. *Outsider Theory: Intellectual Histories of Unorthodox Ideas.* Minneapolis: University of Minnesota Press, 2018.

Eckley, Grace. *Children's Lore in* Finnegans Wake. Syracuse, NY: Syracuse University Press, 1985.

———. *The Encryption of* Finnegans Wake *Resolved.* Lanham, MD: Hamilton Books, 2018.

———. *The Steadfast* Finnegans Wake: *A Textbook.* Lanham, MD: University Press of America, 1994.

Eco, Umberto. *The Open Work.* Trans. Anna Cancogni. Cambridge, MA: Harvard University Press, 1989.
Eide, Marian. *Ethical Joyce.* Cambridge: Cambridge University Press, 2002.
Eliot, T. S. "*Ulysses,* Order, and Myth." In *Selected Prose.* Ed. Frank Kermode. London: Faber and Faber, 1975. 175–79.
Ellmann, Richard. *The Consciousness of Joyce.* New York: Oxford University Press, 1977.
———. *James Joyce.* Rev. ed. Oxford: Oxford University Press, 1983.
Empson, William. *Seven Types of Ambiguity.* New York: New Directions, 1966.
Fauconnier, Gilles, and Mark Turner. *The Way We Think: Conceptual Blending and the Mind's Hidden Complexities.* New York: Basic Books, 2003.
Fitch, Noel Riley. *Sylvia Beach and the Lost Generation: A History of Literary Paris in the Twenties and Thirties.* New York: Norton, 1983.
Flynn, Catherine. "'Circe' and Surrealism: Joyce and the Avant-Garde." *Journal of Modern Literature* 34.2 (2011): 121–38.
Fordham, Finn. *I Do I Undo I Redo: The Textual Genesis of Modernist Selves.* Oxford: Oxford University Press, 2010.
———. *Lots of Fun at Finnegans Wake: Unravelling Universals.* Oxford: Oxford University Press, 2007.
Foucault, Michel. *The Order of Things: An Archaeology of the Human Sciences.* London: Routledge, 2002.
Freud, Sigmund. *The Interpretation of Dreams. The Standard Edition of the Complete Psychological Works of Sigmund Freud,* vol. 4. Ed. James Strachey et al. London: Hogarth Press, 1900.
Glasheen, Adaline. *Third Census of* Finnegans Wake. Berkeley: University of California Press, 1977.
Goldsmith, Kenneth. *Fidget.* Toronto: Coach House Books, 2000.
Goodman, Paul. "Format and Communication." *The Paul Goodman Reader.* Ed. Taylor Stoehr. Oakland: PM Press, 2011. 183–98.
Gordon, John. *"Finnegans Wake": A Plot Summary.* Dublin: Gill and Macmillan, 1986.
Hanaway-Oakley, Cleo. *James Joyce and the Phenomenology of Film.* Oxford: Oxford University Press, 2017.
Harding, Michael. "James Joyce." *Working with Astrology: The Psychology of Harmonics, Midpoints and Astro*Carto*Graphy.* By Michael Harding and Charles Harvey. London: Penguin, 1990. 335–64.
Hart, Clive. "James Joyce's Sentimentality." *James Joyce Quarterly* 41.1 (2003–4): 25–36.
———. *Structure and Motif in "Finnegans Wake."* Evanston, IL: Northwestern University Press, 1962.
Hayman, David. *A First-Draft Version of* Finnegans Wake. London: Faber and Faber, 1963.
———. "Some Writers in the Wake of the *Wake.*" In *In the Wake of the* Wake. Ed. David Hayman and Elliott Anderson. Madison: University of Wisconsin Press, 1978. 3–38.
———. Ulysses*: The Mechanics of Meaning.* Rev. ed. Madison: University of Wisconsin Press, 1982.
Herman, David. "Cognition, Emotion, and Consciousness." In *The Cambridge Companion to Narrative.* Cambridge: Cambridge University Press, 2007. 245–59.
Herr, Cheryl Temple. "Joyce and the Everynight." In *Eco-Joyce: The Environmental Imagination of James Joyce.* Ed. Robert Brazeau and Derek Gladwin. Cork, Ireland: Cork University Press, 2014. 38–58.
Hobsbawm, Eric. "Socialism and the Avant-Garde, 1880–1914." *Uncommon People: Resistance, Rebellion and Jazz.* London: Abacus, 1999.

"Irish Leaders Greet Convention in Chicago." *New York Times*, April 19, 1921. http://query.nytimes.com/gst/abstract.html?res=9907E1DD113FEE3ABC4152DFB266838A639EDE&legacy=true.
Jackson, John Wyse, and Peter Costello. *John Stanislaus Joyce: The Voluminous Life and Genius of James Joyce's Father*. New York: St. Martin's Press, 1997.
James, William. *The Varieties of Religious Experience: A Study in Human Nature*. New York: Modern Library, 2002.
Jameson, Fredric. *Jameson on Jameson: Conversations on Cultural Marxism*. Ed. Ian Buchanan. Durham, NC: Duke University Press, 2007.
Jarnot, Lisa. *Ring of Fire*. Cambridge: Salt, 2003.
Jaynes, Julian. *The Origin of Consciousness in the Breakdown of the Bicameral Mind*. Boston, MA: Houghton Mifflin, 1976.
Joyce, James. *Dubliners*. London: Penguin, 1992.
———. *Exiles*. London: Jonathan Cape, 1952.
———. *Finnegans Wake*. New York: Penguin, 1976.
———. *Letters I*. Ed. Stuart Gilbert. New York: Viking, 1957.
———. *Letters II*. Ed. Richard Ellmann. New York: Viking, 1966.
———. *Letters III*. Ed. Richard Ellmann. New York: Viking, 1966.
———. *Occasional, Critical, and Political Writing*. Ed. Kevin Barry. Oxford: Oxford University Press, 2000.
———. *A Portrait of the Artist as a Young Man*. Oxford: Oxford University Press, 2000.
———. *Selected Letters of James Joyce*. Ed. Richard Ellmann. New York: Viking, 1975.
———. *Ulysses*. Ed. Hans Walter Gabler. New York: Penguin, 1986.
Kenner, Hugh. *Joyce's Voices*. Berkeley: University Press of California, 1978.
Kiberd, Declan. Ulysses *and Us: The Art of Everyday Life in Joyce's Masterpiece*. New York: Norton, 2009.
Kidd, John. "Making the Wrong Joyce." *New York Review of Books*, September 25, 1997. 54–56.
———. "Editor's Preface." Proof for Lilliput Press. August 21, 1994. Unpublished. In the Zurich James Joyce Foundation.
———. "Prospectus: *Ulysses* Unveiled: James Joyce's Secret Numerology." January 1, 1981. Unpublished. In the Zurich James Joyce Foundation.
Knowlton, Eloise. *Joyce, Joyceans, and the Rhetoric of Citation*. Gainesville: University Press of Florida, 1998.
Kostelanetz, Richard. *More Master Minds*. Ridgewood, NY: Archae Editions, 2018.
Lacivita, Alison. *The Ecology of* Finnegans Wake. Gainesville: University Press of Florida, 2015.
Laporte, Dominique. *History of Shit*. Trans. Nadia Benabid and Rodolphe el-Khoury. Cambridge: MIT Press, 2000.
Laqueur, Thomas W. *The Work of the Dead: A Cultural History of Mortal Remains*. Princeton, NJ: Princeton University Press, 2015.
Leader, Zachary. *Revision and Romantic Authorship*. Oxford: Clarendon, 1996.
Lehrer, Jonah. *Proust Was a Neuroscientist*. Boston, MA: Houghton Mifflin, 2007.
Llona, Victor. "I Dont Know What to Call It but Its Mighty Unlike Prose." In *Our Exagmination Round His Factification for Incamination of Work in Progress*. New York: New Directions, 1972. 93–102.
Loehrich, Rolf. *The Secret of Ulysses: An Analysis of James Joyce's* Ulysses. London: Peter Owen, 1955.

Marinetti, F. T. "Destruction of Syntax—Wireless Imagination—Words-in-Freedom." In *Modernism: An Anthology*. Trans. Lawrence Rainey, ed. Lawrence Rainey. Malden, MA: Blackwell, 2005. 27–34.

Mason, Clara. *Mister Germ's Choice*. Singapore: James Joyce Press, 2015.

Mazur, Joseph. *Enlightening Symbols: A Short History of Mathematical Notation and Its Hidden Powers*. Princeton, NJ: Princeton University Press, 2014.

McGann, Jerome. *A New Republic of Letters: Memory and Scholarship in the Age of Digital Reproduction*. Cambridge, MA: Harvard University Press, 2014.

McGee, Patrick. *Paperspace: Style as Ideology in Joyce's* Ulysses. Lincoln: University of Nebraska Press, 1988.

McGilchrist, Iain. *The Master and His Emissary: The Divided Brain and the Making of the Western World*. New Haven, CT: Yale University Press, 2009.

McHugh, Roland. *Annotations to "Finnegans Wake."* 4th ed. Baltimore, MD: Johns Hopkins University Press, 2016.

———. *The* Finnegans Wake *Experience*. Berkeley: University of California Press, 1981.

———. "Recipis for the Price of the Coffin." *A Conceptual Guide to* Finnegans Wake. Ed. Michael H. Begnal and Fritz Senn. University Park: Pennsylvania State University Press, 1974. 18–32.

Mendelsohn, Daniel. *An Odyssey: A Father, a Son, and an Epic*. New York: Vintage, 2017.

Metzinger, Thomas. *The Ego Tunnel: The Science of the Mind and the Myth of the Self*. New York: Basic Books, 2009.

Miller, William Ian. *The Anatomy of Disgust*. Cambridge, MA: Harvard University Press, 1997.

Moholy-Nagy, László. "The Contribution of the Arts to Social Reconstruction." In *Moholy-Nagy*. Ed. Richard Kostelanetz. New York: Praeger, 1970. 19–21.

———. "Literature." In *The Avant-Garde Tradition in Literature*. Ed. Richard Kostelanetz. Buffalo, NY: Prometheus Books, 1982. 78–141.

Montaigne, Michel de. "That to Philosophize Is to Learn to Die." In *The Complete Works*. Trans. Donald M. Frame. New York: Knopf, 2003. 67–82.

Monty Python's Flying Circus: Just the Words. 2 vols. London: Methuen Press, 1989.

Morton, Timothy. *Ecology without Nature: Rethinking Environmental Aesthetics*. Cambridge, MA: Harvard University Press, 2007.

Nolan, Emer. *James Joyce and Nationalism*. London: Routledge, 1995.

Norris, Margot. *The Decentered Universe of "Finnegans Wake": A Structuralist Analysis*. Baltimore, MD: Johns Hopkins University Press, 1974.

———. "Possible Worlds Theory and the Fantasy Universe of *Finnegans Wake*." *James Joyce Quarterly* 44.3 (2007): 455–74.

O'Brien, Eugene. "'Can Excrement Be Art ... if Not, Why Not?': Joyce's Aesthetic Theory and the Flux of Consciousness." In *Eco-Joyce: The Environmental Imagination of James Joyce*. Ed. Robert Brazeau and Derek Gladwin. Cork, Ireland: Cork University Press, 2014. 197–212.

Ordine, Nuccio. *The Usefulness of the Useless*. Trans. Alastair McEwen. Philadelphia, PA: Paul Dry Books, 2017.

O'Sullivan, James. "*Finn's Hotel* and the Joyce Canon." *Genetic Joyce Studies* 14 (Spring 2014), online.

Partnoy, Frank. *The Match King: Ivar Kreuger and the Financial Scandal of the Century*. London: Profile Books, 2009.

Perloff, Marjorie. "Avant-Garde Community and the Individual Talent: The Case of Language Poetry." 2004. http://marjorieperloff.com/stein-duchamp-picasso/avant-garde-community-and-the-individual-talent/. Accessed September 13, 2015.

———. "Avant-Garde Eliot." In *21st-Century Modernism: The "New" Poetics*. Malden, MA: Blackwell, 2002. 7–43.

———. "Becoming a Critic: A Memoir." *Poetics in a New Key: Interviews and Essays*. Ed. Jonathan Y. Bayot. Chicago: University of Chicago Press, 2013.

———. *The Dance of the Intellect: Studies in the Poetry of the Pound Tradition*. Evanston, IL: Northwestern University Press, 1985.

———. "Poetry as Word-System: The Art of Gertrude Stein." In *The Poetics of Indeterminacy: Rimbaud to Cage*. Evanston, IL: Northwestern University Press, 1981. 67–108.

Place, Vanessa. *La Medusa*. Tuscaloosa: University of Alabama Press, 2008.

Rabelais, François. *Gargantua and Pantagruel*. Trans. J. M. Cohen. London: Penguin, 1955.

Raw, Louise. *Striking a Light: The Bryant and May Matchwomen and Their Place in History*. London: Continuum, 2009.

Rawls, John. *A Theory of Justice*. Cambridge, MA: Harvard University Press, 1971.

Read, Forrest, ed. *Pound/Joyce: The Letters of Ezra Pound to James Joyce*. New York: New Directions, 1967.

Rose, Danis. *The Textual Diaries of James Joyce*. Dublin: Lilliput Press, 1995.

Rothenberg, Jerome. *Poetics and Polemics, 1980–2005*. Tuscaloosa: University of Alabama Press, 2008.

Ruiz, Pablo M. *Four Cold Chapters on the Possibility of Literature: Leading Mostly to Borges and Oulipo*. Champaign, IL: Dalkey Archive, 2014.

Sandulescu, C. George. *The Language of the Devil: Texture and Archetype in* Finnegans Wake. Gerrards Cross, UK: Colin Smythe, 1987.

Scholes, Robert. "Introduction to James Joyce's Sentimentality." *James Joyce Quarterly* 41.1 (2003–4): 25–26.

Scholes, Robert, and Richard Kain, eds. *The Workshop of Daedalus: James Joyce and the Raw Materials for* A Portrait of the Artist as a Young Man. Evanston, IL: Northwestern University Press, 1965.

R. J. Schork, "Genetic Primer: Chapter I.6." In *How Joyce Wrote Finnegans Wake: A Chapter-by-Chapter Genetic Guide*. Ed. Luca Crispi and Sam Slote. Madison: University of Wisconsin Press, 2007. 124–41.

———. *Greek and Hellenic Culture in Joyce*. Gainesville: University Press of Florida, 1998.

Senn, Fritz. *Joyce's Dislocutions: Essays on Reading as Translation*, ed. John Paul Riquelme. Baltimore, MD: Johns Hopkins University Press, 1984.

———. Letter to the Editor. *James Joyce Quarterly* 41.1/2 (Fall 2003–Winter 2004): 325–26.

Shakespeare, William. *Twelfth Night, or What You Will*. *The Norton Shakespeare*. 2nd ed. Ed. Stephen Greenblatt et al. New York: Norton, 2008. 1793–846.

Shattuck, Roger. *The Banquet Years: The Origins of the Avant-Garde in France, 1885 to World War I*. Rev. ed. New York: Vintage, 1968.

Shelley, Percy Bysshe. "A Defence of Poetry." In *The Selected Poetry and Prose of Percy Bysshe Shelley*. Ed. Carlos Baker. New York: Modern Library, 1951. 494–522.

Simone, Tom. "'Met Him Pike Hoses': *Ulysses* and the Neurology of Reading." *Joyce Studies Annual* (2013): 207–37.

"Sixteen Years Work by James Joyce: New Novel is 'Endlessly Exciting in its Impenetrability,'" *Irish Times*, June 3, 1939.

Skeat, Walter W. *An Etymological Dictionary of the English Language*. Mineola, NY: Dover, 2005.

Slote, Sam. *Joyce's Nietzschean Ethics*. New York: Palgrave, 2013.

———. "Nulled Nought: The Desistance of Ulyssean Narrative in *Finnegans Wake*." *James Joyce Quarterly* 34.4 (Summer 1997): 531–42.

Swift, Jonathan. "The Lady's Dressing Room." In *Eighteenth-Century Poetry: An Annotated Anthology*. 2nd ed. Ed. David Fairer and Christine Gerrard. Oxford: Blackwell, 2003. 81–85.

———. "A Modest Proposal for Preventing the Children of Poor People in Ireland from Being a Burden to Their Parents or Country, and for Making Them Beneficial to the Publick." In *Gulliver's Travels and Other Writings*. Ed. Louis A. Landa. Boston, MA: Houghton Mifflin, 1960. 439–46.

Tallis, Raymond. "The Neuroscience Delusion," *Times Literary Supplement*, April 9, 2008. http://entertainment.timesonline.co.uk/tol/arts_and_entertainment/the_tls/article3712980.ece?&EMC-Bltn=CUEGU8.

Theall, Donald F. "The Avant-Garde and the Wake of Radical Modernism." In *Contemporary Poetics*. Ed. Louis Armand. Evanston, IL: Northwestern University Press, 2007. 57–66.

The Third Man. Dir. Carol Reed. Screenplay by Graham Greene. London: British Lion Film Corporation, 1949.

Van Hulle, Dirk. *James Joyce's "Work in Progress": Pre-Book Publications of Finnegans Wake Fragments*. London: Routledge, 2016.

Vrselja, Zvonimir, Stefano G. Daniele, John Silbereis, Francesca Talpo, Yury M. Morozov, André M. M. Sousa, Brian S. Tanaka, Mario Skarica, Mihovil Pletikos, Navjot Kaur, Zhen W. Zhuang, Zhao Liu, Rafeed Alkawadri, Albert J. Sinusas, Stephen R. Latham, Stephen G. Waxman, and Nenad Sestan. "Restoration of Brain Circulation and Cellular Functions Hours Post-Mortem." *Nature* 568 (2019): 336–43.

Walsh, Erin. "Word and World: The Ecology of the Pun in *Finnegans Wake*." In *Eco-Joyce: The Environmental Imagination of James Joyce*. Ed. Robert Brazeau and Derek Gladwin. Cork, Ireland: Cork University Press, 2014. 70–90.

Warner, Marina. *Phantasmagoria: Spirit Visions, Metaphors, and Media into the Twenty-First Century*. Oxford: Oxford University Press, 2006.

Wells, H. G. "James Joyce." In *James Joyce: The Critical Heritage, Vol.1 1907–1927*. Ed. Robert H. Deming. London: Routledge and Kegan Paul, 1970. 86–88.

Wiener, Norbert. *The Human Use of Human Beings: Cybernetics and Society*. Boston, MA: DaCapo Press, 1954.

Wilde, Oscar. "The Critic as Artist." In *The Complete Works of Oscar Wilde*. London: Collins, 1991. 1009–59.

———. *The Picture of Dorian Gray*. *The Complete Works of Oscar Wilde*. London: Collins, 1991. 17–167.

———. "The Sphinx." In *The Complete Works of Oscar Wilde*. London: Collins, 1991. 841.

Wilson, Robert Anton. "Coincidance." *Semiotext(e)* 13 (1987): 155–88.

Wittgenstein, Ludwig. *On Certainty*. Trans. Denis Paul and G. E. M. Anscombe. New York: Harper & Row, 1972.

———. *Tractatus Logico-Philosophicus*. Trans. D. F. Pears and B. F. McGuinness. London: Routledge, 2008.

Wood, Michael. "'Avengers: Endgame.'" *London Review of Books*, June 6, 2019. 28.

Žižek, Slavoj. *The Parallax View*. Cambridge: MIT Press, 2006.

INDEX

Abbot, H. Porter 64n23
Abrams, M. H. 107n1
Adorno, Theodor W. 26, 100n10, 120
Alighieri, Dante 9, 70, 134
Amis, Kingsley 83
Anderson, Elliott 11
Anderson, John P. 146–47, 148
Andreasen, N. J. C. 125n2
Andrews, George 126–27
Anyfanti, Alexandra 62n19
Apollinaire, Guillaume 6
Aquinas, Thomas 19–20
Aristophanes 45
Aristotle 27, 45–46, 70, 144
Arp, Jean 6
Austen, Jane 56n3, 60, 61

Ball, Hugo 6
Balzac, Honoré de 52
Barthes, Roland 18n8, 73, 80
Bartók, Béla 6
Beach, Sylvia 83, 126–27
Beckett, Samuel 9, 11, 12, 31n2, 100n10, 132, 141
Beethoven, Ludwig van 148
Behan, Maurice 115
Bellmer, Hans 11
Bennett, Arnold 150
Bergvall, Caroline 10–11, 14
Best, Peter Nigel 138–40, 143, 144, 145, 146
Bichat, Xavier 95
Bishop, John 21n23, 28, 131
Black, Martha Fodaski 131–32
Blanchot, Maurice 33
Blavatsky, H. P. 135

Böhme, Gernot 119
Boland, Harry J. 88
Boldereff, Frances 132–33
Borges, Jorge Luis 7, 17n7
Boyd, Brian 61
Bradstreet, Anne 15, 22n30
Brecht, Bertolt 2, 6
Bricmont, Jean 57n4, 57n5
Broch, Hermann 26–27
Brooke-Rose, Christine 11
Bruno, Giordano 132
Budge, E. A. Wallis 37
Bürger, Peter 4–5, 6
Burgess, Anthony 127–28
Burrell, Harry 128n8
Bush, George W. 64

Cadbury, Bill 115n13
Caesar, Julius 78
Cage, John 11
Cahill, Clinton 8n19
Calvino, Italo 105
Campbell, Joseph 128n8, 129
Carroll, Lewis 70, 75
Cendrars, Blaise 6
Certeau, Michel de 105
Cervantes, Miguel de 16, 18
Charlemagne 3
Cheng, Vincent 88n18
Cixous, Hélène 11
Clinton, Bill 76
Cocteau, Jean 6
Cohen, J. M. 86
Coleridge, Samuel Taylor 18n8
Collins, Joseph 125n2
Conn, Andrew Lewis 13

Connolly, Marshall 81n1
Copland, Aaron 6
Corballis, Michael C. 57n7
Costello, Peter 129n15
Crispi, Luca 129
Crowley, Aleister 149

Danto, Arthur C. 120
Deane, Vincent 78n12
Dennett, Daniel C. 58–61, 63–64, 65–67
Deppman, Jed 33n6, 42n3
Derrida, Jacques 29, 108
Descartes, René 16, 55, 60, 65, 68, 77
de Valera, Éamon 88
Deyab, Mohammed 82n5
Dickens, Charles 17
Dixon, Vladimir 34
Dufrenne, Mikel 119

Eburne, Jonathan P. 149
Eckley, Grace 128–32, 147
Eco, Umberto 108, 148
Eide, Marian 75
Eliot, T. S. 5, 9, 10, 12, 43, 114
Ellmann, Richard 4n5, 34, 35n12, 62n19, 83, 133, 144
Empson, William 113–14, 116
Euclid 37

Fauconnier, Gilles 58
Federman, Raymond 11
Ferrer, Daniel 42n3, 78n12
Fitch, Noel Riley 126n5
Flynn, Catherine 6n13
Fordham, Finn 31, 42n1, 110
Foucault, Michel 7
Francis, Pope 81, 89, 92
Freud, Sigmund 20, 21–22

Gabler, Hans Walter 135
Gilbert and Sullivan xiv
Glasheen, Adaline 60
Goldsmith, Kenneth 13–14
Goldstein, Rebecca 57
Goll, Yvan 6
Goodman, Paul 5
Gordon, John 20–21
Groden, Michael 42n3

Hameroff, Stuart 66
Hamilton, William Rowan 75
Hanaway-Oakley, Cleo 101
Harding, Michael 133–34
Harpham, Geoffrey Galt 107n1
Harris, Frank 51
Hart, Clive 24, 31, 92, 112n6
Hay, Louis 42n3
Hayman, David 9–10, 11, 35, 64n23
Heidegger, Martin 120
Herman, David 62n19
Herr, Cheryl Temple 85
Hindemith, Paul 6
Hobsbawm, Eric 2
Hodder, James 75
Holzman, Wilhelm. *See* Xylander
Homer 8, 61, 99–100, 105
Huelsenbeck, Richard 6
Hume, David 82n3

Jackson, John Wyse 129n15
James, William xiv, 150
Jameson, Fredric 27
Jarnot, Lisa 13
Jaynes, Julian 68
Joyce, James
 Anna Livia Plurabelle 34
 Chamber Music 134
 "The Day of the Rabblement" 73
 Dubliners 24, 43, 47, 63, 91, 96, 101, 104, 109–10, 111n5, 134, 141, 145
 Exiles 87n16, 145
 Finnegans Wake xiii, 1–14, 16–17, 18, 19, 20–21, 23, 25n33, 27, 28, 29, 31–40, 41, 45–54, 57, 58, 62, 63, 64, 65, 66–67, 68, 69–70, 71–80, 85–86, 87–89, 91, 93, 96, 99, 100, 102, 104, 107–21, 123, 124, 126–27, 128–33, 134, 138–41, 142–44, 145, 146–47, 148, 149–50
 Giacomo Joyce 33
 A Portrait of the Artist as a Young Man 16n5, 27, 32, 41, 43, 44, 45, 46, 47, 48–49, 52–53, 62, 64, 65, 79, 82, 89–91, 96, 101, 102, 103
 Stephen Hero 41, 43, 44, 101
 Tales Told of Shem and Shaun 34, 45

INDEX 161

Ulysses xiii–xiv, 12, 13, 16–17, 18, 19,
  20, 21, 22, 23–26, 27, 29, 32, 42,
  43, 44, 49, 50–51, 52, 57, 58, 61,
  63, 64, 65–66, 67, 68, 70, 72, 75,
  82, 83, 84–85, 86–87, 89, 92,
  95–96, 97–100, 101, 102, 103, 104,
  105, 110, 111n5, 123, 125, 128,
  135–37, 139, 141, 142, 144–45,
  148, 149, 150
Joyce, Stanislaus 35n12

Kafka, Franz 6
Kassak, Lajos 6
Kenner, Hugh 21n21, 62
Kiberd, Declan 72
Kidd, John 135–37, 141, 145
Knowlton, Eloise 20
Königsberg, Johannes Müller von. *See*
  Regiomontanus
Kostelanetz, Richard 6, 8n18, 10
Krenek, Ernst 6
Kreuger, Ivar 39n17

Lacivita, Alison 88n17
Laporte, Dominique 84–85, 92
Laqueur, Thomas W. 95n2, 105
Leader, Zachary 42
Lehrer, Jonah 59n11
Leibniz, Gottfried Wilhelm 77
Lernout, Geert 40n19, 78n12, 129
Lewis, Leslie L. 8, 14
Lewis, Wyndham 3
Liddell, Alice 148
Llona, Victor 57
Loehrich, Rolf 144–46
Lukács, György 2

Madonna 146
Marinetti, F. T. 6, 7
Mason, Clara 138
Mayakovksy, Vladimir 6
McGann, Jerome 32, 35
McGee, Patrick 64n23
McGilchrist, Iain 68–70
McHugh, Roland xv, 20n17, 109, 112
McLuhan, Marshall 112
Melville, Herman 60–61
Mendelsohn, Daniel 99n8

Merleau-Ponty, Maurice 90
Metzinger, Thomas 23n28
Milhaud, Darius 6
Miller, William Ian 82n3
Milton, John 24
Moholy-Nagy, László 5–6, 7–8, 9, 14
Montaigne, Michel de 105
Morton, Timothy 116, 117, 119–20
Mozart, Wolfgang 59

Nietzsche, Friedrich 80
Nolan, Emer 73
Norris, Margot 17n7, 18

O'Brien, Eugene 90
O'Connell, Daniel 131
O'Donovan, John 92
O'Hanlon, John 53
Ordine, Nuccio 91
O'Sullivan, James 33n5

Partnoy, Frank 39n17
Pater, Walter 132
Penrose, Roger 66
Perloff, Marjorie 2, 12–13
Place, Vanessa 13
Plato 27, 144
Pound, Ezra 3, 6, 12n30, 86
Proust, Marcel 28–29, 59, 114
Pythagoras 47
Python, Monty 16, 28–29

Quinet, Edgar 147

Rabelais, François 86–87
Rand, Ayn 147
Raphael 27
Raw, Louise 39n16
Rawls, John 79
Recorde, Robert 77
Regiomontanus 77
Ribemont-Dessaigne, Georges 6
Robinson, Henry Morton 128n8
Roche, Maurice 10
Rose, Danis 33, 34, 48, 53, 136n28
Rothenberg, Jerome 3
Ruiz, Pablo M. 80
Rutland, Earl of 125

Sagan, Carl 124
Sandulescu, C. George 140–41, 142–44
Schmidt, Arno 10
Scholes, Robert 24
Schork, R. J. 37, 45
Schwitters, Kurt 6
Senn, Fritz 17n7, 27–28, 64, 125–26, 144, 145–46
Seuss, Dr. 61
Shakespeare, William 21, 22–23, 25, 27, 49, 61, 101, 105, 123, 125, 141
Shattuck, Roger 95n3
Shaw, George Bernard 83, 90, 131–32
Shelley, Percy Bysshe 113
Simone, Tom 62n19
Skeat, W. W. 99
Slote, Sam 19, 51, 75
Smith, Hester Travers 51–52
Socrates 45
Sokal, Alan 57, 59–60, 61
Sollers, Philippe 10, 11–12, 14
Sorrentino, Gilbert 11
Spencer, Herbert 74, 75, 79
Spiegelman, Art 61
Stead, William T. 128, 129–32, 147
Stein, Gertrude 6, 12
Stockwell, Peter 56n1
Stramm, August 6
Stravinsky, Igor 6
Sullivan, Hannah 43
Swift, Jonathan 82, 91, 148

Tallis, Raymond 56, 57, 68
Tejedor Cabrera, José Maria 134

Theall, Donald F. 7
Tolstoy, Leo 2, 4
Turner, Mark 58
Twain, Mark 70
Tzara, Tristan 6

Van Hulle, Dirk 42n1, 129
Varèse, Edgard 6
Verne, Jules 17n7
Vico, Giambattista 9, 20n16, 57, 111
Vonnegut, Kurt 44
Voronca, Ilarie 2
Vrselja, Zvonimir 95n1

Walsh, Erin 88n17
Warner, Marina 117
Weaver, Harriet Shaw 34–35, 37n15, 116
Welles, Orson 148
Wells, H. G. 17n7, 82, 85, 102
Wiener, Norbert 68n28
Wilde, Oscar 49–53, 125
Wilson, Robert Anton 148
Wittgenstein, Ludwig 102, 103–04
Wood, Michael 100n10
Woolsey, John M. 87

Xylander 77

Yeats, Georgie 3
Yeats, William Butler 2

Žižek, Slavoj 22
znore 148–49

www.ingramcontent.com/pod-product-compliance
Lightning Source LLC
Chambersburg PA
CBHW021143230426
43667CB00005B/235